Eco-Translation

Ecology has become a central question governing the survival and sustainability of human societies, cultures and languages. In this timely study, Michael Cronin discusses the profound implications of the ecological crisis for the practice and study of translation, and illuminates the role of translation in building a richer and sustainable future. Ranging across society, economy, technology, culture, and literature, five incisive chapters cover:

- the radically changed environmental circumstances of humanity;
- the ecological relationship between translation and one of the essential means of species survival: food;
- how translation figures in our relationship or lack of relationship with the numerous other species that inhabit the planet;
- the position of technology and translation in an era of ecological vulnerability;
- the role of literature, particularly travel writing, in teasing out the relationship between ecology, travel and translation.

Including discussion of a wide range of issues from climate justice to animal communication to global monocultures, Eco-Translation is key reading for all those working in the areas of Translation, Translation Studies and Environmental Studies.

Michael Cronin is Professor of Translation Studies at Dublin City University. He is the author of *Translation and Globalization* (2003), *Translation and Identity* (2006), *Translation goes to the Movies* (2009) and *Translation in the Digital Age* (2013).

New Perspectives in Translation and Interpreting Studies

Series editors:
Michael Cronin holds a Personal Chair in the Faculty of Humanities and Social Sciences at Dublin City University.

Moira Inghilleri is Director of Translation Studies in the Comparative Literature Program at the University of Massachusetts, Amherst.

The *New Perspectives in Translation and Interpreting Studies* series aims to address changing needs in the fields of translation studies and interpreting studies. The series features works by leading scholars in both disciplines, on emerging and up to date topics. Key features of the titles in this series are accessibility, relevance and innovation.

These lively and highly readable texts provide an exploration into various areas of translation and interpreting studies for undergraduate and postgraduate students of translation studies, interpreting studies and cultural studies.

Cities in Translation
Sherry Simon

Translation in the Digital Age
Michael Cronin

Translation and Geography
Federico Italiano

Translation and Rewriting in the Age of Post-Translation Studies
Edwin Gentzler

Eco-Translation
Michael Cronin

Translation and Migration
Moira Ingheilleri

Eco-Translation

Translation and Ecology in the Age of the Anthropocene

Michael Cronin

Routledge
Taylor & Francis Group

LONDON AND NEW YORK

First published 2017
by Routledge
2 Park Square, Milton Park, Abingdon, Oxon OX14 4RN

and by Routledge
711 Third Avenue, New York, NY 10017

Routledge is an imprint of the Taylor & Francis Group, an informa business

British Library Cataloguing in Publication Data
A catalogue record for this book is available from the British Library

Library of Congress Cataloging in Publication Data
A catalog record for this title has been requested

ISBN: 978-1-138-91683-8 (hbk)
ISBN: 978-1-138-91684-5 (pbk)
ISBN: 978-1-3156-8935-7 (ebk)

Typeset in Sabon
by Taylor & Francis Books

MIX
Paper from
responsible sources
FSC
www.fsc.org FSC® C013604   Printed and bound by CPI Group (UK) Ltd, Croydon, CR0 4YY

For Máirtín and Lasairfhíona, messengers from the future

Contents

Acknowledgement

Writing is always as much about writing with as for. There is no sentence that is not at some level teased into expression in the company of a friend or in the conversation of a colleague. The seed life of books lies in the organic exchange of the random, the haphazard and the inspired that energises the community of scholarship the world over despite the relentless instrumentalisation of knowledge for corporate gain and institutional oneupmanship. It has been my great fortune for over 30 years now to have worked with an exceptional group of colleagues and research students in the Centre for Translation and Textual Studies and the School of Applied Language and Intercultural Studies at Dublin City University. This multilingual and multiethnic community has been a continuous source of support, stimulation and spirited fun through years of teaching, writing and publishing. I would particularly like to acknowledge my gratitude to the Head of School Professor Dorothy Kenny and the Governing Authority of Dublin City University for allowing me to avail of sabbatical leave in 2015–2016 so that I could work on the present volume. In an era when the notion of debt has been colonised by the predatory greed of financiers I would like to acknowledge a more noble version of debt in my gratitude to friends who have done so much to expand my understanding of what is at stake in the present moment, notably, Gavan Titley, Caoimhghín Ó Croidheáin, Barra Ó Séaghdha, Evelyn Conlon, Colin Coulter, Peter Sirr, Fintan Vallely, Kieran Keohane, Carmen Kuhling, Hans-Christian Oeser, David Johnston, Stephen Kelly, Susan Bassnett and Sherry Simon.

If connectedness is the signature tune of translation, then it is a sound that has resonated in many different places and different times in the writing of this book. I would especially like to thank Dr Anthony Cordingley for organising a LABEX Arts H2H Visiting Professorship to Université Paris 8 in 2014 and to Professor Luc von Doorslaer for arranging a Visiting Professorship in Specialised Communication (Translation Studies) to KU Leuven (Antwerp) in 2015. I have also benefited from the kindness and interest of colleagues in the following institutions where I was afforded the opportunity to present some of the ideas and arguments advanced in this book:

Aberystwyth University, Wales; University of Vigo, Spain; Queen's University Belfast; University of Porto, Portugal; University of Prešov, Slovakia; Université de Liège, Belgium; Birkbeck Institute for the Humanities, England; University of

Geneva, Switzerland; New Zealand Centre for Literary Translation, Victoria University of Wellington; University of Manchester, England; Université Bordeaux-Montaigne, France; Universidade do Minho, Braga, Portugal; University of Bologna, Forlì, Italy; Maison des sciences de l'homme, Paris, France; Université Sorbonne Nouvelle, Paris, France; University of Stirling, Scotland; Annual Conference of Mediterranean Editors and Translators (MET), Poblet, Spain; Free University Brussels, Belgium; University of Berne, Switzerland; University of Birmingham, England; University of Leeds, England.

A special word of thanks as always to the unfailingly supportive staff in Routledge, in particular Louisa Semlyen and Laura Sandford.

Books may be private in the execution but they are unavoidably public in the claims they make on the time and attention of those who are closest to us. I want to thank my two children, Máirtín and Lasairfhíona, for their resolute good humour and patience in allowing their father to squirrel away the moments necessary to produce this book and for reminding him each day why the future of the only planet we have matters so much. This book is lovingly dedicated to them. Fionnuala Mac Aodha has been unstinting in her support throughout the writing of this book and her presence has sustained me in every line, the best possible companion on the long trail of doubt and discovery.

Earlier versions of sections of chapters two and five have appeared in *Translation Studies, The Translator, Comparative Critical Studies* and Corinne Fowler, Charles Forsdick and Ludmilla Kostova (eds) *Travel and Ethics: Theory and Practice*, Routledge, 2014, *Amodern*, Anthony Cordingley and Céline Frigau Manning, *Collaborative Translation: From the Renaissance to the Digital Age*, London: Bloomsbury, 2016.

All translations, unless otherwise stated, are my own.

Introduction

Earthlings

'We need a new subject for small talk. The weather has become too interesting.'
(Chrostowska 2015: 158)

His brother, Wilhelm, believed that his mind was 'made to connect ideas, detect chains of things' (Wulf 2015: 87). When the German naturalist Alexander von Humboldt went exploring the Andes, a moss that grew there reminded him of a species from the forests of Northern Germany thousands of miles away. In the mountains near Caracas he found rhododendron-like plants that he compared to flowers he had seen in the Swiss Alps. In Mexico he came across pines, cypresses and oaks that were similar to those in Canada. In the words of his modern biographer, Andrea Wulf, Humboldt believed 'Everything was connected' (88). Connections brought about insights but they also spelled trouble. In Venezuela, for example, in the valley of Aruga at Lake Valencia, Humboldt noticed how once fertile land was being over-exploited and turning barren. The reason? Colour. The global demand for indigo led local people to grow the plant that produced the blue dye. The plant gradually replaced maize and other edible crops grown in the valley. Indigo plants were particularly demanding of the soil so that not only were local people depriving themselves of necessary food crops but the further cultivation of the plant would soon be impossible as a result of soil exhaustion. The dye on the European tablecloth had a long tail of ecological destruction that led to the other side of the Atlantic.

Translation is also 'made to connect ideas' and one of the ideas that has come to the fore in the contemporary world is that of climate change. As this book was being written, over 197 countries came together in Paris to discuss an agreement on limiting carbon dioxide emissions. Between 1990 when the first report by the Intergovernmental Panel on Climate Change (IPCC) alerted governments to the real threat of global warming and 2015 when the governments gathered in Paris, carbon dioxide emissions had not gone down. They had, in fact, risen by 60 per cent (Anderson 2015). What the global gathering demonstrated was the extent both of our interconnectedness and our vulnerability as a species. What we will argue in this book is that translation as a body of ideas and a set of practices is central to any serious or sustained attempt to think about this interconnectedness and vulnerability in the age of human-induced climate change.

Over a decade ago I finished a volume on translation and globalisation with a brief consideration of 'translation ecology' (Cronin 2003: 165–172). My main concern was with the role of translation in giving minority language speakers control over what, when and how texts might be translated into or out of their languages. The notion of translation ecology was subsequently taken up by Chinese scholars who were particularly interested in how the science of ecology could be used to study the contexts and practices of translators (Xu 2009). This has led to regular symposia on the 'eco-translatology', where much focus is placed on ecosystemic notions of selection and adaptation (Liu 2011: 87–90). The approach that is adopted in this work is derived from a broad concept of political ecology understood as the study of the social, cultural, political and economic factors affecting the interaction of humans with other humans, other organisms and the physical environment (Robbins 2011). In taking the term 'eco-translation' first employed by Clive Scott at a lecture given in 2015 in the University of Exeter, I have extended it beyond Scott's understanding of the term to describe the translator's 'psycho-physiological' involvement with the text to be translated (Scott 2015). As used in the current work, 'eco-translation' covers all forms of translation thinking and practice that knowingly engage with the challenges of human-induced environmental change. One of the challenges, indeed, is how to apprehend the agents and objects of this change.

Timothy Morton has coined the term 'hyperobjects' to refer to 'things that are massively distributed in space and time relative to humans' (2013: 1). His examples of hyperobjects are various:

> A hyperobject could be a black hole. A hyperobject could be the Lago Agrio oil field or the Florida Everglades. A hyperobject could be the biosphere, or the solar system. A hyperobject could be the sum total of all the nuclear materials on Earth; or just the plutonium, or the uranium. A hyperobject could be the very long-lasting product of direct human manufacture, such as Styrofoam or plastic bags, or the sum of all the whirring machinery of capitalism.
>
> (1)

Another example of a hyperobject is global warming or climate change. The difficulty with hyperobjects is that humans will experience only part of the hyperobject at any one time and they are impossible usually to grasp in their totality. You could be aware of a series of unusually hot or unusually wet summers or have noted that a small piece of coastline you know well has changed since childhood but the notion of 'global warming' can seem excessively abstract or remote. If you throw away a Styrofoam cup how can you imagine what the world will be like in 400 years' time, the time it will take to biologically degrade the cup? If you plug into an electricity network that is partially powered by nuclear energy, how aware are you that the amortisation rate for plutonium is around 24,000 years? As Morton observes, 'Twenty-four thousand years into the future, no one will be meaningfully related to me. Yet everything will be influenced by the tiniest decisions I make right now' (122). Hyperobjects change our experience of time. The future, in other words, is no longer in the future. It informs the here and now. When we think about the future of translation it involves inescapably the question of climate change which will leave no area of human and non-human being untouched. Translation studies as one of the human and social sciences cannot remain immune to the ecological shift in many humanities and social science subjects. It needs to take seriously the idea that translation and translators do not exist in isolation but that they are 'an inextricable and integral part of a larger physical and living world' (Stibbe 2015: 7). Food security, climate justice, biodiversity loss, water depletion, energy security, linguicide, eco-migration, resource conflicts, global monocultures, are only some of the issues that will be at the heart of environmental debates in the twenty-first century and that will need to be addressed by scholars and practitioners of translation alike. *Eco-Translation* is an attempt to think through some of the assumptions we make about translation and how they may need to be radically re-thought on a planet that, from a human standpoint, is entering the most critical phase of its existence.

Chapter one investigates the radically changed environmental circumstances of humanity and asks why this should be of concern to debates around language, culture and translation. It opens with an examination of the notion of the Anthropocene – the new geological era of human-induced climate change – and looks at the shift in the status of the human from biological to geological agent. This shift in status means that the history of the planet and the history of humanity begin to converge. The long standing division between the human and social sciences and the natural and physical sciences is no longer tenable in a world where we cannot remain indifferent to the more than human. From this new awareness comes a need for the development of a post-anthropocentric identity which naturally affects all human activities including translation. In placing the future of the planet at the centre of our preoccupations, rather than our all too human selves, the chapter introduces the notions of place, resilience and relatedness in the context of the formulation of a new political ecology of translation. These core notions are repeatedly explored throughout the book but in chapter one they provide a context for paying attention to the notion of attention itself. As translation battles for recognition in the increasingly crowded attentionscape of late modernity, how are we to think about what it means to be attended to and what might an 'ecology of attention' mean in terms of what translators do or aspire to do? One of the reasons for desiring the attention of others is to make work visible or have it valued. The difficulty in the contemporary moment is that the products of translation may be visible but not the process. Taking a key concept from social anthropology, the 'logic of inversion', the chapter looks at how the means needed to bring about a translation – human, social, cultural – are often sacrificed to the ends of immediacy, transparency and instantaneity. This tyranny of ends over means relates to the more general concealment of the earth's resources that have made human action possible. The result has been, for example, a long historical indifference to the forms of energy – from human slaves to fossil fuels – which have allowed civilisations to emerge. Part of the task of 'transitology' – the science and art of managing the transition to more sustainable, resilient and viable economies and societies – is to take means seriously because it is they that determine how and in what direction our societies will travel. It is in this context that the chapter concludes by considering translation as a means, a form of energy that is potentially more amenable to the cyclical rationale of recycling than to the linear logic of extractivism, the logic based on a non-reciprocal, dominance-based relationship with the earth.

Chapter two explores in detail the ecological relationship between translation and one of the essential means of species survival, food. The production, distribution and consumption of food has, of course, become a core concern of political ecology, as how food is currently produced, distributed and consumed has enormous consequences in terms of carbon emissions. When we open our mouth, it is usually to eat or to speak or do both. Talking and eating or talking about eating are typically human activities. Humans, however, like the foods they eat, move about. If humans and foods travel in a multilingual world, then translation must be integral to that movement. The chapter considers how food features in representations of migration and how particularly forms of translation practice can work not so much to reveal as to conceal the paths of migration. The concealment of movement is equally at play in the tyranny of transitivity, the notion that translation, like cooking, is a matter of following preordained routines. The actual working through a translation like the preparation of a dish allows the unpredictable, the unplanned for to emerge and it is this excess of effect over intention that brings us to one of the paradoxes of food translation, the more a food is of a place, the more it can seemingly be displaced. The chapter examines the different ways in which we can attempt to capture the relationship between food and place in a way that acknowledges specificity and identity but embeds them in more ecologically attuned notions of connectedness. One of the pressures of food on place is, of course, demand. The more mouths there are, the more that need to be fed. The more mouths there are, however, the more that also want to speak and be understood. In the field of political economy, there is an increasing emphasis on the social consequences of the 'second machine age', the shift towards digitalised and automated forms of production that substitute for higher-level human cognitive activities. One of the activities targeted is precisely to do with the need to speak and be understood, translation. The chapter examines the logic of industrialised food production and aligns this with the ever-increasing demands for translation, more food, more words. If the practices of agro-industry were eventually called into question by the Slow Food movement is there an equivalent movement of resistance to the mass, industrialised production of translated language? Is there a need to develop something like a Slow Language movement? Is language a common good like the land, earth, air and water that has been constantly devalued because it is something that we all share and therefore is not valued? In the context of these questions, the chapter looks at how the description of food, the consumption of food and the preparation of food as they are filtered through translation guide us towards a new translation ecology.

Chapter three looks at how translation figures in our relationship or lack of relationship with the numerous other species that inhabit the planet. Taking a critical look at human exceptionalism, the notion that humans are radically different from and immeasurably superior to other members of the animal kingdom, the chapter goes on to consider the symbolic nature of communication for both organic and inorganic entities in our world. The notion of 'tradosphere' is advanced to capture the different forms of translation implied by the multiple connections between the organic and the inorganic. In order to develop any sense of solidarity with other species in a period of unprecedented mass extinction of other species by humans, inter-species relatedness demands reflection on translation, how to communicate across difference. That this is a challenging task is illustrated by the complexity of different animal communication systems discussed in the chapter. The difficulty of the task, however, does not lessen the responsibility on students and scholars of translation to consider how they might use translation to move towards a post-anthropocentric relationship to the world, vital for any notion of ecological survival. In particular, the chapter investigates the rehabilitation of the animal subject through translation drawing on historical experiences of colonialism where translation in its more enlightened mode offered the possibility of a voice for the oppressed. The need to engage with difference should not mean the annihilation of difference and there is due regard for the dangers of anthropomorphism. Denying difference through the projection of human fantasies is examined in the context of the relationship between translation and the problematic of incommensurability. Dealing with the indeterminacy of meaning has long been a preoccupation of those who practise and study translation and due consideration is given to how this experience might guide us in dealing with inter-species communication. What results from the challenges of the Anthropocene is not only the necessity to engage at a very profound level with the animal world around us but the need to re-examine existing disciplinary tools and ask whether they are any longer fit for purpose. Translation studies as an interdiscipline is well placed to tackle a changing disciplinary environment once it is sufficiently self-reflexive about its own biases and assumptions. One of these assumptions relates to seeing its remit as dealing exclusively with human language. However, not only must this assumption be questioned but the chapter also asks us to consider whether entities other than life-forms need to be factored into a more comprehensive or enlarged understanding of what translation might mean or could do. Implicit in this line of thinking is the necessary humility of 'earthlings', the consciousness of beings who realise that they have only one planet and whose well-being is crucially dependent on the well-being and intelligibility of all the other entities for whom the earth is also home. The humility involves not only the crossing of borders in a move towards empathy and understanding but also a respect for borders in a drive towards respect and sustainability.

Chapter four examines the position of technology and translation in an era of ecological vulnerability. A core argument of the chapter is that there is nothing virtual about the consequences of the virtual. Creating the immaterial worlds of informations and communications technology (ICT) leads to very real, material effects for the environment, in everything from the extraction of precious metals to the constant drain on energy resources. Technology as an indispensable component of contemporary translation practice is deeply implicated in forms of energy dependency that are increasingly unsustainable. Even when the emphasis is placed on energy efficiency, a paradoxical consequence is that the more energy that is saved, the more energy that is sought. In part, the insatiable logic of ICT development is driven by and drives an economic model of endless, material growth. Translation as a practice through localisation that is indispensable in the development of foreign markets for goods and services is closely bound up with an ideology of infinite growth. The chapter examines what are the future possibilities for translation technology in a world where this growth model is no longer sustainable. In particular, the chapter examines the potential for the move from a 'high-tech' to a 'low-tech' translation practice. Part of the motivation for this shift is not only the need to reconsider energy use and resource availability but also to re-examine the position of translators in situations where their labour is not valued or, more critically, remunerated. Any analysis of the contemporary technological moment must address the seemingly unquenchable desire for data accumulation that has very tangible environmental impacts. In the context of this desire, the question is asked whether it is ecologically responsible to pursue a model of endless translation growth. The chapter considers whether less may indeed be more, in particular in the case of the direction of translation. That is to say, a maximalist notion of translation productivity can favour the creation of monolingual monocultures that are deeply inimical to the viability of resilient and diverse knowledge spaces. How these spaces survive in an era of rapid techno-logical development and increased ecological vulnerability is partly related to how knowledge itself is organised. The chapter looks at how alternative models of knowledge organisation impact on the relationship between translation and technology and other critical areas. In considering what kind of transition is necessary to avoid ecological collapse, there can be no gainsaying the fundamental importance of the tools that humans use. It is in the spirit of the re-evaluation of the role of technology in translation that the notion of translation as 'craft' is revived to suggest or explore potential futures for translators and their machines.

Chapter five analyses the role of literature, particularly travel writing, in teasing out the relationship between ecology, travel and translation. The chapter begins with the different representations of minority languages and speakers in contemporary travel accounts and concludes with an exploration of the trans-lation consequences of 'minoritised' migrant languages. As travel writers move through different cultures, they also move within different language worlds and how these worlds are constructed partly depends on the language of narration. That is to say, the world can look like a very different place depending on whether the traveller is the speaker of a global or a lesser-used or less-translated language. Global languages, however, embark on their own translation journeys and the chapter examines the impact of the hidden histories of language contact on a re-engagement with the surrounding world. Landscapes constantly suggest the convergence of the aesthetic and the ethical. It is indeed an ethical concern with the disappearance of landscapes for future generations of children that has animated much debate in contemporary ecology. In the chapter it is suggested that the languages of children themselves, the translation of the world into the multiple dialects of childhood, reveals the transformative energy of translation as a way of both paying close attention to and to transforming the world. If language difference is key to cultural diversity, how these differences and diversity are portrayed will have inevitable consequences for how an ecological sensitivity develops around language and translation. At the heart of this portrayal is a tension never fully resolved between the mobile traveller on the one hand and the immobile resident on the other. Travel accounts in a spirit of ecological open-mindedness may wish to celebrate language diversity but find that the value-system of a highly mobile modernity can result in highly reified and entropic versions of minority languages and cultures. The preference for culturalist rather than political explanations of difference and context mean that whole communities are moved outside the realm of time into the domain of ageless atavism. The issue becomes even more problematic when speakers of minority or minoritised languages find themselves not in picturesque peripheries but at the heart of the contemporary metropolises. Debates around language, translation and integration presuppose notions around 'integration' which are inappropriate, rigid and do not reflect the complex linguistic labour of globalisation from below, the constant language and translation contacts in the cafes, factory floors and markets of modern cities. Of course, if a core value of ecosophy is to make humans alive to the sheer diversity of the living and the non-living, humans need to know how this diversity has been described. Translation is essential to this disclosure of the world. We need to know what people have said about ecosystems before we can respond appropriately. The chapter explores a number of the ethical dilemmas that result from this and the complicated relationship minority languages and indigenous peoples can have with the translation imperative. The age of the Anthropocene is of necessity a Translation Age as it requires all the skills translators can muster to restore a degree of intelligibility to our deeply damaged ecosystems.

Alexander von Humboldt first warned of the environmental consequences of deforestation in French. When the German translator came to put the German's French words into German he felt that he could not let the author's remarks on deforestation go unchallenged. He added a footnote of his own claiming that Humboldt's claims about the harmful effects of deforestation were 'questionable' (Wulf 2015: 213). If the great German naturalist had to put up with translators as climate sceptics, the challenge now is to bring translation to the heart of the dialogue about the future of our shared planet. Any other response would indeed be 'questionable'.

1   Paying attention

For the fiftieth birthday of *The New York Review of Books* the well-known British historian Timothy Garton Ash was invited to comment on what he felt had fundamentally changed in the world since the *NYRB* first appeared on the magazine racks in 1963. Seeing the magazine as a 'light-house at the centre of the Western world' he wanted to show 'how the world has changed under its steady illumination' (Garton Ash 2013: 51). 'Human rights' and a concern with same are first picked out under the sweeping beam of retrospection. He then sheds light on the rise and staggered fall of the US as 'hyperpower', the increased prominence of the Arab world, the inexorable ascension of China and the explosion of 'digital opportunity', the binary revolution that leaves expression gloriously unbound. Not a word, however, about the Stern Review on the Economics of Climate Change. Not a line about the Intergovernmental Panel on Climate Change. No melting ice. No rising sea levels. No acidic oceans. No species loss. For Garton Ash, all is gloriously quiet on the weather front. Our duty in this changing world, if we have one, is to 'remain true to the core values of a modernized Enlightenment liberalism, Western in origin but universal in aspiration' (53).

The Anthropocene

In thinking about translation in the contemporary moment, my argument will be that the 'modernized Enlightenment liberalism' Garton Ash has in mind is no longer effective or persuasive as a means of liberation because of a set of assumptions around what it is to be human which can no longer remain uncontested. We want to begin by sketching out the background to new thinking around the notion of the human and then examine the implications for translation of a move towards what has been dubbed the 'posthuman' (Braidotti 2013). Central to our thesis is an idea that has been borrowed from the Nobel Prize winning chemist Paul Crutzen and his collaborator, a marine scientist specialist, Eugene F. Stoermer, namely, the idea of the 'anthropocene'. Crutzen's contention is that in the last three centuries, the effects of humans on the global environment have escalated dramatically. As a result, anthropogenic emissions of carbon dioxide are very likely to significantly affect the climate for millennia to come:

'It seems appropriate to assign the term "Anthropocene" to the present [...] human-dominated, geological epoch, supplementing the Holocene – the warm period of the past 10–12 millennia' (Crutzen 2002: 23; see also Crutzen and Stoermer 2000: 17 and Steffen, Grinevald, Crutzen and McNeill 2011: 842–867). The Anthropocene is traced back to the latter half of the eighteenth century when analyses of air trapped in polar ice showed the beginning of growing global concentrations of carbon dioxide and methane. Since 1750 as a result of human activities, methane (CH_4) emissions have increased by 150 per cent, nitrogen oxide (N_2O) emissions by 63 per cent and carbon dioxide (CO_2) emissions by 43 per cent. The concentration of CO_2 rose from 280 parts per million (ppm) on the eve of the industrial revolution to 480 ppm in 2013, the highest level for over three million years (Bonneuil and Fressoz 2013: 20). The principal consequence of anthropogenic climate change is that humans have now become capable of affecting all life on the planet. As Dipesh Chakrabarty pointed out a number of years ago, when the collective actions of humans fundamentally alter the conditions of life on the planet they move from being biological agents to becoming a geological force in their own right,

> For it is no longer a question of man having an interactive relationship with nature. This humans have always had, or at least that is how man has been imagined in a large part of what is generally called the Western tradition. Now it is being claimed that humans are a force of nature in a geological sense
> (Chakrabarty 2009: 207)

With this shift in status comes a dual shift in perspective. Firstly, it is no longer possible to speak about the 'environment' as something out there, as a negligible and dispensable externality. The environment is not exterior to but constitutive of who we are. Secondly, it is no longer tenable to conceive of humans as a species apart but as one species among many in relationships of increasingly acute interdependency. Therefore, we must think again about what it is to be human and if we think again about what it is to be human then we must inevitably think again about one of the activities that humans engage in, namely, translation.

Joseph Stalin, in a statement of classical historical orthodoxy in his *Dialectical and Historical Materialism* (1938), claimed that 'changes in geographical environment of any importance require millions of years, whereas a few hundred or a couple of thousand years are enough for even very important changes in the system of human society' (Stalin 1938). Stalin's distinction between natural history and human history had a certain credibility as long as the human remained, in Fernand Braudel's words, a 'prisoner of climate' rather than a maker of it (cited in Crosby 1995: 1185). In the era of the Anthropocene, however, the distinction no longer holds. Once humans move from being biological agents to geological agents, dominating and determining the survival of many other species on the planet, they then become not so much subject to nature as a condition of nature itself. This dominance comes, of course, at the cost of the very survival of humanity. For this reason, trying to conceive of a sustainable future for humans means the convergence of human history with the history of life on the planet to produce a form of 'deep history'. Implicit in the notion of deep history is that thinking about a variety of historical phenomena does not involve an excessive privileging of the printed word. Historical evidence can take other forms. Daniel Lord Smail in *On Deep History and the Brain* points out that the ancient world is unimaginable without archaeological evidence and this also holds for what we now know about the Middle Ages. He adds:

> So what does it matter that the evidence for the deep past comes not from written documents but from the other things that teach – from artefacts, fossils, vegetable remains, phonemes, and various forms of modern DNA? Like written documents, all these traces encode information about the past. Like written documents, they resist an easy reading and must be interpreted with care.
>
> (Smail 2008: 6)

One crucial outcome of the emergence of the Anthropocene is a revisiting of traditional disciplinary divisions or alliances. The findings of biology and geology in the nineteenth century and the greatly expanded timescale of terrestrial existence that ensued led to a division of academic tasks. The geologists would concentrate on the physical history of the planet, the biologists would look at the history of organic life on the planet and historians would devote themselves to the study of what a subsection of these organisms, humans, got up to in their time on the planet (Rudwick 2005). With the sole exception of geography, the social and human sciences increasingly defined themselves in isolation from the natural world whether it was social and cultural anthropology under Durkheim differentiating itself from physical anthropology or psychoanalysis under Freud considering any sensation of deep relation to the natural environment as a belated fusional fantasy from early childhood (Bonneuil and Fressoz 2013: 49–50). As Christophe Bonneuil and Jean-Baptiste Fressoz note:

> On the one hand, the hard sciences which became too *inhuman* with their conception of objectivity and their modern certainties; on the other, human and social sciences which became *anti-natural* by foregrounding as a distinctive feature of humans and human societies the fact of emancipation from natural fate or determination and making society a self-sufficient totality.
>
> (52; their emphasis)[1]

Translation studies, traditionally part of the humanities and social sciences, has shared this general indifference to the more-than-human world. Part of the challenge of the advent of the Anthropocene is how to factor thinking about the natural ecosystems on which humans are dependent for their survival into the ways in which we both conceptualise and practise translation. In other words, if translators by dint of their professional activity have often found themselves straddling the 'two cultures', moving from a text on farm machinery in the morning to an article on museum history in the afternoon (Cronin 1988: 325–329), the implications of the Anthropocene are much more wide ranging in that it is not simply a question of subject matter or polymath curiosity but of a genuine engagement by translation scholars with a host of disciplines from the earth sciences to animal studies.

The notion of the Anthropocene is not, however, without its problems. In John McNeill's *Something New Under the Sun: An Environmental History of the Twentieth-Century World*, the reader is presented with a picture of largely undifferentiated demographic, economic and technological growth that has predictably baleful ecological consequences. In a work of close on five hundred pages only forty are given over to 'ideas' or politics and the rest consist largely of figures, tables and dates (McNeill 2001). The difficulty is that it is not clear for the reader what the specific strategies of the principal agents are in this grand environmental narrative, what choices could have been made differently along the way, who contested what decisions, when and for what reasons? In other words, in the numbers-and-curves stories of environmental change or assessment, the detached, global overview of analysis and assessment results in a relentlessly quantitative, dehistoricised and largely apolitical account of climate change where an undifferentiated humanity becomes the unwitting architect of its own destruction through unrelenting increases in population, GNP, industrial and agricultural output, deforestation and mining.

However, there is nothing inevitable about choices that are environmentally destructive. In 1800, there were indeed 550 steam engines in Europe but there were over 500,000 water mills. Coal was more expensive than hydro power and many industrialists were not persuaded of its added value (Bonneuil and de Jouvancourt 2014: 73). It was the economic recession of 1825–1848 with increasing agitation by textile workers over salaries and conditions and a reluctance by industrialists to invest in public goods (such as dams and other hydraulic facilities) which made the use of coal-powered, steam-driven spinning machines a much more attractive proposition (Malm 2014). More machines meant fewer workers and fewer workers meant fewer demands, notably for wage rises. Therefore, the substantial increase in CO_2 emissions in Britain in the first half of the nineteenth century, which through economic competition, war and imperial domination would start a worldwide trend, was not the blind outcome of the machinery of 'progress' but the cumulative consequence of a set of very specific decisions taken by identifiable socio-economic actors. Similarly, the notion that ecological awareness is only a very recent phenomenon where 'humanity' finally woke up to the environmental consequences of its economic activities does not stand up to scrutiny. In the period from the beginnings of the industrial revolution, for example, to the decade when the movement towards fossil fuels use becomes more marked, awareness of the relationships between humans and their environment or the 'natural world' was widespread (Guha 2000; Fressoz 2012). Already, in the 1820s, Saint-Simon, a champion of 'industrialism' knew what he and his colleagues were doing:

The object of industry is the exploitation of the globe, that is to say, the appropriation of its products to meet human needs, and as, in carrying out this task, it modifies the globe, transforms it, gradually changing its conditions of existence, the result is through industry, humans (outside of themselves in some respect) take part in the successive manifestations of the divinity, and continue in this way the work of creation. From this point of view, industry becomes a cult.[2]

(Saint-Simon 1830: 219).

More than a century later, William Vogt's *Road to Survival* (1948) and Fairfield Osborn's *Our Plundered Planet* (1948) detailing the environmental consequences of specific human activities sold between 20 and 30 million copies. The notion of an unthinking humanity bringing destruction upon itself does not bear up to examination. Environmental risks have been clearly and repeatedly signalled from the time of the industrial revolution onwards. If biology unites human beings in their shared animality, ecology differentiates them in their ability to produce greater or lesser amounts of anthropogenic climate change. Therefore, in reflecting on the translational consequences of the notion of the Anthropocene it is important not to replace an emphasis on the political space of the nation state with a naive version of the bio-political space of the planet that evacuates historical agency and socio-economic responsibility. We should be mindful of history-earth rather than system-earth. Translation as a global activity in the age of the Anthropocene must be apprehended in the specificity of its impacts in different locations over time rather than in terms of undifferentiated, systemic flows that describe much and explain little.

Post-Anthropocentrism

If history is traditionally associated with the longer view, the biologist Edward O. Wilson in *The Future of Life* (2003) sees specific, long-range historical thinking as crucial to curbing humanity, as 'planetary killer, concerned only with its short-term survival' (202). Wilson argues it is only when humans begin to think of themselves as species that they can begin to take the longer view not only as an important exercise in critical self-understanding but as a means of securing the future. For Rosi Braidotti this move towards species awareness is a necessary step towards post-anthropocentric identity. Critical at the present moment is the de-centring of *anthropos*, 'the representative of a hierarchical, hegemonic and generally violent species whose centrality is now challenged by a combination of scientific advances and global economic concerns' (Braidotti 2013: 65). Of course, the critique of humanism and anthropocentrism is not just a fact of environmental awareness. It is explicit in the tradition of 'anti-humanism' that Braidotti references, 'feminism, de-colonization and anti-racism, anti-nuclear and pacifist movements' (16) where the white, sovereign, male subject of Western techno-imperialist thought was singled out for repeated critique. Out of this vision comes a notion of relationality and ontological equality that does not privilege one life form over another.

Louis Borges once grouped animals into three classes: those we watch television with, those we eat and those we are scared of (cited in Braidotti 2013: 68). Another more psychoanalytically inflected way of classifying these relationships might be the oedipal (you and me on the same sofa), the instrumental (you will end up by being eaten) and the fantasmatic (how exotic, sleek, dangerous you are). In Braidotti's view a post-human ethics implies an end to forms of 'anthro-polatry' which not only obscure emergent forms of species thinking but consign all other species to dangerous, destructive and ecologically untenable forms of subordination. For her, 'becoming animal' is a way of realising the irretrievably embodied, material nature of our existence on a planet that we share with innu-merable other species that we continue to destroy in vast numbers. The current rate in the loss of species diversity alone is similar in intensity to the event that 65 million years ago wiped out the dinosaurs (World Resources Institute 2005; Shubin 2008: 17–19).

The backdrop to the end of anthropolatry is the rise of geo-centrism, the notion that the planetary must now be figured into all our thinking. This includes everything from the Great Coral Reef and the Gulf Stream to the future of the honey bee. In Braidotti's interpretation of Spinoza's monism, she emphasises not so much the tyranny of oneness or the narcissism of separateness that is often associated with monism as the freedom of relationality, '[monism] implies the open-ended, inter-relational, multi-sexed and trans-species flows of becoming through interactions with multiple others' (Braidotti 2013: 89). Being 'matter-realist' to use her term is to take seriously our multiple connections to natural and material worlds. If we conceive of the notion of subjectivity to include the non-human then the task for critical thinking is, as Braidotti herself admits, 'momentous'. This would involve visualising the subject as 'a transversal entity encompassing the human, our genetic neighbours the animals and the earth as a whole, and to do so within an understandable language' (82).

So where does translation, which on the face of it appears to be a pre-eminently human activity, fit into this notion of the post-human or, more importantly, what does translation studies gain from being situated in a post-anthropocentric perspective? If we bear in mind what Braidotti has to say about new, emergent forms of subjectivity, 'a transversal entity encompassing the human, our genetic neighbours the animals and the earth as a whole', the emphasis is clearly on extended forms of relatedness. Fundamentally, it is a more generous or extended form of relatedness that defines the emergent, post-human moment. Herein lies a paradox for translation as it is frequently understood. On the one hand, translation is seen to be all about relatedness as it brings together people and languages and cultures, crossing the chasms of cultural suspicion and historical aversion. The first principle of the PEN Charter adapted at its congress in Brussels in 1927 on the initiative of John Galsworthy was, 'Literature knows no frontiers and must remain common currency among people in spite of political or international upheavals' (Rotondo 2011). The principle, of course, has no currency if there are no translators to put it into effect. On the other hand, translators have been keen to deny relatedness of a kind in their desire to emphasise the value or distinctness of their profession. This denial is part of a much larger conceptual galaxy that needs to be briefly defined if we are to understand how ecologically inflected notions of collaborative translation could prove to be profoundly subversive of dominant ways of thinking about the translation subject.

Dany-Robert Dufour in *L'Individu qui vient* (2011) locates contemporary understandings of the individual subject in a series of decisive shifts in the powerful stories that the West has been telling itself for centuries (Dufour 2011: 57–83). One of these stories originates in North Africa and is the response of one man, Augustine, Bishop of Hippo, in modern-day Algeria, to contemporary events. Augustine was greatly troubled by the different factors that had led to the sack of Rome in 410AD. He concluded in his monumental work *The City of God* that the sack of Rome was, in fact, a playing out of a struggle that would bedevil humanity to the end of time. The conflict between the City of God and the City of Man was based on two competing forms of love. The first involved the love of God to the point of expressing contempt for the self (*Amor Dei usque ad contemptum sui*). The second was a love of self to the point of expressing contempt for God (*amor sui usque ad contemptum Dei*) (Augustine 2003: XIV, 28, 1). The lives of believers occasioned the endless playing out of this tension between *Amor Dei* and *amor sui* that were seen to be radically distinct and in deadly opposition to each other. It is paradoxically in the Augustinian tradition that Augustine's opposition comes to be undone. Blaise Pascal in one of his most famous *Pensées*, fragment 397, argued the following:

> If you gain, you gain all.
> If you lose, you lose nothing.
> Wager, then, without hesitation that He is.
>
> (Pascal 1993: 187)[3]

Implicit in the Pascalian wager is the notion that self-interest can have divine consequences, or as he puts it, in fragment 106, 'la grandeur de l'homme, [c'est] d'avoir tiré de la concupiscence un si bel ordre' (102). Pierre Nicole, the pupil and friend of Pascal, in his *Essais de morale* (1671) will take Pascal's reasoning further and argue that the only way of truly reforming the world and driving out the forces of evil is to develop in everyone an '*amour-propre éclairé*' which through the use of reason will be able to distinguish its true interests from its false ones (Nicole 1999). John Locke, the great liberal theorist, will translate the *Essais de morale* into English in 1680 and renders 'l'amour propre éclairé' by the 'harmless self-love'. Adam Smith, an admirer of Locke, will, of course, make the notion of self-love central to his *Inquiry into the Nature and Causes of the Wealth of Nations* (1776) where he argues that it is not the benevolence of the butcher or the baker that we depend on for the supply of meat and bread for our dinner but on the interest they have in their own self-enrichment. We appeal not to their humanity but to their selfishness (Smith 2010: 12). Individual pursuit of self-interest rather than harming or destroying the community leads through the invisible hand of the market to collective prosperity and well-being. A new regime of value, therefore, emerges in opposition to the Augustinian rejection of the *amor sui* where the self is not only not to be castigated but to be celebrated as the touchstone of legitimacy and the engine of progress. Revolutionary notions of democratic citizenship and Romantic notions of expressive originality further strengthen the link between self and worth. In the words of L'Oréal's famous 2009 advertising campaign, because I am worth it, so much of what is outside of the I is worthless.

It is against this dominant regime of value that one has to situate the attempts to think about the translator as the forgotten agent of history or as the undervalued scribbler cowering behind a cloak of invisibility whose contribution to global societies and cultures needs to be foregrounded and celebrated (Simeoni 2008: 13–26; Venuti 2008). Drawing attention to the individual achievements of translators (Delisle 1999, 2002) is a way of restoring a literary or political or social identity to translators in the context of a dominant episteme which denigrates or does not value or recognise the faceless anonymity of the mass or what Negri and Hardt have called the 'multitude' (Hardt and Negri 2005). If translators are commonly neglected or obscured in cultural and political histories then a narrative of heroic individualism appears to be the only way of ensuring both professional recognition and remuneration and an acknowledgement of historical dues. Whatever about the death of the author it is difficult to celebrate the death of the translator when translators have been entombed by indifference for centuries. The individual assignation of identity and value in the liberal, utilitarian paradigm would seem then to be in obvious tension with the collective embrace of the relational that is seen as part of the utopian promise of translation. In other words, there is a clear contradiction between what I have termed elsewhere the 'messianic tradition' in translatorial self-representation (Cronin 2013: 89), the idea of translation as a collective project of mutual understanding and the regimes of value that have been dominant in Western modernity for more than three centuries.

Place, resilience, relatedness

What I would like to propose is that we situate value elsewhere and consider how different forms of translation might be situated within a post-humanist ecology of translation. That is to say, is there a way of attaching value to what translators do that does not involve the sacrifice of a sense of collective responsibility? Three potential principles underlying this emergent ecology would be the principles of place, resilience and relatedness. Just as the ecology movement has stressed the importance of locally produced foodstuffs as a way of drawing on local traditions in the context of preventing long-term damage to the planet (and we will see more about this in chapter two), one could argue that a similar commitment to the situatedness of place and the preeminence of context within the framework of a global sensibility must underline any form of translation practice considered from an ecological perspective. The alternative to a McDonaldisation of the word with the mass production of translated language is an awareness of the place sensitivity of language and usage as a way of globally allowing for the flourishing of creativity and difference. For example, during the humanitarian catastrophe that followed the Haiti earthquake in 2010, one of the major problems for the search and rescue teams was language. The teams themselves were multilingual and the survivors they were searching for were predominantly speakers of Haitian Creole. The mobile phone network was still functioning so messages indicating location could be sent out but the question was who would understand them? The solution was to set up a collaborative translation network where messages posted on a site could be read by Haitian Creole speakers around the world. These speakers were frequently bilingual and translated the messages into the different languages of the members of the search and rescue teams (Biewald 2010). It was the globally collaborative nature of the translation that saved lives but it was collaboration that was firmly predicated on understanding the specific nuances and forms of usage of language. In other words, collaboration here was not to do with the massification but with the diversification of language. It was through understanding the language of a particular place that the particularity of place could be mapped for rescue and survival in the context of the global enablement of mobile, digital technologies.

More generally, it can be argued that a place-based rather than ethnos-based sense of identity allows for the inclusion of all speakers of a language, both natives and newcomers. In this way, the focus of our translation activity, as in community interpreting, is firmly on the communities of speakers of a language in a particular place rather than positing a set of ethnic attributes which somehow map on to the translation situation, irrespective of where particular speakers and translators happen to find themselves. Translating from Turkish into German in Berlin is not comparable to translating from Turkish into English in London (Mandel 2008; Issa 2005). An ecological notion of translating *in situ* means that place not race becomes the marker of collective significance and collective emancipation, through the provision or denial, for example, of community interpreting services. This notion of place-based translational politics is all the more significant as a standard trope of xenophobic populism and its hostility to the provision of translation and interpreting services is the elaboration of a fantasy vision of place (always, everywhere monolingual) which parallels a fantasy vision of the polity (ethically and culturally homogeneous). This place-based translational politics is, of course, inclusive not exclusive of other places in the sense of the broader ecological awareness of the connection between voice, place and belonging in different contexts and different situations. As Naomi Klein has noted with regard to activists fighting the depredations of the fossil fuels industry, 'What is clear is that fighting a giant extractive industry on your own can seem impossible, especially in a remote, sparsely populated location. But being part of a continent-wide, even global, movement that has the industry surrounded is a very different story' (Klein 2014: 322). In a similar sense, the local and global dimensions to struggles for language and translation rights are mutually reinforcing in the context of a political ecology of translation, adding a further meaning to the notion of 'collaborative' translation.

A second principle of translation ecology is the principle of resilience. Resilience is generally understood as the capacity for individuals, cultures and societies to withstand stress or catastrophe. Where might we situate translation and more particularly ecologically inflected translation within the framework of resilience? If resilience is all about drawing on the resources of difference to deal with the unexpected is there a sense in which too much translation uniformises and that the only way of safeguarding difference is not more translation but less? Emily Apter has recently argued in *Against World Literature: On the Politics of Untranslatability* (2013), that too much value is placed on the virtues of circulation and anything which resists or blocks the circulation of meaning is seen as an immediate object of suspicion. Her concerns lie principally with a notion of world literature that erases difference or sifts out the foreign or the unsettling in the name of easy consumption. In this way, world literature mimics a free market fantasy of the endless, frictionless circulation of goods and information. In this massification of the written word, there is no room for difficulty or opacity. The untranslatable in this context is the world party pooper. It is the resistance of language to univocal meaning, the countless historical, political and cultural associations of words that trouble any easy traffic between languages. Apter, drawing on Barbara Cassin's *Dictionary of Untranslatables: A Philosophical Lexicon* (2014), gives various examples of words that are resistant to simple rendering. There is famously the Portuguese *saudade* which means variously nostalgia, longing, yearning, torpor, moral ambiguity, loneliness. The Russian word *pravda* which is conventionally translated in English by the word 'truth' exists in a complex echo-chamber of reference. Depending on the context, the word can allude to 'democratic cosmopolitics, the topology of exile, solidarity with persecuted minorities and refugees, Russian Saint-Simonianism and Russophilic world-views' (Apter 2013: 34). The untranslatable becomes a way of thinking about the specificity of languages and cultures, a call to attend to the singularity of written expression in particular places at particular times. One of the paradoxes of untranslatability, of course, is that you need more translation not less. You have to try harder to understand what the other is saying, devote more resources to the effort and value successful translation all the more when it is achieved, precisely because it is so difficult. An essential element in Apter's thinking on this subject came from her involvement with the English-language translation of Barbara Cassin's *Vocabulaire européen de philosophie*. The explicit model for Cassin's project was Émile Benveniste's *Le vocabulaire des institutions indo-européennes* (1969). Benveniste used his encyclopedic knowledge of ancient and classical languages to trace the evolution and separate developments of different institutions in the ancient world. Comparing, for example, the different appellations for 'king' in Persia, Rome and Greece allowed him to explore the radically different concepts of sovereignty that emerged in the different civilisations. The idea behind a 'Vocabulaire' or a Lexicon as opposed to a dictionary is, of course, that it can be added to or is open-ended. It does not pretend to the inclusive exhaustiveness of the dictionary or encyclopedia. The question that might be asked is why did the English-language translation reverse the order of presentation and give pride of place to the word 'dictionary', a notion which is undermined by the democratic incompleteness of the initial project? The inversion is primarily political. By giving pride of place to the notion of the 'untranslatable' consigned to the sub-title in the original, the co-editors Apter, Lezra and Wood were signalling an instability at the heart of language which has a fundamental bearing on how any knowledge structure (dictionary, encyclopedia) might want to make sense of the world. More to the point, this instability is often invisible to the primary target readership of this publication, English speakers.

As Emily Apter notes in her introduction, the increasing tendency across the world to make English the official language of instruction in science, technology and business means that 'students increasingly naturalize English as the singular language of universal knowledge, thereby erasing translation-effects and etymological histories, the trajectories of words in exile and in the wake of political and ecological catastrophes' (ix). Faced with *desengaño* or *sprezzatura*, an English speaker might reach for the dictionary or Google but in the case of 'consensus', 'conservative', 'performance', 'whole', 'instinct', 'law', 'style', 'duty'? All of these words appear as entry topics in the *Dictionary* with complex, knotted histories of interactions, shifts and transformations across languages but these histories rarely trouble the monolingual hubris of the Anglophone world. Once the italics, the manacles of otherness, are removed, the word can forget everything about its past life in another language and enjoy the amnesiac embrace of plain speaking.

It is this preoccupation with the untranslatable that becomes readily apparent in particular forms of collaborative translation activity. A case in point is the online discussion fora used by translators and language professionals. For example, in a WordReference.com Language Forum, the request for a French translation of 'cream cheese' generated twenty-five separate posts (WordReference 2005: 1–2). One post claimed that 'crème de fromage' existed in French and also 'crème de gruyère' but another Senior Member 'Claude 123' responded 'No, no, no, Cream Cheese is a North American reality; it has nothing to do with Fromage fondu. In Quebec the "Comité intergouvernemental de terminologie de l'industrie laitière" has adopted Fromage à la crème as an equivalent.' This post prompted a response from another Senior Member, 'Rodger', 'Sorry Claude123, it's a french [sic] reality! Called Saint Moret.' A debate then ensued about the appropriateness of 'fromage frais' as a translation with further references to the *Office de la langue française*, a contribution from a Senior Member 'williamtmiller' who works for a French cheese company where 'cream cheese' is translated as 'Fromage Frais Fondu' or 'Fromage Frais à Tartiner' and a discussion as to whether Saint Moret really tastes like cream cheese. What is apparent in the range and intensity of the discussion is that the participants are both testing and defining the limits of what can be said in French to capture a culinary reality that originated in the United States in 1872 as an attempt to recreate the French cheese Neufchâtel.

The attempted cultural translation of a French food product leads over a hundred years later to a polemical effort to retranslate the product, this time linguistically, back into French. What the online collaborative debates reveal is that the more language resists translation, the more it invites translation. So we can advance the idea that the ability of language to survive and flourish over time and adapt to a multiplicity of pressures – the principle of resilience – lies in the endless unveiling of the incommensurable in language which calls for new translations, new accommodations, new ways of rendering what can only be rendered with difficulty. As James Hopkins points out, the ability to 'spontaneously, continually, and with remarkable precision and accuracy' interpret one another 'seems fundamental to our co-operative and cognitive lives' (1999: 255). In this respect, questions of untranslatability, incommensurability and resilience are central to the communicative regimes that are the daily reality of global cities with their linguistically and culturally mixed populations.

The third principle of ecology is one that emerges frequently in public pronouncements concerning translation, namely, the principle of relatedness. It is something of a truism that translate relates to historical contexts, languages and cultures. All these forms of relatedness are solely situated in the realm of the human. However, we want to relate relatedness here to a more unexpected form of relatedness, namely relatedness to the non-human. An area which is largely neglected in translation studies is intersemiotic communication. With the exception of research in the field of sign language interpreting (and even here, it could be contended that sign language interpreting is simply a form of interlingual interpreting), intersemiotic communication often emerges as the poor cousin of Jakobson's famous tripartite division of the translation task (Jakobson 2012: 127). A core concern of ecology is that we are not alone on the planet and that we are responsible for species destruction on an unprecedented scale. Our food and farming practices have resulted in conditions of existence for other sentient beings which are frequently barbaric and inhumane (Schlosser 2001). This principle of relatedness draws on a post-humanist, post-anthropocentric idea of relatedness where humans see inter-species relatedness as central to new, more ethical forms of behaviour (Braidotti 2013). If this relatedness is to become a reality we must invest heavily in that hugely neglected area of translation studies, intersemiotic communication, to see how translation would feature, for example, in emerging new disciplines such as Animal Studies. Works such as Henry Gee *The Accidental Species: Misunderstandings of Human Evolution* (2013) and Thomas Suddendorf *The Gap: The science of what separates us from animals* (2013) or Raymond Corbey's earlier work *The Metaphysics of Apes: Negotiating the animal-human boundary* (2005) point to the enormous potential of translation studies in exploring forms of collaboration that would radically transform our species-based understanding. It is this potential we will consider in detail in chapter four. Thinking about how we might move outside anthropocentric assumptions in translation studies and relate to other species involves a radical point of departure for an area of enquiry that has previously only considered forms of relatedness in human terms.

Attention

Relating to others, whether human or non-human, implies, first and foremost, paying attention to them. Are you all sitting still and paying attention? The familiar injunction of the schoolmistress has become the watchword of the new economy. If the notion of economy is based on the management of scarce resources, attention in a media-saturated world has become the most precious resource of all. Already in the mid-1990s Michael Goldhaber was arguing that with the emergence of digital technologies, traditional factors of production would decline in importance relative to that of attention (Goldhaber 1996a; 1997). Thomas Davenport and John Beck in *The Attention Economy: Understanding the New Economy of Business* predicted the monetisation of attention where the attention of consumers would be so sought after that they would be supplied with services free of charge in exchange for a few moments of their attention (Beck and Davenport 2001: 213). We would be paid to pay attention. This is, in a sense, what has happened with Google where users can use extremely powerful search engines seemingly free of charge.

From the point of view of an economics of attention, two challenges immediately present themselves. The first is how to protect attention from information overload to ensure an optimal allocation of this scarce resource (the vogue for time management courses) and the second is how to extract the maximum amount of profit from the capture of this scarce resource (Kessous, Mellet and Zouinar 2010: 366). It is in the second sense, of course, that search engines come at a price. For Google, the user is the product and her attention span has a lucrative exchange value. The more she pays attention, the more Google gets paid for her to pay attention. What these developments highlight is a fundamental shift in economic emphasis from production to promotion. In information-rich environments, a series of media gates exist to filter information to potential users or consumers. Not all of these media gates have the same power co-efficient. An ad in a local college newspaper will not reach the same audience as an ad on prime time television. If the absolute cost of diffusing information has fallen dramatically over the centuries – it is substantially cheaper to post a blog in the twenty-first century than to print a book in the sixteenth – the cost of getting past the filters of preselection has risen exponentially (Falkinger 2007: 267). In other words, as societies are more and more heavily invested in various forms of mediation, from the rise of the audiovisual industries to the emergence of digital technologies, it is less the production of goods and services than the production of demand through the capture of attention that absorbs increasing amounts of resources. Getting people to take notice is the main income generator for what McKenzie Wark has famously dubbed the 'vectorialist class' (McKenzie Wark 2004).

Contrary to a popular misconception McKenzie Wark argues that information is never immaterial. It must always be embodied at some level. The vectors are the hard drives, the disks, the servers, the cables, the routers but also the companies and investment funds that are needed for information to be stored, archived, retrieved and to circulate between humans in space and time (McKenzie Wark

2012: 143). The importance of this class in the United States is borne out by the figures cited by Erik Brynjolfsson and Andrew McAfee in their *Race Against the Machine* where they point out that the share of income held by equipment owners continues to rise as opposed to income going to labour. While payrolls have remained flat in recent years in the US, expenditure on equipment and software has increased by an average 26 per cent (Brynjolfsson and McAfee 2011: 45).

There is a sense, of course, in which gaining people's attention may be a central feature of the new economy but is not necessarily novel in human experience. People have been trying to get others to sit up and take notice for millennia. As Richard Lanham points out in *The Economics of Attention: Style and Substance in the Age of Information* (2006), the central thrust of the art and science of rhetoric for more than two millennia has been to find ways of soliciting the attention of audiences. Lanham argues that much of what has been debated under the heading of 'style' in literary criticism, art history, aesthetics has largely been a matter of how writers and artists have sought to corner the attention of their readers or viewers in a field of competing media or stimuli. That the late moderns have not been the first to deal with the consequences of information overload is clear from the experience of Renaissance humanists and seventeenth century philosophers who were both excited and bewildered by the informational munificence of the printing press. One such scholar, Richard Burton, author of *The Anatomy of Melancholy* (1621) detailed this media invasion:

> I hear news every day, and those ordinary rumours of war, plagues, fires, inundations, thefts, murders, massacres, meteors, comets, spectrums, prodigies, apparitions, of towns taken, cities besieged in France, Germany, Turkey, Russia, Poland &c., daily musters and preparations, and such like, which these tempestuous times afford, battles fought, so many men slain, monomachies, shipwrecks, piracies and sea-fights, peace, leagues, stratagems, and fresh alarms [...] New books every day, pamphlets, currantoes, stories, whole catalogues of volumes of all sorts, new paradoxes, opinions, schisms, heresies, controversies in philosophy and religion &c.
>
> (Burton 1927: 14)

Tables of content, indices, references, bibliographies were among the devices employed at a textual level to filter this informational excess and, at an epistemological level, an interest in Cartesian style methods came from a wish to make sense of this abundant 'news' (Blair 2010). Any attention to regimes of attention will necessarily have to relativise its arguments in the light of previous historical experiences but it is nonetheless evident that the advent of digital technologies have added a significant new dimension to what Davenport and Beck call the 'attentionscape' (Beck and Davenport 2001: 49) of late modernity.

A problem not mentioned by Burton but implicit in the spread of his interests is language. There is no way to make sense of the 'towns taken' and the 'cities besieged' in France, Germany, Turkey, Poland and Russia if there are no means of obtaining and translating the information from the cities and towns that have fallen or that remain under siege. In other words, you can only pay meaningful attention to what you can understand and translation in a multilingual world is central to the task of language mediation. That translation is a constituent part of information-rich environments is borne out by the exponential growth of the localisation industry (Jimenez-Crespo 2013). The demands for translated data in globalised markets are apparently insatiable. In 2012, Common Sense Advisory estimated the size of the translation service industry to be $33.5 billion and a report by IbisWorld claimed that translation services are expected to keep on growing and reach $37 billion in 2018. These predictions tally with the forecast by the US Bureau of Statistics that the translation industry is likely to grow by 42 per cent between 2010 and 2020 (Pangeanic 2015: 1). The translation service provider Pangeanic concluded that, '[g]lobalization and an increase in immigration will keep the industry in demand for the coming years despite downwards costs pressures on the services' (2). Of course, a central rationale for investment in translation is the shift in emphasis, that we mentioned earlier, from production to promotion. In globalised markets, with attention an increasingly scarce resource, one way to make people sit up and pay attention is to offer them products in their own language. 'Legibility' of supply encourages expansion of demand. This is the rationale behind the typical sales pitch from a web localisation company such as Language Scientific: 'More than 1/3 of all internet users are non-native English speakers[...]As companies look to expand into new markets, reach a global audience and increase international sales, the benefits of website localization are clear' (Language Scientific 2015).

One of the consequences of this upward shift in translation demand on the foot of attention capture in globalised markets is the emergence of a new kind of scarcity, not only of attention but of translators. The response of the language services sector to growing demands for translation has been the accelerated interest in the technologisation of the word. As Pangeanic put it in their promotional literature, '[t]he advent of machine translation technologies should partly address the lack of qualified, professional translators coping with ever increasing amounts of data' (Pangeanic 2015: 2). Computer-assisted translation, machine translation, translation memories, wiki-translation, all in their various ways invoke technology in dealing with the ever expanding demand for translated text. Indeed, already in 2006, Alan Melby made a prediction that he himself admitted was 'a bit scary', namely, that 'in the future, the only kind of non-literary translator who will be in demand is one who can craft coherent texts that, when appropriate, override the blind suggestions of the computer' (Melby 2006).

The move towards translation automation in the global attentionscape raises the question of attentional asymmetry that has already being identified in existing audiovisual media. As the German theorist Georg Franck points out, there is a strict asymmetry between the attention the media offer and the attention they receive. The media use the tools of technical reproduction to diffuse information while users pay for every piece of information they receive with live attention, an attention guaranteed by the 'artisanal' and cognitively laborious sensory apparatus of our ears, eyes and brains. The standardised, industrialised media product can be delivered by means of automated technology on a scale that allows for the capture of a substantial attention 'mass' (typically quantified by TAM ratings (Franck 2014: 61)). A less dramatic and more banal example is the time it takes to write an e-mail message which is automatically distributed across a mailing list and the amount of time cumulatively that will be spent either reading or discarding it. It is this discrepancy between automated and live attention that leads Yves Citton to posit a notion of 'attentional capital gain':

> Collecting enormous quantities of information through a small amount of attention being multiplied by the technical devices of automation, cultural industries benefit from an enormous capital gain which results from the difference between attention given and attention received.
>
> (Citton 2014: 97; his emphasis)[4]

Implicit in the offer by Systran, the noted architects of machine translation systems for the European Union, is the exchange of the automated translation of the system in exchange for the 'live' attention of the user: 'Instantly understand foreign language content or make your message understood in languages other than English. How? With SYSTRAN products' (Systran 2015).

This attentional capital gain that results from the difference between the dead attention of technical reproduction and the live attention of legibility or reading through translation to make sense of the foreign message is, of course, a key generator of (advertising) income in the informational economy. Are there, however, different ways of construing the notion of translation, legibility and attention in late modernity? In particular, is there a way of thinking through the relationship between translation and legibility against the backdrop of automation that is not beholden to a scenario of repeated expropriation and disenfranchisement?

Focusing on the economics of attention inevitably implies a certain set of assumptions, notably the maximisation of profits through the minimisation of costs in the context (real or imagined) of market competition. In the standard neo-classical paradigm, the economy is primarily concerned with the optimal management of scarce resources. The ends to which these resources are employed are normally outside its area of competence. However, a notion of attention which is solely concerned with means and not ends is scarcely viable as a theory of attention because attention is invariably bound up with value.

William James in his *Principles of Psychology* (1890) pointed out how a notion of attention that was purely passive was unable to account for the ways humans pay attention. James is critical of the British school of Empiricism (Locke, Hume, Hartley, Mills and Spencer) for not treating of the notion of 'selective attention'. He argues that because their main concern is showing that 'the higher faculties of the mind are pure products of "experience"', experience itself must be thought of as 'something simply *given*' (his emphasis). James goes on to claim:

Attention, implying a degree of reactive spontaneity, would seem to break through the circle of pure receptivity which constitutes 'experience,' and hence must not be spoken of under penalty of interfering with the smoothness of the tale.

But the moment one thinks of the matter, one sees how false a notion of experience that is which would make it tantamount to the mere presence to the senses of an outward order. Millions of items of the outward order are present to my senses which never properly enter into my experience. Why? Because they have no interest for me. My experience is what I agree to attend to. Only those items which I notice shape my mind – without selective interest, experience is an utter chaos. Interest alone gives accent and emphasis, light and shade, background and foreground – intelligible perspective, in a word. It varies in every creature, but without it the consciousness of every creature would be a gray chaotic indiscriminateness, impossible for us even to conceive.

(James 1890: 402–403)

Out of the '[m]illions of items of the outward order' we choose to pay attention to certain items and not to others. Attention inescapably involves value as attention itself implies a choice determined by particular ends (safety, sanity, satisfaction) that are believed to be important. In the circular relationship of attention and value, subjects value that to which they pay attention and pay attention to that which they value. Ends cannot, therefore, be discounted in any credible attentionscape. The purely economistic representation of attention prevents us from asking the most basic question, to what ends are directed the attention that will decide our future or, put another way, if our future is strongly determined by those things to which we might pay attention to in the present (for example, public transportation in our cities), then must not the underlying value systems of our 'selective attention' be a matter of explicit and sustained public debate?

If the making legible of a text or an environment (or both) demands at the very least a deployment of our attention, an 'experience that I agree to attend to', then this attention is only intelligible in terms of present or future-oriented values. For this reason, Aurélien Gamboni has proposed the idea of an 'ecology of attention' as opposed to an economy of attention (Gamboni 2014). From the point of view of an ecology of attention, attention is always a form of interaction and these forms of interaction are, by definition, relational. That is to say, attention implies a relation between attending subjects and the objects or persons to which they attend. This idea of relation can be linked to the ecosophical notion of relationism advanced by Arne Naess which posits that individuals do not pre-exist their relationships. Peoples and organisms cannot be isolated from their environment. Speaking about the interaction between organisms and their environment is a fallacy because the organism is already an interaction (Naess 1989: 78; see also Citton 2014: 45). Articulating attention within the ecosophical notion of relationism means taking seriously the new forms of economic practice detailed by the economics of attention but embedding these more broadly in an ecology of attention that discusses questions of values, ends and sustainability. More specifically, for theorists like Citton, the notion of an ecology of attention brings together different forms of ecology:

> The *biophysical* ecology of our environmental resources, the *geopolitical* ecology of our transnational relations, the *socio-political* ecology of our class system, the *psychic* ecology of our mental resources all depend on the *media* ecology which determines our modes of communication.
>
> (Citton 2014: 46; his emphasis)[5]

Media ecology at one level could be considered to be the most superficial of the different forms, being merely the reflection of the four others (superstructural) but at another, it can be construed as the most fundamental (infrastructural) because it decides to what we will (or will not) pay attention. How is translation to be conceived of in this ecology of attention and what are the implications for reading the (culturally, socially, politically) illegible?

Visibility

In Chimamanda Ngozi Adichie's *Half of a Yellow Sun* (2006), the heroine Olanna wonders how the friends of her new partner Odenigbo are reacting to her. In particular, she is not sure what Miss Adebayo thinks of her:

> Neither was she sure of Miss Adebayo. It would have been easier if Miss Adebayo showed jealousy, but it was as if Miss Adebayo thought her to be unworthy of competition, with her *unintellectual* ways and her too-pretty face and her mimicking-the-oppressor English accent. She found herself talking more when Miss Adebayo was there, desperately giving opinions with a need to impress.
>
> (Ngozi Adichie 2006: 51)

Olanna is caught between how she is perceived and how she wants to be perceived. She battles against false perceptions that she feels betray who she actually is. In a sense, what Olanna is articulating to herself is a notion of authenticity running from Rousseau to the Romantics to Sartrean existentialism which views appearances as deceptive and as irrelevant to any proper or authentic sense of self (Taylor 1992). In the economy of attention, however, visibility is everything. If attention is the hard currency of cyberspace then Michael Goldhaber argues that attention flows do not simply anticipate flows of money but that they eventually end up replacing them. In attentional capitalism, attention is fast becoming the hegemonic form of capital (Goldhaber 1997). For Yves Citton the ontology of this attentional capitalism is the ontology of visibility which measures the 'extent to which someone exists on the basis of the quantity and quality of other's perceptions of them' (Citton 2014: 75).[6] From the quantity of

YouTube hits to the number of Twitter followers, value is heavily invested in forms of visibility that accrue attention capital. On the website for the state government of Victoria in Australia, future entrepreneurs are encouraged to think of social media as fundamental to their very existence, 'your business can now use social media to tell your story, and demonstrate your expertise on a global scale in real time with very little cost' (Business Victoria 2015). Young graduates are repeatedly reminded of the importance of having a strong web profile and getting on to virtual networks like LinkedIn. If attention is the currency of 'semiocapitalism' (Berardi 2010) then what are implications for translation? How is the ontological status of translation affected by new regimes of visibility?

The title of Lawrence Venuti's 1995 work *The Translator's Invisibility* articulates a long-standing concern with the marginal or peripheral situation of the translator. Venuti's contention was that 'translation continues to be a largely misunderstood and relatively neglected practice, and the working conditions of translators, whether they translate into English or into other languages, have not undergone any significant transformation' (Venuti 2008: ii). He explicitly used the term 'visibility' to capture the historical and contemporary predicament of the translator:

> 'Invisibility' is the term I will use to describe the translator's situation and activity in contemporary British and American cultures. It refers to at least two mutually determining phenomena: one is an illusionistic effect of discourse, of the translator's own manipulation of the translating language, English, in this case; the other is the practice of reading and evaluating translations that has long prevailed in the United Kingdom and the United States, among other cultures, both Anglophone and foreign-language.
>
> (1)

Venuti's examples are primarily situated within print culture and within the cognitive economy of the post-Gutenberg world. However, the notion of 'visibility' for translation has gained rather than lost traction as we examine translation in the context of post-print or digital culture. If we consider the earlier contention that a significant shift in economic activity has been from production to promotion, then translation products must, by definition, become part of the attentional arms race where more and more resources are devoted to capturing the attention of readers in the crowded virtual agora of 'world literature'. The pressures are all the greater in that as Franco Berardi has pointed out there is a fundamental tension between cyberspace and cybertime. If cyberspace is potentially unlimited, as even the humble memory stick increases exponentially in capacity, cybertime is not. Cybertime – the finite, organic, physical elaboration of information – is bound by real limits. The temporality demanded by this elaboration slows down the operations of our mind as it seeks to invest information with effective forms of meaning (Berardi 2010: 44, 71). The digital has opened up vast possibilities for the dissemination of translated literature in cyberspace but the difficulty is contending with the attentional economy of cybertime, the making visible of a writer or a literature in translation that must compete in the electronic agora.

The anxiety around visibility becomes manifest in the language of promotion itself. In January 2013 the Flemish Literature Fund which supports the funding of translations of Belgian Dutch-language literature co-organised an event in the United Kingdom under the heading 'High Impact: Literature from the Low Countries'. Flanders House London and the Netherlands Embassy in the United Kingdom presented what they described as 'High Impact', an event involving six top writers from the Low Countries on tour to six cities for six nights of readings and debates to showcase the best 'High Impact' literature from Flanders and the Netherlands in English translation. The authors were the Low Countries literati:

> all prize-winners and best-sellers back home, all writing in Dutch but from two different countries – Belgium and the Netherlands ... Now for the first time, and in a unique collaboration, six of the best Dutch-language story-tellers are coming together for a rock star-style tour of six English cities.
>
> (Flemish Literature Fund 2015)

The language of institutional ranking ('high impact') with the implicit background of the metrics of visibility (the optics of hits, citations, visits) is fused with the more conventional politics of spectacle ('a rock star-style tour of six English cities'). If the English public knows little about its Dutch-speaking neighbours, then resources must be mobilised to achieve the maximum visibility in the crowded Anglophone attentionscape.

Translation is the indispensable ally in the viability of the operation as both the literature itself and associated promotional activities on the website or elsewhere will be met with puzzlement, or worse, indifference, if audiences have no idea of what is going on. Put differently, what the Flemish Literature Fund is attempting to do is to create zones of legibility, in both a literal and metaphorical sense, for Dutch-language literature in the English-language literary landscape. This politics of legibility is, as I have argued elsewhere (Cronin 2013: 111–113), part of the incorporation of literary translation into forms of brand nationalism, where state-funded agencies seek to promote positive images of cultural capital as part of a soft power strategy in international relations. In the widespread culturalisation of economic advantage in everything from tourism to high-end consumer goods, capturing the scarce resource of attention through various forms of cultural performance is seen to guarantee more tangible forms of economic reward (see Bradley and Kennelly 2009) thus justifying public expenditure on the activities in the first place. Cultural legibility shadows forms of economic accountability and vice versa. As the British Council argues in its public rationale for global involvement in English-language education and the arts, 'In these ways, the British Council builds links between UK people and institutions and those around the world, helping to create trust and lay foundations for prosperity and security around the world' (British Council 2015).

Logic of inversion

There is a paradox, however, that haunts translation in this new political economy of attention and that is the attention that is or is not paid to translation itself. If translation as made explicit by the localisation industry is essential to attention-gathering in the global age, what kind of translation is envisaged? If in the time-space compression of global competitiveness, economic advantage consists in taking the waiting out of wanting, then how will translation be configured? One place the answers to these questions can be found is in *A Strategy for American Innovation: Driving towards Sustainable Growth and Quality Jobs* (2009) issued by the Office of the President in the United States. At the end of the document under the heading 'Catalyze Breakthroughs for National Priorities', there is an explicit recommendation for investment in 'automatic, highly accurate and real-time translation between the major languages of the world – greatly lowering the barriers to international commerce and communication' (Office of the President 2009: 22). This first statement of commitment to developing fully operational MT systems, that has been reiterated subsequently, pre-supposes a notion of translation as invisible, automatic and instantaneous. In the de-regulation of language ('lowering barriers to international commerce'), translation becomes the invisible hand in the market of communication. In order to consider the deeper implications of this conceptualisation we want to briefly consider the distinction the anthropologist Tim Ingold establishes between 'transport' and 'wayfaring'. Ingold argues that human existence is not fundamentally place-bound but place-binding:

> It unfolds not in places but along paths. Proceeding along a path, every inhabitant lays a trail. Where inhabitants meet, trails are entwined, as the life of each becomes bound up with the other. Every entwining is a knot, and the more that lifelines are entwined, the greater the density of the knot.
>
> Places, then, are like knots, and the threads from which they are tied are lines of wayfaring. A house, for example, is a place where the lines of its residents are tightly knotted together. But these lines are no more contained within the house than are threads contained within a knot. Rather, they trail beyond it, only to become caught up with other lines in other places, as are threads in other knots. Together they make up what I have called the *meshwork*.
>
> (Ingold 2011: 149; his emphasis)

Transport is primarily concerned with destination. If wayfaring is a development along a way of life, transport is primarily about carrying people or goods across, from location to location, leaving their basic natures unchanged, 'for in transport, the traveller does not himself move' (150). Only when travellers reach their destination do they begin to move. One consequence of the privileging in the contemporary moment of transport over wayfaring is what Ingold terms the 'logic of inversion' (69). This is the procedure whereby movement is reduced to a static point in space. If, for example, I draw a circle on a piece of paper, there are two ways of conceiving of this circle. One is to consider it as the trace of a trail, the story of a movement with a pencil. The other is to see the circle as a bounded point with an inside and an outside. The pathway in this view becomes a place in space. The inversion lies in the folding of the object in upon itself so that it is delineated and contained within a perimeter, set off against the surrounding world, with which eventually it is destined to interact. The memory of the continuous movement of the line in the world that brought it into being is lost. What becomes illegible in Google's 'Translate this page' is the continuous movement of language in the world that produces one or the other translation option. Translation is conceived of as a form of transport rather than as way-faring, as primarily destination-oriented, a process of straight information transfer from point A (language A) to point B (language B) in networks of international communication.

It is precisely this logic of inversion that an ecology of translation must set out to challenge. Just as the major critique of an economics of attention was that it privileged means at the expense of ends without which the notion of attention was meaningless, similarly, to see languages as purely instrumental without considering the ends to which they are employed is to allow strategies of legibility to be employed in ways that may be deeply damaging to human flourishing. Mary Louise Pratt and Vicente L. Rafael have detailed how the 'weaponization' of language in contemporary forms of warfare, notably in counterinsurgency practices, is rooted in instrumentalist concepts of translation and foreign language learning (Pratt 2009: 1515–1531; Rafael 2012: 55–80). More broadly, it can be argued that what an ecology of translation must seek to do is to make available or communicable the commons of language itself. In his 12 axioms of attentional ecosophy, Yves Citton lists as axiom number 12 *Apprendre à valoriser les propriétés de fond* (Learn to value background properties) (Citton 2014: 260). Part of the project of political ecology has been to make subjects aware of the importance of the 'commons', the water, air, climate, traditional knowledge and know-how, those things that are shared and because they are shared are 'grounds' rather than 'figures' in individualistic regimes of value. They are not the focus of attention because in neo-classical or neo-liberal regimes of thought they do not 'figure'. Paying attention to what is in the background is re-calibrating attentiveness to produce new regimes of value that prize what we have in common if only because it is these things that ensure our common survival.

Language is one of those things that humans hold in common and although or because it is what humans use to speak about the figures of their attention (every time we open our mouth it is to talk about what, for some reason or another, has caught our attention) its role can too often be perceived to be the neutral, background medium that facilitates the plain speaking of information exchange. The logic of inversion which feeds the automated, instantaneous paradigm of language transfer keeps language firmly in the background. Reco-vering the Language Commons is about developing an ecology of translational attention that brings the wayfaring of language and cultural movement to the fore. In other words, in the contemporary digital moment, it is about exploring translation practices in everything from translators' blogs to fansubbing to see how attention is drawn to the processual complexity of language and culture as they move across global attentionscapes. This ecology of translational attention is also concerned with how routinised, unreflective or narrowly utilitarian notions of language impoverish the Language Commons and deplete the expressive resources of future generations.

Transition

If the ecology of translational attention has not received the attention it should, it may be something to do with the nature of the act of translation itself, a trait that it shares with ecology in the present moment, namely the importance of the transitional. Blaise Pascal in his *Pensées* was not particularly hopeful about the constancy of affection. One day you wake up and the other is no longer the beloved but a complete stranger:

> He no longer loves the person he loved ten years ago. I think: she is no longer the same nor is he. He was young and she also; not she is totally different. He might still love her as she was then.
>
> (Pascal 1993, II, 123)[7]

For the French philosopher the fickleness of human affections demands the durability of divine love. Underlying Pascal's description of the hapless lovers is a particular way of viewing events which is central to Western ontology. One moment the couple are in love, the next they are not. I am sitting or I am standing but I cannot be doing both at the same time. Otherwise, I am in the realm of the paradoxical. The work of *logos* is to determine. The more the object is determined, the greater the sensation of the object's existence. As Hegel notes, as long as pure Being is indeterminate, it is indistinguishable from pure nothingness. It is a pure void. There is nothing to see. Hence, the great movement in Western art in the early and late Renaissance, as E.H. Gombrich has pointed out, to give weight, heft and substance to the world through the determinations of the artist's brush (Gombrich 2007). The difficulty is what to do with or how to think about transitional states.

Aristotle in his *Physics* tries to offer a definition of the colour grey and claims that it is black with respect to white and white with respect to black (V 224b). There is a distinct uneasiness here about what is neither black nor white but something in between. The ontological fixation makes thinking about certain phenomena difficult or problematic. One of these phenomena is, of course, translation which, by definition, is bound up with the transitional, with moving from one state to another. But there are others. Can we say there is an exact moment when people fall out of love? Is there a precise minute or hour or day when I begin to grow old? Am I young at 11.55am and middle-aged at 12? At what specific time did we enter the age of the Anthropocene? Answering any or all of these questions is not easy and suggests that our own specific conceptual traditions may not always be adequate to the experiences that are the lot of all humans. The French sinologist François Jullien advocates the usefulness of looking at other traditions as a way of both revealing blind spots in how we interpret the world and locating repertoires of thinking that allow us to capture important dimensions to subjective and social experience. In his case, he draws on the Chinese term, biàntōng, – which can be variously translated as 'to accommodate to circumstances', 'flexible', 'to act differently in different situations' (Jullien 2009: 26–27) – as a way of thinking about transition in a way that is not beholden to Western ontological assumptions. The two characters that make up the word refer to modification-continuation. At one level, these are opposites but at another each is the precondition of the other. It is thanks to the 'modification' that the process engaged does not exhaust itself but is renewed and can 'continue' and it is thanks to the 'continuation' that the modification can communicate itself, can make sense in the context of the overall process. By way of illustration, Jullien selects one of the abiding themes of classical Chinese art, the passage of the seasons:

> Between winter and spring or between summer and autumn, the 'modification' takes place, when the cold changes and becomes warmer or the warm, colder; as for 'continuation' this can be seen going from spring to summer or from autumn to winter, when warm becomes warmer and or cold colder. Each moment of modification or continuation alternates but even the moment of 'modification' by repairing through the other the factor that is exhausting itself, benefits the other and allows for the whole process to continue.
>
> (27)[8]

From this standpoint, it is not defining Being or substance (winter, spring, summer or autumn) that matters but rather the actual process of change itself. What the binomial term with its polar opposites attempts to account for is the nature and coherence of the transition just as each word I am writing is new (modification) but I am still (I hope) making sense (continuation). Thus, to return to Pascal's example the focus is not on the subject, the lover who no longer loves or is loved, but on the process that leads to this state of affairs or rather that the process itself becomes the true subject of enquiry.

Pascal Chabot in his *L'Âge des transitions* (2015) has argued for the development of a new discipline or interdiscipline of 'transitology', the science and art of managing the transition to more sustainable, resilient and viable economies and societies in order to avoid the irrevocable destruction of the ecosystem. At the heart of late modern culture is what he sees as a toxic cult of maximisation:

> Maximization is a monoculture. Obsessive, it becomes dominant and hegemonic. When only growth is valued, everything else remains in the shade.

Quality, conviviality, pleasure, pride in a job well done, all this is left way behind the main objective. Always seeking the maximum means seeking nothing else. But, it also involves singling out one parameter, for example, a firm's turnover, or television viewing figures or the lowest price for a piece of clothing, and subjecting everything else to the realization of this one aim.

(Chabot 2015: 41)[9]

Chabot, however, warns against what he calls after Gandhi the elitism of means over ends. As the Indian leader once remarked, there is no road to peace, peace is the road. In other words, he is sceptical about forms of political debates that are excessively focused on 'values' as forms of societal ends. It would generally be hard to find a party anywhere in the world that did not profess a belief at some level in democracy, equality and justice. Consensus about ends is widespread. And for that reason, increasingly meaningless. The real differences emerge in the means used to realise those ends. Political struggle shifts from a conflict around the pre-eminence of ends to rivalry around the appropriateness of means. A society can agree that it is a good idea for its citizens to able to move about freely, so free movement is an end, but how? Petrol-driven private cars? Airplanes? Helicopters? Public transport? Trams? Cars? Bicycles? Depending on the choices made, roads are built or abandoned, railways are laid or pulled up, cyclists live or die, pedestrians get to work or lie in intensive care, health expenditure rises or falls. If means, for example, fossil fuels, have changed the world, the logic is that changing the world involves changing the means. It is in this context that translation takes on a particular importance as translation is pre-eminently the 'means' used to bring a work of literature into another culture, to sell a product to speakers of a different language or to convey an important body of thought or set of beliefs into a foreign setting. The ontological fixation and the privileging of ends over means must explain, in part, the long recorded marginalisation of translation practice in the West (Venuti 2008).

Energy

By focusing on means, however, a transitional movement can make clear where choices lead or are likely to lead – and this is the value of history in tracing the trajectories of these outcomes – but it can also open up the black box of corporate or political power by revealing what means (human/environmental) are used to put the burger on your plate or the coat on your child's back or the iPhone in your pocket. Part of this investigation as we shall see in more detail in chapters two and three is to investigate what translation means are used to drive industrialised food production or the exponential growth of consumerist cultures. In other words, translation as means can become complicit in a culture of extractivism, a culture which has been defined by Naomi Klein in the following terms:

Extractivism is a non-reciprocal, dominance-based relationship with the earth, one purely of taking. It is the opposite of stewardship, which involves taking but also taking care that regeneration of life and future life continue [...] It is the reduction of life into objects for the use of others, giving them no integrity or value of their own – turning living complex ecosystems into 'natural resources', mountains into 'overburden' (as the mining industry terms the forests, rocks and streams that get in the way of its bulldozers).

(Klein 2014: 169)

Extractivism has long been bound up with the history of imperialism, the peripheries feeding the imperial workshops of the world. Relating to the world 'as a frontier of conquest – rather than as home' fosters a particular kind of colonial irresponsibility where there is 'always somewhere else to go to and exploit once the current site of extraction has been exhausted' (170). It is indeed in the context of the ideology of extractivism that we might think about the notion of energy itself. If we reflect on the notion of energy for a moment what is noticeable in the history of thought is a striking silence about the sources of energy.

Whether the slaves as primary energy source of Greco-Roman society or fossil fuels as the main energy staple of the developed world, not many theorists or thinkers in the Western tradition, until recently (Mitchell 2011), have dwelt on the energy sources that power political, economic or social practices. The slave or the steam engine rest in the realm of the unspoken or the unsaid. Slaves, hydrocarbons and nuclear power have the common property of being means. Humans fixated on ends have often been reluctant to speak of them. They remain obscured, concealed in the black box of power. However, as Chabot argues, transitional thought has a different aim: 'bring to light the invisible, reveal the hidden, understand what we consume so as not to become victims of what we consume'[10] (Chabot 2015: 89). If we are defined, in part, by the type of energy that we consume, might we think again about how translation itself is both complicit in the production of particular types of energy but also how translation is itself a form of 'energy' that drives political, economic and cultural systems? Is there a sense in which translation both as practice and as an end product that can be consumed (by being read on page or screen or absorbed through a headset at a conference or on a conference call at a hospital) is a form of energy that drives particular forms of exchange and transformation in our societies? If we bear in mind Jullien's argument around 'silent transformations' and the need to move away from a specific kind of ontological fixity, we might begin to think about translation less in terms of matter and more in terms of energy. This call for a re-evaluation of a particular Western ontological prejudice leads to the reconsideration of another, the secondary position or status of energy in many strands of Western philosophical thinking. As Chabot points out:

This secondarity of energy is typically Western. Unlike the East which has traditionally thought about becoming rather than being, the energies of metamorphosis rather than the stability of substance, subtle fluids, breaths, and chakras rather than about organs and their functions, European thought has only accorded energy a secondary position on the margins of its categories of thought. Its main concern is with the mind-matter opposition which is the primary point around which the collective unconscious is organised.

(106)[11]

Leaving aside the dangers of essentialising East/West distinctions, Chabot's contention is none the less plausible that many schools of thought in Asia have over the centuries privileged thinking about energy over substance (see Allen 2015). There are, however, thinkers in the Western tradition who did take notions of energy and becoming seriously, most notably, Henri Bergson. Bergson argued that humans were not just consumers of various forms of energy which allowed their brains to function and their bodies to survive but they possessed a mind which had on the face of it a peculiar property, 'The mind has a force which can extract more than it contains, give back more than it gets, give more than it has' (Bergson 1959: 838).[12] The mind itself possesses a form of energy that is pre-eminently productive. It creates concepts, ideas, information that were not there before. The creativity of mental energy faces, however, the potential road blocks of language. For Bergson, one of the dilemmas for humans was that language broke up the continuum and the fluidity of experience into crude fragments. Only intuition and the imagination working through art allow humans, in the words of the literary historian Helen Carr, to 'make contact with the ceaseless flux of being' and to renew their contact with the difficult, shifting mutability of experience. As Carr notes, it was this credo of creative energy that drove the architects of European modernism in the early twentieth century:

> Philosophers, artists and writers of the period were coming to understand the world in similar terms: the dead cloak of convention, rationality, factuality, measurement, hid the vital, dynamic, pulsing nature of human life; the rational conscious ego was unaware of its unconscious passions and desires; the unruffled surface hid its tumultuous depths.
>
> (Carr 2009: 162)

Reflecting on translation as an integral part of an ecological revolution of means, a form of creative or transformative energy which brings into being what has not been there before, we might consider two translation moments, one the translation of a particular poem, the other, the operations of cultural mediators in a specific urban setting.

Aucassin et Nicolette is a thirteenth-century *chantefable* written in the dialect of northeastern France. A *chantefable* was a story told in alternating sections of verse and prose. The verse was sung and the prose recited. The American poet William Carlos Williams in his autobiography speaks of discovering the text with his fellow poet, Hilda Doolittle (H.D.): 'I discovered in those days [1905–6], the wonders of *Aucassin and Nicolette*, the prose and the verse alternating' (Williams 1958: 52). Walter Pater in *Studies of the History of the Renaissance*

(1875) had been an enthusiastic champion of the work in translation and he particularly recommended Andrew Lang's rendition of the text in a footnote to the 1893 edition of his influential work (Pater 1893: 10). Ezra Pound who had read an American pirated edition of the translation was similarly enthusiastic. Writing in *The Spirit of Romance* in 1910 he claimed that the story 'owes its immortal youth purely to the grace of its telling [...] Andrew Lang was born in order that he might translate it perfectly, and he has fulfilled his destiny, bringing into his English all the gay, sunlit charm of the original' (Pound 1910: 83–84). For Williams, the 'grace of its telling' was primarily in the form of the romance with the intermingling of poetry and prose which would suggest possibilities for his own poetic creations. Walter Pater, too, had commented on the mixture of poetry and prose but goes on to argue that:

> here, as elsewhere in that early poetry, much of the interest lies in the spectacle of the formation of a new artistic sense. A novel art is arising, the music of rhymed poetry, and in the songs of Aucassin and Nicolette, which seem always on the point of moving into true rhyme, but which halt somehow, and can never take flight, you see people growing aware of a new music in their possession, and anticipating how pleasant such music might become.
>
> (Pater 1893: 13)

The direction that Pater suggests for the romance, rhymed poetry, is not the path chosen by three admirers of Lang's translation, Williams, H.D. and Pound. They will, however, be drawn by the blurring of categories and the need for the 'formation of a new artistic sense' and the search for a different kind of music in poetic language. In other words, there is a distinct sense that the translation is bringing forward or to fruition forms of poetic expression that had not existed before. Lang's translation of the thirteenth-century romance can be said to 'give back more than it gets, give more than it has' in its energetic intervention in the lives and writings of three major American modernists. This shock of the new in translation is allied to the notion we advanced in an earlier work, the 'negentropic translational perspective' (Cronin 2006: 129). The emphasis here is not on the specific entropy of the alleged inadequacy of translation to the task of carrying particular texts across into different languages and cultures or the general entropy of the putative failure of translation to address the challenge of linguistic and cultural homogenisation but to examine how new forms of expression and practice emerge through specific negentropic acts of translation which, in turn, foster the persistence and development of cultural diversity. It is important to note here, however, that the shock of the new referred to above involves a text from the thirteenth century written in the almost extinct dialect of northeastern France. One could argue that translation repeatedly breaks with the *linear* logic at the heart of conventional understandings of progress and development narratives and points to the *cyclical* logic of ecological regeneration.

The preoccupation with commemoration that is particularly prevalent in contemporary Western societies (West 2015) provides a clue to the enduring hold of a linear logic that is troubled by translation. Cultures of commemoration are deeply implicated in an understanding of what constitutes a historical event. There is non-being one moment, being the next. One minute the troops are going over the top of the trenches, the next minute, they are dead. The historical event has the dual advantage of structuring narrative and creating dramatic tension, essential components of the mythologising moment. Cultures of the event are driven by the mythologising impulse. And no event beats death. The notion of being towards death is, of course, a recurrent staple of the European philosophical tradition, what Jullien has described as 'this fascinating, apocalyptic, culminating moment, *towards* which, everything converges and will suddenly be resolved, where finally tearing apart the veil the longed for Truth will be revealed' (Jullien 2009: 60).[13] This is hardly surprising in that death represents a kind of absolutising of the ontological alternative – the Hamletic to be or not to be. Moreover, the Incarnation, when the Word is made Flesh, culminates in the death of Christ on the cross, *mythos* and *logos* conjoined in an apocalyptic moment of revelation where time is radically configured to embrace the linear, forward step of *anno domini*. Christ cannot die on the cross twice so the Good News is about singularity not repetition. What, however, if we shift our conceptual grid and move away from the ontological conservatism of event-based linear logic and begin to think about cyclical progresses of regeneration? Just as Williams, H.D., Pound and Pater will, in a sense, recycle Lang's translation of a late medieval text are there ways in which translators or translation networks recycle the cultural, social or political energies in a society?

Antwerp in Belgium in the nineteenth century was a city that was predominantly Dutch-speaking but where the language of education and culture was mainly French. This situation would change in the twentieth century with the political movement in favour of the language rights of the Dutch-speaking majority and the advent of Dutch monolingalism in the Flemish city. Reine Meylaerts and Maud Gonne explore the role of 'cultural mediators' in the context of a city riven by linguistic, cultural and political tensions. Meylaerts and Gonne define these cultural mediators as individuals who undertake a range of discursive transfer techniques:

> They are multilingual authors, self-translators, or translators who translate, adapt, plagiarize, summarize, censor, manipulate etc. in various ways a variety of products of allophone linguistic communities: poems, novels, songs, theatre plays, opera librettos, serial novels. In this way, they serve as discursive bridges between these linguistic communities.
>
> (Meylaerts and Gonne 2014: 136).

They are active in a variety of intercultural and inter-artistic networks and they are often, though not exclusively, 'hybrid' persons, 'who develop transfer activities in several geo-cultural spaces' which considerably sharpen their 'international and intercultural consciousness' (136). Meylaerts and Gonne go on to argue that the lives and activities of these cultural mediators demonstrate that:

The complex transfer practices that characterize multilingual contexts cannot be fully understood by translation studies' classical binary concepts (author vs. translator, original vs. translation) since they prevent us from seeing the complexity of both the mediators' role and their mediating practice.

(136)

What these mediators are engaged in is a process of allowing ideas, thoughts, conceptions, proposals, art forms to circulate from one linguistic and cultural space to another but also in a negentropic way to generate at a meta-level the city or urban community, in this instance, as a translation zone where linguistic and cultural energies circulate. By considering the wide range of discursive transfer techniques or the 'complex transfer practices' in multilingual contexts, what we are being asked to consider is not so much the substantive identifiable products of translation (though these, as we shall see, are very important) as the actual flow of translational energies across different forms from magazine editorship to bilingual criticism to self-translation and translation. The actual production of translations which is focused on in more canonical forms of translation history (in line with the substantive ontology of Western thinking) can tend to occlude the *translation continuum*, those range of discursive transfer practices engaged in by mediators, which is better captured by a means-centred, energy-focused notion of fluid exchange. In the case of the cultural mediators from Antwerp singled out by Meylaerts and Gonne, Georges Eekhoud (1854–1927) and Roger Avermaete (1893–1988), their translation work *sensu stricto* takes on its importance in the context of a wide range of writerly and language activities in and between the two languages of the city and that takes in everything from chairing meetings of editorials boards to writing novels in one language about communities speaking another. Both Eekhoud and Avermaete engage in forms of self-translation. Eekhoud, writing under a telling pseudonym Gabriel d'Estrange, together with the Flemish Dutch-language author Jules Hoste, produces a novel in serial form eventually published in book form as *Brusselsche Straatzanger: Vaderlandsche roman uit de XVIe eeuw* (1897). This is translated by the authors themselves into French around the same time and published under the title *Le petit mendiant ou le chanteur des rues bruxellois, grand roman patriotique du XVIè siècle*. Avermaete's debut novel in Dutch, *Een voorbeldige vrouw* (1924) is his own translation of a novel he wrote in French and published under the title of *Une épouse modèle* a year earlier. Eekhoud's writing in French, his primary language of expression, was often viewed negatively by Francophone critics as tainted by the exotic traces of Flemish dialects. As one critic put it, 'one might say that the author thinks in Flemish and translates himself into French'[14] (Gauchez 1910: 31). Avermaete, on the other hand, strives to avoid any 'typically Antwerpian language mixture' and '[t]he language of both versions, the Dutch and the French, is strikingly pure, without any language interferences' (Meylaerts and Gonne 2014: 143). What we have, in both instances, are examples of materials, previously written in one language, either Dutch or French, and recycled into another through the medium of self-translation. The target language of translation may to a greater or lesser extent reveal the traces of the translation but what concerns us here is that translation can be viewed as a *renewable*, a form of cultural and linguistic energy that can be recycled through different forms and that adds to rather than depletes the linguistic and cultural resources that a society has at its disposal. This is not to predict specific outcomes for the translation process itself. That is to say, the ultimate effects of the activities of cultural mediators may be to sharpen or make more precise the definition of boundaries and prepare the way for the dominance of one language rather than the other, as ultimately happened in the Antwerp of Eekhoud and Avermaete. This does not detract, however, from the fact that the 'complex transfer practices' themselves are negentropic practices that point to translation as a form of renewable cultural energy. These practices allow materials to circulate between languages and cultures even if the substantive outcomes of these forms of circulation are always dependent on the social, political and economic forces at play in the city and the wider society. What we will now move on to consider is what happens when a fundamental source of energy – food – becomes entwined in the twin logics of translation and ecology.

Notes

1 D'un côté, le territoire des sciences dures qui se firent par trop *inhumaines* avec leur conception de l'objectivité et leurs certitudes modernes; de l'autre celui des sciences de l'homme et de la société qui se firent *anti-naturelles* en mettant en avant comme le propre de l'Homme et des sociétés humaines le fait de s'arracher aux déterminations et fatalités naturelles et en conférant à 'la société' sa totalité autosuffisante.

2 l'objet de l'industrie est l'exploitation du globe, c'est-à-dire l'appropriation de ses produits aux besoins de l'homme, et comme, en accomplissant cette tâche, elle modifie le globe, le transforme, change graduellement les conditions de son existence, il en résulte que par elle, l'homme participe, en dehors de lui-même en quelque sorte, aux manifestations successives de la divinité, et continue ainsi l'oeuvre de la création. De ce point de vue, l'industrie devient le culte.

3 Si vous gagnez, vous gagnez tout. Et si vous perdez, vous ne perdrez rien. Gagez donc qu'il est, sans hésiter.

4 En collectant de gigantesques masses d'attention à l'aide d'une petite quantité d'attention multipliée par des dispositifs techniques d'automatisation, les industries culturelles bénéficient d'une énorme PLUS-VALUE ATTENTIONNELLE, résultant de *la différence entre l'attention prêtée et l'attention reçue*.

5 L'écologie *biophysique* de nos ressources environnementales, l'écologie *géopolitique* de nos relations transnationales, l'écologie *socio-politique* de nos rapports de classes, l'écologie *psychique* de nos ressources mentales dépendent toutes de l'écologie *médiatique* qui conditionne nos modes de communication.

6 'degré d'existence d'un être à la quantité et à la qualité des perceptions dont il fait l'objet de la part d'autrui.'

7 Il n'aime plus cette personne qu'il aimait il y a dix ans. Je crois bien: elle n'est plus la même, ni lui non plus. Il était jeune et elle aussi; elle est tout autre. Il l'aimerait peut-être encore, telle qu'elle était alors.

8 La 'modification' intervient de l'hiver au printemps, ou de l'été à l'automne, quand le froid s'inverse et tend vers le chaud, ou le chaud vers le froid; la 'continuation',

quant à elle, se manifeste du printemps à l'été, ou de l'automne à l'hiver, quand le chaud devient plus chaud ou le froid plus froid. L'un et l'autre moment alternent, de modification ou de continuation, mais même celui de la modification, en réparant par l'autre le facteur qui s'épuise, opère au profit de son autre et sert à la continuation d'ensemble du procès.

9 La maximilisation est une monoculture. Obsessionnelle, elle devient dominante et hégémonique. Quand la seule croissance est privilgiée, les autres paramètres restent dans l'ombre. La qualité, la convivialité, le plaisir, le goût du travail bien fait, tout cela passe loin derrière l'objectif premier. Chercher toujours le maximum, c'est obliger à ne chercher rien d'autre. Mais, c'est ensuite, abstraire d'un système complexe un seul paramètre, par exemple le rendement pour une entreprise, ou l'audience pour une télévision, ou le prix le plus bas pour un vêtement, et soumettre le fonctionnement de l'ensemble à ce seul objectif.

10 'porter au jour l'invisible, montrer l'enfoui, comprendre ce que nous consommons pour n'en être pas les victimes.'

11 Cette secondarité de l'énergie est typiquement occidentale. Contrairement à l'Orient traditionnel qui a pensé le devenir plutôt que l'être, les énergies de métamorphose plutôt que la stabilité de la substance, les fluides subtils, les souffles et les chakras plutôt que les organes et leurs fonctions, la pensée européenne n'accorda à l'énergie qu'une place seconde en marge de ses catégories. Le principal, pour elle, reste l'esprit et la matière, dont l'opposition constitue le noeud majeur sur lequel l'inconscient collectif se greffe.

12 'L'esprit est une force qui peut tirer d'elle-même plus qu'elle ne contient, rendre plus qu'elle ne reçoit, donner plus qu'elle n'a.'

13 'ce point culminant, fascinant, apocalyptique, *vers* quoi, tout converge et se dénouera subitement: où se révèle enfin, déchirant le voile, la Vérité attendue.'

14 'l'auteur [...] pense, dirait-on, en flamand et se traduit en français.'

2 Eating our words

David Inglis and Debra Gimlin have no doubts about what food means for humans: 'Food lies at the very heart of human existence. Just as the individual person must eat, so too does any form of social order have to organize the production, distribution and consumption of foodstuffs' (Inglis and Gimlin 2010: 3). Greater concern in cultural analysis in recent decades with notions of the body, materiality, situatedness and discourse has meant that much is brought to the table of culinary inquiry:

> we grapple with concerns about the animate and the inanimate, about authenticity and sincerity, about changing familial patterns, about the local and the global, about whether sexual and alimentary predilections tell us anything about ourselves, about colonial legacies of the past for those of us who live in stolen lands, about whether we are eating or being eaten.
>
> (Probyn 2000: 3)

Our mouths can, of course, be used for two activities, eating and talking. It is no surprise then that a notable characteristic of human communities is the ready association of cuisine and chat. What Alastair Pennycook and Emi Otsuji dub 'commensality' (2015: 114), eating together, is rarely conducted in silence, unless there is a specific religious prescription to forego conversation. Not only do humans talk while eating but they talk a great deal about eating. The rise of celebrity chefs such as Jamie Oliver, Gordon Ramsay and Nigella Lawson, the success of television shows like *Masterchef* or *Come Dine with Me*, the record sales of cookery books, are evidence of the relentless appetite for talk about appetite. When Elspeth Probyn mentions the 'local and the global' in the context of food, she is pointing up the inescapable paradoxes of the globalisation of food with the proliferation of ethnic 'eateries' in urban centres the world over and the consequent dissemination of dishes and foodstuffs across the planet. Given that many languages are spoken on the planet what are the translation consequences of the movement of food across languages? From the standpoint of an ecology of translation, in what ways are the fortunes of translation bound up with the economy and organisation of global food production? Do we need to differentiate between a culinary cosmopolitanism that is bound up with upwardly mobile practices of the consumption of ethnic food and the 'multi-culturalism of the home – where "home-building" may be constructed around the preparation of particular dishes representative of certain migrant community cultures' (Pennycook and Otsuji 2015: 117)? Ghassan Hage's phrase 'eating the other' (1997: 126) captures the ambivalence of food consumption in the contemporary moment where the translation (spatial, cultural and linguistic) of food across borders creates any number of ethical dilemmas from the fragilisa-tion of local ecologies through industrialised food production to the gendered, insecure, low-paid occupations of migrant workforces with limited access to translation or the dominant language of the host community. It is in the context of food and migration that we might begin to examine the role of eco-translation in thinking about food and language in our contemporary world.

Migration

In 1991 in Orléans, Jacques Chirac, then Mayor of Paris, spoke at a dinner for supporters of his party, *Rassemblement pour la République* (RPR). He eventually got round to the subject of immigration. He conjured up the scenario of a Frenchman and his wife, both working, living in the Goutte d'or district of Paris, and who together earned 15,000 francs. They see on the same floor in their social housing block:

> a whole family, squashed in, with the father, three or four wives, and around twenty kids, and who gets 50,000 francs in welfare benefits, without, of course, working! [*applause*] If you add to that the noise and the smell, well the French worker loses his rag.[1]

> (Chirac 2014)

If the French worker is put out by the sounds and smells of his migrant neighbours, his self-interest reminds him that they are a necessary part of his world. So Chirac later in the speech speaks in glowing terms of the immigrants who run the local convenience stores in French cities: 'Most of these people are people who work, good sorts. If we didn't have the corner shop of our Kabyle grocer, open from 7 in the morning until midnight, we wouldn't have anything to eat in the eve-nings.'[2] Chirac's notorious phrase 'le bruit et l'odeur' subsequently became an iconic tagline for French racism and xenophobia and was the title of a song and an album released by the French rock group Zebda in 1993. When Éric Pittard in 2002 released his film on the 1998 riots in Toulouse, he chose as his title *Le Bruit, l'odeur et quelques étoiles*. However, what is striking about Chirac's remarks is not so much the perverse logic and the cynical populism of his arguments as the centrality of food to his fantasmagoric construction of the migrant other. Bad Migrants cook up foul-smelling stews with their compa-triots in overcrowded ghettoes (*l'odeur*) and Good Migrants (*l'épicier kabyle*) are the indispensable part of the food chain without whom the honest labourer would go hungry. In both instances, Chirac uses food as a way of demonising or glorifiying the other, a natural metaphor to translate the delusional logic of rejection and the unpalatable fact of dependency. What we will suggest in this chapter is that the Mayor of Paris and future French President's choice of image was not accidental and points to a long-established connection between food and migration. More specifically, we will examine how translation operates as a strategic factor in the triangular relationship between food, mobility and culture and how in the age of the Anthropocene, the ecological dimension is key to our understanding of this relationship.

Intralingual translation

From the perspective of Roman Jakobson's tripartite definition of the tasks of translation, intersemiotic and intralingual translation have remained the poor cousins in translation analysis. It is interlingual translation or translation 'proper' (Jakobson 2012: 139) which has remained very much at the heart of the theorisation of translation and intralingual translation generally receives scant if any attention. It is intralingual translation that is very much to the fore, however, in the manner in which language is mobilised in translation to make a crucial difference in the way food or cooking is presented and culturally assimilated. One recent example of the effectiveness of a translational shift has been the meteoric success of the British celebrity chef Jamie Oliver whose television shows, books and successful restaurant chain meant that by 2007 he was already included in *The Sunday Times* list of the 50 richest Britons under the age of 30 and in 2010 he was confirmed as the most influential figure in the British hospitality industry. In his campaign in Britain for a shift to healthier eating in school canteens or his journeys to the United States to encourage people to move away from an excessive dependency on fast food, Oliver has become synonymous with a crusading style of food ecology emphasising the importance of fresh, organic, locally grown produce (Oliver 2013). An integral part of the effectiveness of Oliver's gospel is the vigorous embrace of a vernacular that eschews the formal registers of language, specialised food terminology and foreign appellations to distance food and the preparation of food from the sniffy prerogatives of class privilege. In *Jamie's Great Britain* Oliver inducts the reader into the secrets of making 'Baby Yorkshire puds (creamy smoked trout & horseradish pate)'. The introductory remarks are resolutely informal: 'This is dead quick, so easy and absolutely perfect for a starter – just whack it right in the middle of the table so everyone can help themselves. Your guests will be fighting over it, I promise' (Oliver 2012: 58–59). The tone throughout is deliberately conversational with a studied avoidance of a language specific to the art of cooking. The repeated use of diminutives, 'puds', 'Yorkies', or the studiedly imprecise use of measurements, 'a little thimble', 'a little rapeseed oil', 'a few more chopped chives', or the careful enfolding of colloquialisms into the narrative of the recipe, 'whack it right in the middle of the table', 'It's very important that this mixture has a bolshie attitude', all create a sense of a democratisation of access that is vouchsafed in the language used.

One could argue, of course, that what is happening in the language of food writing is a variation on what happened in the realm of travel writing where the shift from 'modes and manners' narrative to that of the sentimental traveller meant a move away from the objective language of topographical and statistical description of foreign places to the privileging of highly subjective responses to place (Elsner and Rubiés 1999: 1–56). In the construction of the cook as a sentimental, post-Romantic subject, however, one crucial element in food writing is the nature of language itself which carries the dual burden of class and alterity. Indeed it is the perceived connection between the two prestigious forms of ethnic difference – foreign language and foreign food – signalling significant social and cultural capital, which arguably prompts the predominantly intralingual translation at work in Oliver's cookbooks. What is notable, in this context, is the desire to domesticate the otherness of food so even when a non-English term like *pâté* is used in the description of the dish, the diacritics are removed and the word remains stubbornly unitalicised as if the word is reluctant to draw attention to its troubling difference.

This domesticating drive has to be situated in the context of Oliver's explicit embrace of Italian cooking, which, presumably in opposition to the *haut bourgeois* connotations of Michelin-style French cooking, is perceived to be reassuringly demotic:

> Since I was a teenager I've been besotted by the love, passion and verve for food, family and life itself that just about all Italian people have, no matter where they're from or how rich or poor they may be. And that's what I'm passionate about – good food for everyone, no matter what.
>
> (Oliver 2006: 12)

In his book of Italian recipes the names of dishes are first given in English and then in Italian, so a Sicilian recipe is first given as Street Salad and in parenthesis, *Insalata di Strada*. Here the order of translation is reversed with the translation occupying pride of place and the original added as a parenthetical afterthought. The offering of a simple, unvarnished translation 'Street Salad' is partly in opposition to the untranslated menu offerings of yore where the cultural capital of foreign language acquisition meant that the barrier to understanding what the menu meant was a metonymic reminder of other more damaging barriers in wider society. This sense of the untranslatable as a class putdown is captured in the comment of the American inter-war years political satirist, Will Rogers, who railed at French cooks, 'that put a liquid overcoat, and a non-pronounceable name, on a slice of horse meat and have an American wondering if it's breast of veal or Angel food cake' (Rogers 1931: x). The language as much as the 'liquid overcoat' (gravy) served to conceal rather than reveal. In a sense, what the relentless pursuit of a domesticating, intralingual translation strategy attempts to do is to further a vernacularisation of food culture through a repeated domestication of unfamiliarity. So when Oliver describes the scene in the market in Parma he wants to make it appear different but not so different that you would be leery of eating the salads:

> In Palermo there's a night market called Il Borgo, where all the locals gather to eat at little stalls selling things like chickpea fritters, boiled baby octopus and some stuff that you wouldn't want to eat, like gizzards, spleen and other dirty wobbly things! A lot of the veg stalls have massive cauldrons of boiled potatoes and artichokes to serve to their customers – I guess you could say this is the original fast food – and they tasted absolutely brilliant.
>
> (Oliver 2006: 64)

In not naming the 'dirty wobbly things', the Naked Chef is gently parodying the culinary xenophobia of his implied readership but his overall translation strategy is one that has profound consequences in terms of the acceptance of foreign cooking traditions and ingredients into a particular culture. What underlies Oliver's intralingual translation practice is a paradigm that situates the cooking of others at a spatial remove. In other words, substantial Italian migration to the United Kingdom with the subsequent importation of a particular food culture (Fortier 2000) or the globalisation of Italian dishes (pizza) through the emergence of hybrid Italo-American food cultures (Diner 2003; Levenstein 2003; Ziegelman 2011) troubles a narrative of foreignness that requires domestication. Acknowledging the other to be already there through migration and to having profoundly altered indigenous diets (the ubiquity of pasta on the shelves of British supermarkets) complicates any easy assumptions about translation as a practice of transfer or a carrying across. Intralingual translation in combatting particular forms of exclusion (*haute cuisine* and Michelin snobbery) can practise other forms of exclusion (migrant cooking is never here but over there) that are no less insidious for being cheerily familiar. From an ecological perspective, the connections are concealed in an imaginary reconstruction of Here and Over There. The disavowal of connectivity leads to another form of thought that is equally hostile to more open forms of connectedness, the tyranny of transitivity.

Recipes for disaster?

When Giorgio Vasari in the second edition of *The Lives of the Artists* decided that he would pay attention to what the Venetians were doing, he noted something different about Titian (Tiziano Vecellio). Titian was indeed a great master but a master of a peculiar kind:

> Although many have been with Titian to learn, the number of those whom one could truly call his disciples is not large; so that he has not taught much, but has imparted more or less to each one according to what they have known what to take from his own paintings.
>
> (Vasari cited in Hale 2012: 605)

The scene in Titian's studio may not be radically unlike the setting of many translation classrooms. One of the great disappointments of the life of a student of translation is translation pedagogy. We do not mean by this incompetent instructors, poorly prepared class materials or overcrowded seminar rooms. What we have in mind is the initial expectation that translation is basically a set of recipes, a set of carefully coded instructions that if followed to the letter will produce the perfect translation soufflé. Of course, an instructor, teaching technical translation, for example, into English can point to certain recurring grammatical features of technical English such as use of the passive voice, nominalisation, use of the third person, empty verbs, the present tense and so on. Part of the enduring popularity of contrastive stylistics on translation courses for the French-English language pair, for example, was to do with the manner in which the seemingly systematic formal shifts in translating from one language to the other (English predominantly verbal, French predominantly nominal) could be paraphrased into failsafe formulae while rendering a text in one language in another. The difficulty is that few texts satisfy the prescriptive expectations of these translation recipes and very quickly the instructor must resort to other modes of instruction.

In a sense, the horizon of expectation in the translation pedagogy class with the default paradigm of the recipe somewhere in the background is hardly surprising in view of a deep rooted Aristotelian prejudice that informs both cooking and translation alike. From an Aristotelian perspective in order to create anything you have to bring together form (*morphe*) and matter (*hyle*). In this hylomorphic model of creation, form came to be seen as imposed by an agent with a particular design in mind and matter itself was passive and inert, that which was imposed upon (Kirby 2011). The extraordinary success of Albertian principles in architecture, the rise of the printing press and the Faustian energies unleashed by mass production seemed to be incontrovertible proof of the validity of the hylomorphic model where the architect's blueprint, the printer's hot plate and the manufacturer's cast were the tangible proof of the power of a preconceived design to be imprinted many times over on supine matter (Cronin 2013: 67–69). In this transitive model of production, human activity is regarded as the instrumental outcome of preconceived plans.

What happens in the translation classroom, however, troubles this semantic regime of identicality. Each student may have an idea of what the translated text should look like but no two students will produce exactly the same text or, if they did, we would immediately suspect plagiarism. The instructor going into the classroom, even if armed with a fair copy, will in a great many cases find that the work of collaborative translation will throw up translation possibilities that he or she had ignored. No fair copy survives the contact with other translators intact. It is this pedagogical experience that brings us back to Titian's studio and the kitchens of his Venetian residence in the Biri Grande. As James Elkins points out in his volume on *What Painting Is* painters have always been very similar to alchemists. Alchemy, in Elkins' words, is the 'old science of struggling with materials, and not quite understanding what is happening' (Elkins

2000: 19). Painters have always done this, struggling with their knowledge of substances to try and produce something new. The social anthropologist Tim Ingold takes Elkins' reasoning somewhat further and argues, 'As practitioners, the builder, the gardener, the cook, the alchemist and the painter are not so much imposing form on matter as bringing together diverse materials and combining or redirecting their flow in the anticipation of what might emerge' (Ingold 2011: 213). We could add to this list the translator who brings together the materials of language, combines and redirects their flow in the anticipation of what might emerge.

The difficulty is that credit has accrued in the Western tradition to the hylomorphic model as opposed to the 'textility of making' (211) proposed by Ingold. What the popularity of programmes like *Come Dine with Me* or *Masterchef* attest to, however, is the repeated failure of the hylomorphic model which indeed accounts for the narrative interest of these programmes. It is because recipes are never enough, no matter how diligently they are followed, that what the contestants may have planned in their head has no guarantee of ending up on the plate. It is in the actual making of the food, in the weaving into being, so to speak, of the dish, that the textility of cooking becomes apparent. In this respect, cooking and translation are practices that run counter to predominantly hylomorphic conceptions of human activity and to the tyranny of transitivity that has long dominated Western notions of production.

The anti-hylomorphic logic of cooking and translation equally informs debates around migration and integration. A reason for the persistent inclusion of language in citizenship tests in many countries in Europe and the rejection of translation services for migrants is that mastery of the host language facilitates integration. A leitmotif of populist agitation around migration is that immigrants, or in particular, referring back to Chirac's earlier remarks, certain kinds of immigrants, racially profiled, refuse to or are unwilling to 'integrate' fully into the society. The author and commentator Zia Haider Rahman writing in *The Sunday Times* sees all 'hope of escape lost in translation':

> It's a shocking figure: more than £100m was spent in the past year on translating and interpreting for British residents who don't speak English. In the name of multiculturalism, one Home Office-funded centre alone provides these services in 76 languages [...] The financial cost is bad enough, but there is a wider problem about the confused signals we are sending to immigrant communities. We are telling them they don't have to learn English, let alone integrate. Worse by isolating them linguistically, we have created communities that are now incubators for islamo-fascism.
>
> (Rahman 2006)

As the editorial writer put it in *The Irish Times* of 6 October 2007, 'Use of a common language is the most potent tool in facilitating integration within any society'. Host language use and proper integration become fused in the disavowal of translation. However, the difficulty lies in deciding what it is that one is being integrated into. In other words, is integration a hylomorphic operation where the authorties have a *morphe* of citizenship (language and background knowledge tests) which is then impressed upon the *hyle* of the migrant subject to produce the final product of the integrated citizen? Is it not precisely this kind of hylomorphic logic that is contested by translation where the paths of movement from one culture to another are multiple and continuous and cannot be reduced to the fallible recipes of the authoritarian faircopy? Does not the textility of cooking itself reveal the flawed transitivity of hermetic models of integration as in the case of the role of Korean and Chinese migrants from former Japanese colonies whose peddling of thin wheat-flour noodles by the 1990s had paved the way for the 4.5 billion servings of instant ramen every year in Japan, that is, 40 servings per head per year (Laudan 2013: 310)? What the food-translation nexus points to in the context of migration is that rigidly construed understandings of integration falsify the intrinsic permeability of language, culture and identity. This nexus becomes not only more relevant in the context of potentially dramatic increases in the number of climate refugees on the planet (National Geographic 2016) but also in terms of how meaning and ecology become central to the problematic of food translation.

Mutability

It is not uncommon for organisers of academic conferences to propose extracurricular activities for the participants. If a conference was held in Bologna they might organise a class on how to make a *piadina*. The reason would be obvious. This particular type of flatbread is traditionally associated with the Romagna region and in particular with Forlì-Cesena, Ravenna and Rimini. If the conference was held in Dublin, participants might be invited to make their own coddle, a stew-like dish made from salty bacon, pork sausages and potatoes or if it was in Marseilles, participants might try their hand at making the famous fish stew known as *bouillabaisse*. Underlying all of these dishes is the notion of an association with place. They are organically connected with a specific area or region. Thus, the distinctness is as much to do with spatial and temporal location – a particular place, a particular history – as it is to do with the ingredients and manner of preparation of the dish. Indeed, it is the very connection to place that underlines the notion of the *appellation d'origine contrôlée* with respect to wines. If a sparkling wine is not produced in the Champagne region of France it cannot be called champagne. The concept has now been extended to cheeses, butters and other forms of agricultural produce. Among the items listed in the Unesco Register of Items of Intangible Cultural Heritage is the Mediterranean diet defined as

> a set of skills, knowledge, rituals, symbols and traditions concerning crops, harvesting, fishing, animal husbandry, conservation, processing, cooking, and particularly the sharing and consumption of food. Eating together is

the foundation of the cultural identity and continuity of communities throughout the Mediterranean basin.

(Unesco 2014)

The Mediterranean diet is linked on the Unesco register to Cyprus, Croatia, Spain, Greece, Italy, Morocco and Portugal. What is implicit in the control of origin is that there are limits to *translatio*. It is, in fact, the very untranslatability of these items of food and drink that constitute their specificity. Champagne that is not produced in Champagne is not champagne. The very fact that food words often appear as calques in a language – burrito, kebab, pizza, *un hamburger, le christmas pudding* – would appear to testify to the almost ontological link between food and non-translation.

When we look, however, at the beverages menu of one of the world's most successful fast food chains we notice something odd. The American company Starbucks turns out to be one of the most zealous promoters of the Italian language on the planet. A customer will typically be presented with a list of drinks that includes Caffe Americano, Caffe Latte, Cappuccino, Caramel Macchiato and Cinnamon Dolce Latte. The accents may be missing and the juxtaposition of caramel and *macchiato* might fill a native-born Italian with a mixture of horror and puzzlement but there is no gainsaying the implicit connection between branding and zero translation. The distinctiveness of the product is that the name remains in Italian. The only translation consists in paraphrase, where the composition of a drink might be described in definitional terms as, for example, 'espresso with steamed milk, topped with a deep layer of foam'. One could argue, then, that what we have in this example, is the omnipresence of a foreignisation translation strategy in the lives of the millions of Anglophones on the planet who take in the undigested remainder of the foreign language each time they sip their rapidly cooling *latte*.

The very prevalence of the Italianate appellations for Starbucks global brands which involves forms of pseudo-translation such as the trademarked *frappuccino* (coffee blended with ice and other various ingredients and usually topped with whipped cream) points up a seemingly paradoxical feature of translation that lies at the heart of the relationship between food, language and ecology. In effect, it is the untranslatability of the food or drink item which becomes the very condition of its translatability. It is because champagne is only produced in one area of the globe that it is drunk all over the world. A precondition of migration, then, is an apparent refusal to integrate, to become other, to lose control of one's origins. Distinctiveness of identity underpins universality of distribution in much the same way as the viral spread of the Irish Pub even if, in the case of the Irish alehouse, there is no legal constraint with respect to the region of production. If we look more closely at this seeming paradox other features of translation emerge which link the activity more directly to aspects of contemporary ecology and society. These aspects might be loosely grouped under the headings of mutability, commensurability and identity.

Bruno Latour has referred to scientific facts as 'immutable mobiles', where the specific configuration of facts and context must be held in steady state if they are to reach their destination safely and make sense on the receiving end (Latour 1987). Analogous to the scientific example is the case of the Portuguese merchant ships wending their way from and to Lisbon and Calicut in the fifteenth and sixteenth century which managed to retain their shape because a network was established which remained stable. The network enabled the ships to move and be maintained so that when the vessels anchored in the Indian or Portuguese ports they were to all intents and purposes the same ships.

By way of contrast with the immutable mobile is the 'mutable mobile' exemplified by the Zimbabwe bush pump (de Laet and Mol 2000: 225–263) and which we discussed a number of years ago (Cronin 2006). The reason for the success of this kind of water pump is that it is never quite the same from one village to the next. Bits break off and other bits are added on, the set-up varies from one village to the next. In other words, there is no stable network working hard to keep everything exactly in the same place, the pump changes shape but still the pump remains recognisable as the Zimbabwe bush pump. So the object moves not because a particular configuration keeps its shape invariant but the pump is itself a fluid object. The version of space through which the object moves is a fluid one, namely, one where the connections holding the object change gradually and incrementally (bits are added on, bits break off) which means that the object is both the same (recognisable as the bush pump) and different (configuration changes from village to village). There are obvious parallels here with translation where translation is about communicating in the words of Aram A. Yengoan 'simultaneously both difference and similarity of meaning' (Yengoan 2003: 41). As Maria Tymoczko has argued in her 'metonymic' theory of translation, translation almost invariably involves selecting some features over others which then metonymically stand in for the whole text. In other words, translators break bits off and add bits on, as they carry the text from one field of language and culture to another (Tymoczko 1999: 55). Is there a sense in which the intensely migratory nature of food cultures that would seem to be defined by their inherent resistance to migration relates to the status of food as mutable mobile?

The most common complaint of Italians abroad, whether as long-term migrants or passing tourists, is that what passes for a *cappuccino* or an *espresso* is a joke just as you would be hard put to find an Irishman or woman who has a good word to say about the pint of Guinness they might consume in Nairobi or Adelaide. They suspect that what the rhetoric of the untranslated conceals is the fact of translatability. Food is not an immutable mobile but a mutable mobile. The meat, the sauce, the pasta, the water that will be used to produce a *spaghetti bolognese* will differ from London to Toyko to Cape Town even if the term in Roman letter or Japanese characters suggests immutability. Migration, mobility involves mutability. There is no *translatio* without transformation, translation. To put it differently, the fiction of the untranslated masks the inevitability of the translated and the status of both food and translation as subject to the regime of the mutable mobile. Indeed, part of the competing discourse around the offering and the presentation of food is to do with an enduring ideology of non-translation or immutability where restaurants will claim to offer 'authentic' Indian or Italian or Lebanese or Chinese cuisine. Or food critics will promote a return to original flavours or recipes or traditions (as demonstrated by the upsurge in interest in French 'regional' cooking (Willan and Ruffenach 2007)), where forms of metropolitan or social mediation are dismissed as corrupt, mutable translations of the basic, immutable culinary text.

More particulary, as we have argued elsewhere (Cronin 2013: 67–69), given the extraordinary prestige enjoyed by the semantic regime of identicality in Western modernity, it is not surprising that whether it is a question of food or translation, there is a persistent desire to control origins to mask the Original Sin of Translation. In the context of food ecology, the industrial paradigm of McDonaldisation at its inception, for example, was the replication of the identical. Its promise was the same standard of burger no matter where it was consumed. Big Mac fed off a fantasy of zero translation which was inevitably dispelled by the global spread of the product which induced different forms of local translation. Mobility, migration brought mutability inevitably in their wake. As Rachel Laudan notes, it now becomes possible to navigate the globe via different declensions of the hamburger:

> A bulgogi burger? Seoul. A rice-bun Mosburger? Tokyo. A McTempeh burger? Jakarta. A McPork burger with Thai basil? Bangkok. A mutton burger? Delhi. A shammi kebab burger? Pakistan. A burger on a bap? Edinburgh. A McGarden burger? Stockholm. And a McHuevo? Well, it must be Montevideo, Uruguay.
>
> (Laudan 2013: 308)

Notions of mutable mobiles and fluid spatiality connect translation and cooking to forms of migration that are by definition types of transformative practice. Law and Mol observe that:

> A topology of fluidity resonates with a world in which shape continuity precisely *demands* gradual change: a world in which invariance is likely to lead to rupture, difference, and distance. In which the attempt to hold relations constant is likely to erode continuity. To lead to death.
>
> (Law and Mol 2003: 6; their emphasis)

Situating translation in the context of migration and food as a mutable mobile that operates within a topology of fluidity puts paid to the conventional habit of dismissing translation as being nothing more than a synonym for loss, deformation, poor approximation and entropy. This entropic view of translation finds expression in numberless conference papers where the default value is that translation is an immutable mobile. Two texts are then compared to show that indeed the text has moved to another language and culture (it is mobile) but that it has failed to remain immutable (bits have been added and taken off, it is not the same). Locating translation as an essential element of any concept of what it means to cook in a globalised, migratory world means avoiding the originary fetishism of food as a mutable immobile and acknowledging its status as a thoroughgoing mutable mobile.

Food ecology

Wendy Espeland and Mitchell Stevens have pointed out that commensuration is central to contemporary forms of capital commodification and the functioning of modern bureaucracies. From key performance indicators to the emphasis on deliverables and impact, it does not count if it cannot be counted. Espeland and Stevens note that the efficiency of bureaucracies and economic transactions depends on a standardisation between disparate things which reduces the relevance of context. In other words, 'commensuration transforms qualities into quantities, difference into magnitude' (Espeland and Stevens 1998: 323). One area, of course, where commensuration in all its forms became most immediately obvious was in the industrial production of food. We noted earlier in the case of McDonalds the relentless drive towards standardisation in the fast food industry (see also Schlosser 2001). What is equally noticeable, on the other hand, with the emergence of the Slow Food movement (Petrini 2007) is a reaction to the relentless homogenisation of the production and consumption of food. We might argue that what we have with respect to incommensurability in food translation – the untranslatable that generates endless translation which we saw with the example of 'cream cheese' in chapter one – is an invitation to consider food and translation in the context of political ecology. The connection to place implicit in the notion of the '*origine contrôlée*' echoes a concern with place already evoked in the previous chapter.

The notion of place has attracted much attention in recent years as theorists try to account for notions of specificity and difference in the high tide of liquid modernity. The geographer Doreen Massey has challenged the ready equation of place with particular communities as the traditional notion of bounded and coherent social groups becomes ever more difficult to sustain in practice (Massey 1994). The linguists Ron Scollon and Suzanne Wong Scollon suggest the notion of 'geosemiotics' which offers an 'integrative view of these multiple semiotic systems which together form the meanings which we call place' (Scollon and Scollon 2003: 12). For the sociologist Saskia Sassen, the recovery of place is about 'recovering the multiplicity of presences in this landscape' (Sassen 2005: 40). What these various perspectives on place share is an opposition to the notion of place as a mere instantiation of space, a location on a surface where things happen. Places are sites of action and interaction, 'articulated moments in networks of social relations and understandings' (Massey 1991: 28). The notion of place, then, as implicated in the dual coordinates of space and time, is emergent, not given. From a translation point of view it is constructed out of what Pennycook and Otsuji have called the relationship between 'location' and 'locution'

(Pennycook and Otsuji 2015: 85). The notion of place and moreover the specificities of place are seen not as the sacred repository of the immutable, as an essentialist bulwark against the corrosion of change. Place is a dynamic construction which is not formless (it has a shape, a specificity) but whose forms are nascent and negotiated not pre-ordained or decreed. Nowhere is this more apparent than in the relationship between food and place where any attempt to locate food must bear in mind prior histories of *translatio*, of the movements across and through space, culture and language.

Yuval Noah Harari highlights the global subtexts to 'ethnic' cuisine. In an Italian restaurant, he argues, you might expect to find spaghetti in tomato sauce, in Polish and Irish restaurants copious servings of potatoes, in an Argentinian restaurant many kinds of beefsteaks, in an Indian restaurant plenty of dishes flavoured with chilies and in a Swiss café thick, hot chocolate smothered in cream:

> But none of these foods is native to those nations. Tomatoes, chilli peppers and cocoa are all Mexican in origin; they reached Europe and Asia only after the Spaniards conquered Mexico. Julius Caesar and Dante Alighieri never twirled tomato-drenched spaghetti on their forks (even forks hadn't been invented yet). William Tell never tasted chocolate, and Buddha never spiced up his food with chilli. Potatoes reached Poland and Ireland no more than 400 years ago. The only steak you could obtain in Argentina in 1492 was a llama.
>
> (Harari 2011: 188–189).

Martin Page notes how the Portuguese mariners brought the method of frying fish in egg batter, *tempura*, to Japan, which the Portuguese had learned earlier from the Roman conquerors of their lands (Page 2002: 42). The fowl served up at the traditional British Christmas dinner owes its name, Turkey, to the adoption by the Ottoman Empire of the 'Spanish Chicken' the Spanish *conquistadores* had come across in the New World (Tapper and Zubaida 2011: 6). Most national cuisines are recent creations and have resulted either from the breakup of modern empires or are 'forged from hierarchical traditional imperial cuisines, particularly Christian, Islamic and Buddhist-Confucian, in which rank, not nation, determined what an individual ate' (Laudan 2013: 324). In arguing for place in an ecology of food translation, we are advancing the case for specificity, and the legitimate defence of that specificity as a contributory element to diversity, but as these food examples show, the notion of the specific or the local is grounded in a profoundly ecological sense of interconnectivity. When *tempura* makes its way into Japanese cuisine, when it is spatially, culturally and linguistically translated into the Japanese home, it becomes a significant and meaningful part of Japanese local food culture but it is precisely the *translated* nature of its presence that reveals a relatedness or a connectedness to elsewhere that resists closure. Lawrence Buell suggests the term 'ecoglobalist affect' to capture the affective dimension of an environmentality in literature which is border-crossing in nature and whose scope is ultimately planetary but which is equally typified by an 'emotion-laden concern with the near at hand physical environment defined, at least partly, by an imagined inextricable linkage of some sort between that specific site and a context of planetary reach' (Buell 2007: 232; see also Kato and Allen 2014). Ecoglobalist affect is to do with valuing place but place as incorporating not repudiating connectedness.

Just as the ecology movement has stressed the importance of locally produced foodstuffs as a way of drawing on local traditions to prevent long-term damage to the planet, one could argue that a similar commitment to situatedness of place and the preeminence of context must underline any form of translation practice considered from an ecological perspective. Investing time and energy in language and cultural acquisition and devoting resources to mother tongue maintenance is essential to a properly complex engagement with place whether that be a small rural community or a vast, urban metropolis. Cultivating polyglossia and intercultural competencies are central to a translational ecology of place. It is this polyglossia and these competencies that in revealing the translational connectivity of place – the foodstuffs, the cooking methods, the cooks that have arrived from elsewhere and been translated into local conditions – make the relational complexity of a site all the more to be prized.

As we have already noted, incommensurability leads to more translation, not less. The more language resists translation, the more it invites translation. Therefore, it is possible to advance the idea that the ability of language to survive and flourish over time and adapt to a multiplicity of pressures – the principle of resilience we mentioned in chapter one – lies in the endless unveiling of the incommensurable in language which calls for new translations, new accommodations. The arrival of new communities, new languages, new foods, generate precisely those kinds of pressures which release the creative potential of the incommensurable.

A core concern of ecology is that we are not alone on the planet and that we are responsible for species destruction on an unprecedented scale. Our food and farming practices have resulted in conditions of existence for other sentient beings which are frequently barbaric and inhumane (Tester 1991). From an ecological standpoint, the principle of relatedness must draw on a post-anthropocentric conception of relatedness. In this conception, inter-species relatedness is central to new, more ethical forms of behaviour (Braidotti 2013). Humans are, of course, not the only species to migrate. Human activities have an enormous impact on the migratory possibilities of other species and our food practices through history have determined the movements of very large numbers of species on the planet (see Wilson 2003). If this relatedness, however, is to become a reality we must invest heavily in intersemiotic translation, to see how translation would feature, for example, in emerging new disciplines such as Animal Studies.

Richard Tapper and Sami Zubaida in their introduction to *A Taste of Thyme: Culinary Cultures of the Middle East* describe the conditions under which food cultures flourished in the Muslim Middle Ages:

Specific forms of 'high cooking' for the upper classes, distinct from the staples of the common people, develop under conditions of diversity of ingredients (based on more advanced agriculture and trade), and a sizeable class of relatively prosperous and adventurous eaters, who adopt an aesthetic approach to food. Writing facilitates the recording, transmission, and ultimately the cumulative refinement of recipes and menus.

(Tapper and Zubaida 2011: 3)

Food is as much a matter of context as of necessity. These contexts are, of course, multiple, but it is significant that Tapper and Zubaida note the convergent effects of economy (agriculture and trade) and technology (writing, agricultural techniques, modes of transportation). It is the conjoined influence of both that allow for the emergence of specific food cultures in the zones of Islamic influence at a particular period. Claudia Roden notes, for her part, that '[t]here is a lot more to food than eating and cooking' and observes, among other things, that '[i]t has a language' (Roden 2011: vii). If food has a language then food that travels must travel through language. Translation, variously understood, needs to be part of our attempt to try to understand how what happens to food in cultures. However, we cannot separate out a notion of translation from precisely those factors – the economy and technology – which have such a decisive influence on contemporary food production and consumption. Nor can these factors be considered as something existing outside the earth's existing and diverse ecosystems.

Technology, translation and food

Erik Brynjolfsson and Brian McAfee in *Race Against the Machine* (2011) and *The Second Machine Age* (2014) point to the increasing disjuncture between economic growth and job creation in many contemporary economies. Even when certain economies such as the US economy began to recover after the Great Recession of 2008, although the growth figures were up, employment statistics remained consistently depressed. The revenue worth of firms and economies were growing but the workforce was not. Increasingly, it is the failure to hire rather than the tendency to fire which is generating joblessness, particularly where populations are growing. Between 2000 and 2010 the population of the United States grew by 30 million. It would be necessary to create 18 million jobs just to create the same percentage of people in the population working as in the year 2000. However, in that period overall employment growth was close to zero (Brynjolfsson and McAfee 2011: 35).

For Brynjolfsson and McAfee the explanation lies in what they call the 'Great Restructuring', the marked shift towards digitalised and automated forms of production in areas which previously would have been seen as the province of the human (9). These are areas involving advanced mental abilities such as pattern recognition capabilities and high-level communication skills. Of the two examples they offer, one relates to driverless cars and the other is to machine translation in the form of the Geofluent chat translation tool from Lionbridge Technologies which allows for automatic translation of messages to call-centre staff in English, French, Spanish, German, Italian, Portuguese, Russian, Arabic, Traditional and Simplified Chinese, and Japanese. The tool promises global communication without tears by improving time to problem resolution and time to purchase for customers:

> The ability to quickly and cost effectively engage and support customers in global markets through an online chat session, regardless of the languages spoken by either the customer or the agent, can increase international revenue, reduce in-country infrastructure and support costs, and build customer satisfaction.
>
> (Lionbridge 2016)

Brynjolfsson and McAfee claim high levels of user satisfaction with the service but do not elaborate on the criteria for satisfaction (other than a vague mention of the ability to carry out 'meaningful action' (Brynjolfsson and McAfee 2011: 15)) or on the specific nature and therefore complexity of the material translated. But their imprecision is not the point. The larger claim about the shift to the automation of higher-level cognitive activities is borne out by the shift in the distribution of income and the advances in technology itself.

In the US, the home of Lionbridge Technologies, the share of income held by equipment owners continues to rise as opposed to income going to labour. While payrolls have remained flat in recent years in the US, expenditure on equipment and software has increased by 26 per cent (45). The expenditure is all the more understandable in view of the exponential growth in software capability. Technological progress is often benchmarked against Moore's Law and the geometrical progression in processing capacity Gordon Moore predicted in *Electronics Magazine* in 1965. However, a much more significant marker of advance is software development itself. Martin Grötschel in a study of computers' ability to handle a standard optimisation problem noted that between 1988 and 2003, effectiveness had improved 43 millionfold. Processors had improved by a factor of 1,000 in the period under study but the algorithmic power of software had increased by a factor of 43,000 (Grötschel 2010).

Brynjolfsson and McAfee draw on a legend around the origins of chess to explain what they believe is happening in the contemporary economy. One of the earliest versions of the story is contained in the *Shahnameh*, an epic poem written by the Persian poet Ferdowsi between c. 977 and 1010 CE (Ferdowsi 2007). When the creator of the game presented his creation to the ruler of the country, the latter was so pleased he asked the creator to name his prize for the invention. The wily inventor asked for one grain of wheat on the first square, two on the second square, four on the third one and so on, doubling the amount each time. The ruler was surprised at what seemed to be modesty of the creator's demands until he realised that it took his treasurer a week to work out how much it would cost him. The inventor ends up with $2^{64}-1$, which is a pile of grains of wheat higher than Mount Everest. In one version, the ruler has the creator beheaded for his ingenuity, in another he is rewarded with the kingship.

The exponential increases in processing and algorithmic capacity means that for Brynjolfsson and McAfee the economy in terms of the automation of higher-level cognitive tasks has now moved into the second half of the chessboard. Not only is the connection between economic value and job creation sundered but predicting limits to computing innovation becomes more problematic as the pace of growth intensifies.

The singling out of translation as one of those activities which is being colonised in the second half of the informatics chessboard echoes well-rehearsed anxieties among translator scholars about the future of the profession in the digital age. Ignacio García has argued that translators are caught 'between the Scylla of crowdsourcing and the Charybdis of machine translation' and that 'the pie for professional translators seems to be shrinking, and the price per word pushing downwards' (García 2010: 4). He further notes that:

> The era of the professional translator as a language-transfer expert is nearing its end. Translation as a skill – which, as with all skills involved in writing, takes a long time to develop – is on the rise; translation as a profession is not. With language-transfer skills alone, the professional will collide with non-professionals taking their jobs.
>
> (6)

Technology then or the Great Restructuring, in the words of Brynjolfsson and McAfee, is affecting translation in profound and important ways. We can think about this in terms of how the profession has responded both in the present and in the past to technological change in terms of thinking through the relationship between translation and technology (Cronin 2013). Alternatively, we can consider how particular domains of human activity, closely related to translation, have responded to technologisation and how these responses in turn recalibrate or resituate the response of translation as a profession and a discipline to the Second Machine Age.

If we return to the core concern of this chapter, one of the primary difficulties faced by both food providers and translator providers is the problem of spiralling demand. The United Nations Food and Agriculture Organisation estimates that the world will have to grow 70 per cent more food by 2050 just to keep up with population growth. One of the predicted consequences, however, of climate change is that the world's arable land will become more difficult to farm (Freedman 2013: 72). Already, the consequence of changing diets and food fashions is that consumers want fresh fruits and vegetables of whatever kind all the year round. Thus, not only is the amount of food required increasing but so is the distance it has to travel. In 1998, 193,700 tons of avocados were shipped to US distribution centres, 75 per cent were grown domestically and 25 per cent were imported mainly from Mexico and South America. By 2012, 713,900 metric tons of avocados were shipped to US distribution centres, 32 per cent were grown domestically while 68 per cent were imported, again mainly from Mexico and South America (Fischetti 2013: 80). If we turn to translation, the demands for translated data in globalised markets are apparently insatiable. In 2012, Common Sense Advisory estimated the size of the translation service industry to be \$33.5 billion and a report by IbisWorld claimed that translation services are expected to keep on growing and reach \$37 billion in 2018 (Pangeanic 2015). These predictions tally with the forecast by the US Bureau of Statistics that the translation industry is likely to grow by 42 per cent between 2010 and 2020 (Pangeanic 2015: 1). The translation service provider Pangeanic concluded that '[g]lobalization and an increase in immigration will keep the industry in demand for the coming years despite downwards costs pressures on the services' (2).

A classic response of the agricultural sector to growing demand for food was the instigation of the 'green revolution'. The beginnings of the revolution are often associated with Norman Borlaug, a scientist with an interest in agriculture. In the 1940s, during field research in Mexico he developed new disease-resistant, high yield varieties of wheat. The combination of the new wheat varieties and mechanised agricultural technologies meant that Mexico changed from importing half its wheat requirements to becoming a net exporter of wheat by the second half of the century. The development of a new variety of rice, IR8, that produced more grain per plant when grown with irrigation and fertilisers was to prove crucial in averting the risk of famine in India in the 1960s. The principal feature of the Green Revolution was the development of high yield varieties of crops that were bred specifically to respond to fertilisers and produce an increased amount of grain per acre planted (Swanson 2009).

The response of the language services sector to growing demands for translation has been the accelerated interest in the technologisation of the word. As Pangeanic put it in their promotional literature, '[t]he advent of machine translation technologies should partly address the lack of qualified, professional translators coping with ever increasing amounts of data' (Pangeanic 2015: 2). Computer-assisted translation, machine translation, translation memories, wiki-translation, all in their various ways invoke technology in dealing with the ever expanding demand for translated text. Indeed, already in 2006, Alan Melby made a prediction that he himself admitted was 'a bit scary', namely, that 'in the future, the only kind of non-literary translator who will be in demand is one who can craft coherent texts that, when appropriate, override the blind suggestions of the computer' (Melby 2006). The computer, firmly established in the second half of the cognitive chessboard, is increasingly called upon to address the hunger for more (translated) language as global societies and cultures diversify in human (migration) and material (globalisation) terms.

Slow language

What of the response to the increasing industrialisation of the production of food and language? How have the strategies developed as a reaction to the growing demand for material (food) and symbolic (language) nutrition impacted on societies? There are many answers to such questions but we might single out one response to the mass production of food, the birth of the Slow Food movement in Italy. In 1986, a demonstration was held to protest at the opening of a McDonald's outlet near the Spanish Steps in Rome. The initial aim of Carlo Petrini and his fellow activists was 'to defend regional traditions, good food, gastronomic pleasure and a slow pace of life' (Slow Food 2015). As the movement gained momentum an International Slow Food movement was officially founded in Paris and it is now present in 160 countries worldwide. Slow Food's policy strategy is outlined in a document entitled *The Central Role of Food*, ratified at the Sixth Slow Food International Congress in Turin, Italy in October 2012. In this document, they lay out the principles of the movement and argue that:

> In the course of time, what first appeared simply as a clever insight – the central role of food as a point of departure for a new form of politics, for a new economy and for new social relations – has become a shared certainty.
>
> (Slow Food 2012: 4)

The main target of their critique has been the industrialisation and massification of food production with the attendant environmental consequences:

> Paradoxical but true, today we are living through a moment in history in which the main threat to the life of so many species is precisely the production of food, the element indispensable for life.
>
> Large-scale food production, agroindustry, monoculture, chemical agriculture – these are the main culprits of the disaster. Sustainable local agriculture based on native techniques and species, which does not make indiscriminate use of chemicals, which does not waste water resources and which is concerned about more than just quantity – this is an effective tool to correct the current situation.
>
> (Slow Food 2012: 11)

Food security, understood as access to a variety of quality foods, is threatened by agricultural systems based on large-scale farming, involving a limited number of products and with little or no connection to local cultures. It is estimated that the global food system now accounts for between 19 and 29 per cent of world greenhouse gas emissions (Klein 2014: 78). Food has effectively become a commodity on which it is possible to gamble and speculate. Above all, 'like other commodities, it has to circulate rapidly and unhindered. In the consumer society in which we live, it is unthinkable for the production-consumption-disposal-production cycle to stop' (19). Allied to the Slow Food movement is *La Via Campesina*, a global network of small farmers with 200 million members who see agroecology as one of the solutions to solve the climate crisis. Agroecology involves the integration of trees and shrubs into livestock fields, the use of solar-powered drip irrigation that delivers water directly to plant roots, the practice of intercropping that involves planting two or more crops near each other to maximise use of light, water and nutrients, the use of green manures and quick-growing plants that help prevent erosion and put back nutrients in the soil (Stone 2014). Olivier De Schutter, UN Special Rapporteur on the Right to Food from 2008 and 2014, has argued that the defenders of industrialised agriculture who claim that local organic agriculture could not feed a planet of seven billion humans fail to understand that agroecological methods outperform the use of chemical fertilisers in boosting food production where the disadvantaged live,

> to date, agroecological projects have shown an average crop yield increase of 80% in 57 developing countries, with an average increase of 116% for all African projects. Recent projects conducted in 20 African countries demonstrated a doubling of crop yields over a period of 3–10 years.
>
> (De Schutter cited in Klein 2014: 135)

Agroecology is a globalised network of local agricultural responses to the planetary problem of food production. If we consider the figures quoted earlier about the growth of the translation services industry and the response of the localisation industry in the form of more extensive deployment of translation technology, it becomes possible to think of food (Agribusiness) and language (Localisation) as partaking of similar industrial strategies to assuage the material and symbolic hunger of humanity.

Is there an equivalent of the Slow Food movement in the area of translation? Has there been a movement that has called into question the potential consequences for language ecology of the mass production of translated language? Is there a perceived need for the establishment of a Slow Language movement and what might it look like in the area of translation? Marilyn Chandler McEntyre in her *Caring for Words in a Culture of Lies* argues that like water, soil, animal and plant species and food systems, words are another precious, shared resource that urgently require good stewardship:

> Like food, language has been 'industrialized'. Words come to us processed like cheese, depleted of nutrients, flattened and packaged, artificially coloured and mass marketed. And just as it takes a little extra effort to and intention to find, buy, eat, and support the production of organic foods, it is a strenuous business to insist on usable, flexible, precise, enlivening language.
>
> (McEntyre 2009: 16)

For McEntyre, the omnipresence of language in our aural environment (television, radio, piped music) and the intense investment in text-based technologies (surfing the internet, sending e-mails, texting on smartphones) means that our 'environment is glutted with words, sung, spoken, written, to be consumed thoughtlessly like disposable products' (18). The all-pervasiveness of the language of advertising, the prevalence of 'spin' in political discourse and the damaging consequences of the use of unexamined metaphors are pointers both to the uncontrolled inflation of language in the private and public lives of people and the toxic effects of this productivism. Thoughtless hyperbole (a child's slightest effort is described as 'terrific'), inappropriate metaphor (using the word 'family' to describe a corporation's workforce) and alarming instances of figurative slippage (the description of war as a 'job' we have to finish) are but some of the effects noted by McEntyre. She advocates among other practices of good language stewardship the need to 'savor and linger over words; that we taste with delight and taken in slowly' and she goes further, arguing that '[m]aybe we need a slow language movement like the slow-food movement that would encourage us to "cook" and "eat" and digest the sentences we share with one another' (83).

It is in the area of food translation itself that we can begin to imagine what a 'slow language' movement would look like, not so much because it needs to come into being but that it already, in some sense, exists. That is to say, food translation points to particular forms of translation practice that would be central to any attempts to formulate a new translation ecology.

The first level at which this operates is what might be described as the translational productivity of food items. This is most immediately apparent in discussions on online forums often generated by migrants and expatriates who are at loss to find a ready equivalent in the host culture for an ingredient they use in the preparation of food. We saw one such example already in chapter one with an American in France trying to find an equivalent for 'cream cheese'. In another such example on a special interest forum for food on the Lonely Planet site, 'bjd' wanted to know was 'creme fraiche [*sic*]' the same as 'sour cream' adding:

> What's the difference? Here in France, nothing is called 'sour cream', so I have been using 'crème fraîche' as a substitute for years. In Quebec, I guess they call it 'crème aigre' or 'crème sure [*sic*]'. But I have noticed lately (including in a very recent post by Fieldgate) that in English people are saying creme fraiche [*sic*]. So, is it very different from sour cream?

The reply to this post from 'textibule' is emphatic, mixing artisanal observations and the virtual imprimatur of Wikipedia:

> Very different, I'd say. I've met expats here in France over the years who have tried to make their own sour cream by adding lemon juice or vinegar or whatever to crème fraîche, but getting the sour cream thing right seems difficult.

From Wikipedia:

> Crème fraîche is a soured cream containing 30–45% butterfat and having a pH of around 4.5. It is soured with bacterial culture, but is less sour than U.S.-style sour cream, and has a lower viscosity and a higher fat content.

European labeling regulation disallows any ingredients other than cream
and bacterial culture.

The name 'crème fraîche' is French, but similar soured creams are found
in much of northern Europe.

The debate is moved outside the French-English language pair by posts from
Poland and Sweden. The Polish contributor named 'piaczka' adds 'Sure can,
bought some smietana [*sic*] 12% today to add to the cheesecake I'll be making
later this evening (greetings from Poland)'. The Swedish post from 'fieldgate'
invokes the Swedish variety of sour cream in order to try and answer the initial
question posed:

> As textibule said, they're very different.
>
> Here in Sweden we have both. Creme fraiche [*sic*] goes under the French
> name, while sour cream is called 'gräddfil' (in free translation 'cream
> sour'). Creme fraiche [*sic*] is much thicker with fat contents 30–34%. That
> makes it good for cooking, like full cream, although there is a difference in
> density and the taste (regular cream is sweeter). Sour cream, or Swedish
> gräddfil, are like Polish śmietana. The fat contents is 12% and the taste is
> mildly sour. It's mostly used in dishes that are not cooked. It can't be used
> in cooking as it would curdle, unless you mix it, before cooking, with other
> ingredients and in certain proportions.

A contributor named 'iviehoff' takes an even more global view of what is at
stake in the discussion:

> As textibule said, they're very different.
>
> Soured cream is not a well-defined substance, it varies around the world.
> Creme fraiche [*sic*] is a soured cream. It is different from other soured
> creams because it uses a different bacterial culture from others and may
> have a different fat content. Different areas of the world use different cultures
> and different fat contents, which results in the variety of soured creams to
> be found around the world.

What becomes quickly obvious is the extent to which even rendering an
apparently simple ingredient such as 'sour cream' into another language and
culture becomes problematic. The attempt to find an equivalent in the other
language is in effect a form of slowing down where attention focusses on the
definitional field of 'sour cream' and the forms of sour cream found in other
languages and cultures. What is striking in the discussion is that the act of
translation foregrounds the buried cultural and linguistic complexity of items that
are frequently taken for granted in the culture of origin. In a concluding post
'field gate', for example agrees with 'iviehoff' that 'Soured cream is not a well-
defined substance' but adds, 'It is, where it's commonly used and has its own
name, like gräddfil in Sweden, or śmietana in Poland'. However, the realisation

of the specificity of the Swedish and Polish varieties is relational, that is to say, it is the act of probing terms through translation which makes manifest what is peculiar to Swedish or Polish sour cream. As the countless online postings and blogs on the translation of food items demonstrate, food translation is an area where the preparation of food, in McEntyre's words above, 'encourage us to "cook" and "eat" and digest the sentences we share with one another', if only because we are not exactly sure what we share with one another and how translation itself might enrich or make more complex the act of sharing.

The second level at which food translation intersects with an emergent translation ecology is, as we have already noted, through a renewed interest in the significance of place or of the local for the production and consumption of food. In *The Central Role of Food* it is argued that 'the local dimension respects the needs of the land, and we can actively support this dimension through the act of producing or choosing the food we eat' (Slow Food 2012: 19). A notable forum for the expression of this 'local dimension' is the elaboration and presentation of food rituals in literature. Understanding culinary codes in literary texts entails both how they signify within the literary texts and how they refer to aspects of social practice from outside the textual world. In the first novel of Naguib Mahfouz's 'Cairo' Trilogy (*Bayn al-Qasryan*, 1956 [*Palace Walk*, 1990]), the boys in the family sit down to eat breakfast with their father. As Sabry Hafez notes, the detail of the morning meal is eloquent:

> The dishes eaten at breakfast reveal the social background of the family and even its national identity. Eggs, *ful mudamas* (brown beans), cheese, pickled limes and peppers and hot loaves of flat round bread for breakfast put the family into the upper stratum of the middle class, while the presence of *ful mudamas* fried in ghee and loaves of flat round bread makes it unmistakably Egyptian, for *ful mudamas* is as Egyptian as bacon and eggs are British.
>
> (Hafez 2011: 265–266).

Understanding the full significance of what is on the table implies a degree of local knowledge that is acquired over time. Thus, one of the recurrent challenges for translators is to decode the language of food in terms of what it tells them about the social setting, cultural background, situation in time (past, present, future), religious or folk beliefs and relationship to the erotic or the aesthetic. Such understanding is not acquired rapidly and points to the necessarily prolonged immersion in a language and culture before the codes are to become in any way legible. This, then, is the other sense in which food translation demands the deceleration of attention, the slowdown of immersive understanding. This is where what we have called elsewhere the 'durational time' (Cronin 2008: 270) of translational understanding and competence comes into conflict with the 'instantaneous' time of industrialised provision. The slow time of effective language acquisition and knowing cultural absorption, exemplified by the linguistic density and cultural complexity of the languages of food in different cultures, point to the ecological necessity of time, care and attentiveness in doing justice in translation to the nuance of local detail.

A third element in the folding of food translation into translation ecology is the implications of the practice for the way in which it subverts conventional representations of translation. We have noted in chapter one how Tim Ingold's notion of the 'logic of inversion' captures a particular dynamic where the labour of translation is concealed in the final translation product. The logic commonly informs the sales pitch of language service providers: 'Instantly understand foreign language content or make your message understood in languages other than English. How? With SYSTRAN products' (Systran 2015). The promise of immediate language transport underlying the marketing hype becomes a common trope in the era of Google Translate. The notion of carrying across words or ideas from location to location would appear to lie easily with the etymological promise in the Anglophone world of *trans-latio*, across-carrying. Indeed, it is arguably the perception of translation as a form of transport that leads to a particular logic of inversion where the translation product is privileged over the translation process. The focus is on destination. How the translation gets there or what happens on the way is of no particular interest. The basic nature of the message, like the traveller seated in the jet plane, should remain unchanged.

When we look at what translators say about what is involved in food translation, a different view emerges, one that challenges the perverse logic of inversion which would put paid to the prehistory of movement and demonstrates a recurrent ecological sensitivity to context. Brett Jocelyn Epstein in an article on translating recipes writes about the difficulties she encountered while working as a project manager for the translation of two Australian cookbooks into Swedish. A major problem was that a number of the ingredients were specific to Australia or to Asian countries near Australia and were difficult to find in Sweden. The publisher's suggested solution was simply to find substitutes. Epstein argued that in introducing substitutes throughout the book without alerting the reader 'the recipes are being changed much more than a translation warrants' (Epstein 2015). The solution, in the end, was to include the original ingredients and a list of possible substitutes. Epstein argues that the substitutive practice itself must be embedded in a wider practice. She claims that translators should stick as closely as possible to the original and if ideas for substitutions are being offered, the translator must explain why.

> Also, the translator or another person connected to the project should try to cook recipes both in their original form and in the version with substitutions, to make sure that the tastes, appearances, smells, and other salient features are preserved.
>
> (Epstein 2015)

For Epstein the practice of translating food is one that involves a whole series of heuristic exercises destined to test the particular outcomes of the choices made or offered in the translation. In other words, there is no way of knowing in advance if particular substitutes are going to work when they are not tried out in the kitchen.

Epstein makes similar observations about the problem of measurements. Cup or grams? Tablespoons or ounces? Measurement practices vary from one food culture to the next. She advocates adapting to the measurement norms of the target culture but warns that this domestication strategy can have unintended consequences. It is not enough to go to www.onlineconversion.com, type in the numbers from the source text and write down what the website offers as a solution. Two cups would be 4.7317 dl, but no one has ever read a recipe that calls for 4.7317 dl flour. In the strategy that she favours, 'Complete replacement means that either the translator or another expert tests all the recipes and shifts the measurements so that instead of 4.7317 dl flour, the recipe calls for 5 dl flour.' Again, the emphasis is on translation as a line of enquiry, a probing of the possibilities of replacement. The translation is a line of movement that feels its way through language and culture, a form of linguistic and cultural wayfaring.

In this respect, it can be more helpful to think of translation not as a '*network* of transport' but as a '*meshwork* of wayfaring' (Ingold 2011: 151; his emphasis). That is to say, the translation of recipes foregrounds an activity that does not involve isolated, discrete points of language and culture, joined by lines of translation, as in the classic network model but more an activity that generates its own momentum and often unpredictable outcomes in its journeying from one food culture to another. The meshwork is open-ended and the praxis of the translator continues on and through any particular task as part of the lifework of the translator. It is precisely this activity that subverts the logic of inversion by pointing to the lines of movement (cooking, experimentation, doubt) that trouble any notion of translation as a discrete, bounded object. These lines in the context of translation ecology and food can lead us in surprising directions.

Intersemiotic translation

As animal breeding and grazing continues to feature in food production in many parts of the world, a central aspect of food cultures is our relationship to animals and other species. Frans de Waal, a pioneer in primatology and one of the leading experts in the area of primate behaviour, claims that it is easier than before to broach the area of human/animal commonality: 'the climate is totally different, and there's a much greater openness to seeing us as animals, as Darwin always wanted and as many other people wanted' (cited in Kenneally 2008: 50). Part of the renewed impetus for the interest in forms of animal communications come from the growth in recent decades in evolutionary linguistics, the branch of linguistics that investigates the origins of human language (Christiansen and Kirby: 2003). Investigating areas of division and overlap in the evolution of communication systems among different species inevitably invites questions as to what are the possibilities and conditions for communications between species.

Investigators such as Sue Savage-Rumbaugh who has been involved for many years in Ape Language Research (ALR) seek to develop interactive forms of communication through language with bonobos. What motivates the research is not the offering of conscious or unconscious cues for the production of unidirectional behaviour but the desire to realise forms of translation through language that make effective or meaningful communication between species possible (Savage-Rumbaugh, Shanker and Taylor 1998). In other words, an implicit concern in animal language research is what might be meant by the notion or practice of translation as it applies or operates between humans and other animals. In this respect, conceptualising the role of translation studies in food cultures means engaging with the vexed question of intersemiotic translation.

From the early technology of the curing of meats and the cooking of food to the scribal transcription of translations using pen and parchment, the fates of food and translation have been intimately bound up with the forms of technology they employ. In the contemporary moment, the Race Against the Machine has produced a wide range of reactions, notably in the area of food production. What is emerging is an explicit and consistent challenge to particular forms of organisation and consumption that are deemed to be both toxic in the short term and unsustainable in the long term. What we are arguing is that food translation – translation of food items, recipes, textual representations of food events – is the bridgehead towards an emergent political ecology of translation that is motivated by concerns around sustainability, resilience and placedness and inspired by paradigms of wayfaring and meshwork that challenge technicist logics of inversion, logics which obscure the labour of the many for the profit of the few. This growing ecological sensibility allows further for a radical re-ordering of the relationship between humans and those others concerned by the global production of food – animals – a communicative re-ordering that must have translation at its centre.

The English poet Robert Macfarlane writes about his fascination for writers who use language as a way of paying specific attention to the landscape. He argues, 'for all of these writers, to use language well is to use it particularly: precision of utterance as both a form of lyricism and a species of attention' (Macfarlane 2015a: 4). As we enter the Second Machine Age with potentially dramatic consequences for translation it is time for translation scholars to consider other areas of human activity that have been profoundly affected by technologisation and to ask whether one of the appropriate responses to change lies in the buried ecologies of specific forms of translation practice. It is more especially a concern with 'precision of utterance' as 'a form of attention' that can point the way to a transformative vision of the possibilities of a translation in the moveable feast of the post-anthropocentric. But what of those other species that have more often been victims than guests at the feasts of the human? In the next chapter, we will consider how translation might conceive of or relate to the non-human.

Notes

1 'qui voit sur le palier à côte de son HLM, entassée, une famille, avec un père de famille, trois ou quatre épouses, et une vingtaine de gosses, et qui gagne 50.000 francs de prestations sociales, sans naturellement travailler! *[applaudissements]* si vous ajoutez à cela le bruit et l'odeur, eh bien le travailler français sur le palier devient fou.'

2 'La plupart de ces gens-là sont des gens qui travaillent, des braves gens; on est bien content de les avoir. Si on n'avait pas l'épicier kabyle au coin de la rue, ouvert de 7 heures du matin à minuit, combien de fois on n'aurait rien à bouffer le soir.'

3 Translating animals

They all agreed. This is when Kay started to act strangely. 'She had been amazingly altered, they felt, by a course in Animal Behaviour she had taken with old Miss Washburn (who had left her brain in her will to Science) during their junior year' (McCarthy 2009: 2–3). After she took the course, nothing was ever the same again. Kay no longer dressed the same way. She no longer used the same language. And her opinions were decidedly different. For the group of young American graduates from Vassar College, New York in Mary McCarthy's novel *The Group* (1963) talking about as opposed to the animals is a risky business. Translation studies would appear to be haunted by a similar nervousness as animals other than the human have been remarkably silent in its brief history. They are not even spoken about, much less spoken to. This silence is all the more unsettling in that the earth has entered the sixth mass extinction of plants and species in the last 500 million years:

> Although extinction is a natural phenomenon, it occurs at a natural 'background' rate of about one to five species per year. Scientists estimate we're now losing species at 1,000 to 10,000 times the background rate, with literally dozens going extinct every day.
>
> (Center for Biological Diversity 2015)

In effect, this means that as many as 30 to 50 per cent of all species would possibly be wiped out by the middle of the twenty-first century. Previous mass extinctions were primarily the result of asteroid strikes, volcanic eruptions and natural climate shifts. In the present instance, human activities are responsible for up to 99 per cent of species loss through habitat loss, the introduction of exotic species and global warming. Due to accelerated changes in the biosphere and the fact that every species' extinction potentially leads to the extinction of others bound to that species in a complex ecological web, species loss is set to increase exponentially as ecological systems unravel (Thomas et al. 2004: 145–148). In the context of this unprecedented (in origin) species destruction, what has translation to offer as a way of thinking about species survival and how might the discipline be altered by a move away from its foundational anthropocentrism?

Human exceptionalism

Before we answer this question, it may be useful to reflect briefly on the relation of a history of human exceptionalism to how humans have thought and continue to think about themselves. In addition, we also need to consider how reconfigured notions of the 'natural' world challenge the primacy accorded to communication as a distinctive attribute of humans. In an interview with the journalist Pierre Gaultier the French philosopher Alain Badiou is scathing about ecology as the new opium of the people:

> To be affirmationist is refusing to be bullied by manoeuvres around 'nature'. It is necessary to state clearly that humans are an animal species that try to go beyond their animal nature, a natural group that tries to de-naturalise itself.[1]
>
> (Gaultier 2009)

Liberation for humans is conditional on forsaking their animality. The farther humans can move from the constraints of their animal condition, the more they enter fully into evolved forms of humanity. The promise of liberation is the emancipation from the merely animal. If Badiou offers a version of Promethean Marxism as a way of breaking the bonds of animality, Ray Kurzweil proposes a vision of the post-animal future more in keeping with the business model of Silicon Valley. For Kurzweil, the Singularity is that point in the near future when the total processing capacity of the world's informatics networks will result in a dramatic collapse of the current anthropological paradigm and lead to the emergence of a higher form of machinic consciousness resulting from the fusion of biology and technology. A specific human consciousness could be uploaded to the Net to be downloaded in the future and integrated into purely artificial or synthetic bodies (Kurzweil 2005; Sonny 2013). In the digital future, human finitude and animal mortality are a thing of the past.

In both of these versions, the choice is clearly laid out for humans, they can choose between the animals they were or the machines they will be. The term that is repudiated, the common denominator of exclusion, is the animal. Central to the discourse of human exceptionalism is the fetishisation of difference. What makes humans human is what they do not have in common with animals. Identity and definition flourish not in commonality but in dissimilarity. For Val Plumwood this repudiation of commonality is the signature tune of an entire culture. The distinctive feature of western culture, and indicative of its ecological failure, is the notion that humankind is radically different and apart from the rest of nature and from other animals:

> This idea, sometimes called Human Exceptionalism, has allowed us to exploit nature and people more ruthlessly (some would say more efficiently) than other cultures, and our high-powered, destructive forms of life to dominate the planet.
>
> (Plumwood 2007)

However, if we turn to the deep history of Chakrabarty and Smail mentioned in chapter one, we arrive at a markedly different notion of the relationship between the human and animal or between the human and the non-human. For Chakrabarty, the possibility of the destruction of the human species through ecological wantonness makes the writing of history problematic as history assumes a continuity of human experience from the past into the present and on into the future. The experience may, of course, change, but without humans, there is no more human history to be written. Only by looking at the long, 'deep history' of the planet can we begin to make sense of why humans have made a difference and how the planet itself is making a difference which could see humans disappear in a mass extinction triggered by human activities (Chakrabarty 2009: 197).

Making sense of that deep history is the structuring principle behind Michel Serres' 'Great Story' (*grand récit*), his narrative of the beginning of the universe until now. This story is comprised of four major events. The earliest event is the origin of the universe itself, the Big Bang that ushers in being. The next event is the expanding and cooling that leads to the emergence of material bodies and galaxies. Then there is the event, more in the realm of biology than astrophysics, where life appears on earth, with the capacity of RNA to duplicate itself and the emergence of multi-cellular organisms. The most recent event is the emergence on earth of *Homo sapiens* and other humanoid species (Serres 2003). As Christopher Watkin notes:

> Properly speaking, these different stages in the story do not form a succession, as if each needed to stop for the next to begin. The universe is still cooling; the earth is still developing and new planets forming; life on earth, and quite probably elsewhere, is still diversifying and proliferating, and human beings are still evolving. It is better not to think of a succession of chapters [...] but one story told by four voices in counterpoint, each successively joining the collective narrative at a specific moment.
>
> (Watkin 2015: 173)

'Nature' is what holds these voices together, nature understood as that which is born, which marks a before and an after, which tells a story of events that are contingent and unpredictable. Humans are part of this story but they do not define it. There is no grand teleological design with humans as the culmination and end point. What is of interest is where humans come in this narrative rather than what makes them distinctive from other beings.

The German theorist Günther Anders noted that one of the responses to the dislodging by Copernicus of humans from the centre of the solar system was an obsessive concern with history, namely human history. The geocentric fall from grace was compensated for by the anthropocentric elevation of the human subject (Anders 2007: 11–18). In the age of the Anthropocene this form of hubris is no longer viable. What becomes apparent is not disjunction but connectedness. Exploring what is held in common becomes a strategy for survival, a precondition for any notion of flourishing. In Serres' Great Story all forms of being have in common that they receive, process, store and emit information. Rowan Williams, the Welsh poet and theologian, argues that the tendency to perceive matter as 'dead' or 'mindless', the passive object of human action, fails to acknowledge the idea of matter itself as inherently symbolic, 'in the sense that it is structured as a complex of patterns inviting recognition and constantly generating new combinations of intelligible structures' (Williams 2014: 103). Taking the example of the genetic code and the genome, Williams claims that implicit in both is the notion that there are genetic material regularities that can be identified as significant by other material receptors:

> A gene is not a small item, not even in the rather refined sense in which we could still just say this of an atom, but a shorthand symbol for a pattern of recurring elements within the ensemble of genetic material activating cell tissues; but it *becomes* a pattern only when there is a receiving and decoding 'partner'.
>
> (102; his emphasis)

For Williams, it is no accident that the life sciences in general, and biology in particular, are littered with linguistic metaphors. Language is the natural inte-grating factor in the evolving material universe. Rather than examining material processes, in a largely mechanical fashion, to establish what language is, it is more useful to attend to language to show us what matter is:

> language exhibits a pattern of cooperative agency in which the structure of life or action in one medium is rendered afresh (translated) in another. The material universe appears as an essentially *symbolic* complex. It is an exchange of 'messages', a universe of coherent process and temporal stability, of form and motion, an *intelligible* universe, because the unfolding story of material evolution leads to speech, to the expression and sharing of intelligible structure, both a communicating of information and a reinforcement of mutual human cohesion which allows more and more creative 'negotiating' with other parts of the environment.
>
> (102)

Ironically, it is the very prevalence of language that can often blind us to the sym-bolic nature of the universe. As the British nuclear physicist David Bohm points out, 'the "subject-verb-object" pattern of many languages leads us to think of active subjects exercising their agency over passive or inert objects' (Bohm 1981: 28). The active semiotics of the organic and the material is obscured by the grammatical hubris of human agency.

Tradosphere

In Serres' account we shift from the idea of 'storytelling' as a human metaphor to account for the non-human world to human storytelling itself as a metonym of a much wider story that encompasses the non-human world. As Christopher Watkin observes:

> to see human storytelling as a metonym of a much broader phenomenon is, as Serres remarks, to decenter narrative with relation to the human, as nature wrests from us our claim to an exclusivity of language use [...] It may be that we can only have access to the Great Story if we translate it into our language, but in that we are no different from any other information processor.
>
> (Watkin 2015: 176).

In this version of ecosemiotics, the world in which humans find themselves is always and everywhere in what might be termed a *tradosphere*. By tradosphere we mean the sum of all translation systems on the planet, all the ways in which information circulates between living and non-living organisms and is translated into a language or a code that can be processed or understood by the receiving entity. By advancing the notion of tradosphere we want to draw attention to two facets of translation activity that demand our attention.

Firstly, whether we look to deep history or the Great Story, we are confronted by a narrative of human/non-human connectedness. The human is inconceivable without the non-human other. That connectedness is based, however, on a practice of translation. We claim to understand our world or to have access to it and to the beings that inhabit it and constitute it through our ability to be able to translate the information they transmit into a language – and this can be the language of mathematics, cosmic physics, molecular chemistry or marine biology – that we purport to understand. Secondly, the tradosphere like the biosphere is in a constant state of evolution and in a time of ecological crisis is susceptible to a series of risks that can threaten its very survival. The biosphere can typically be threatened by climate change, exponential human population growth, biotic impoverishment, reduction of biodiversity or renewable resource depletion, to name but a few factors. In the case of the tradosphere, the principal danger comes from the collapse of translation systems that allow humans to interact in a viable and sustainable way with other sentient and non-sentient beings on the planet. The use of the term 'tradosphere' rather than 'infosphere' here is deliberate in that we have in mind a non-anthropocentric form of communication. In communicating with others, in trying to understand what it is an organism or non-sentient object is expressing, the point is not anthropomorphic projection but communication across and in the full knowledge of radical difference.

Translation is, as Benjamin famously pointed out, a task, a form of labour. Alexander Bogdanov, the general editor of the three-volume translation of Marx's *Das Kapital* into Russian between 1907 and 1910, argued that, 'Nature is what people call the endlessly unfolding field of their labor-experience' (cited in McKenzie Wark 2015: 18). Bogdanov gives the example of energy as something which emerges from the resistance of nature to labour. Energy is not *in* coal or oil but emerges out of the activity of labour on these materials. It is not a thing-in-itself but is a co-production of nature and human labour. Labour in this instance translates material into a form that is understood by humans but this activity of translation meets with resistance. Coal or oil remain obdurately other. It is precisely this translational recognition or acknowledgement of otherness that makes the tradosphere inescapably part of the realm of ethics. That is to say, if we are to take up the challenge from chapter one to develop a translation ecology for 'a transversal entity encompassing the human, our genetic neighbours the animals and the earth as a whole' (Braidotti 2013: 82), then at the heart of our engagement with our genetic neighbours and the earth must be an ethical concern for the well-being and sustainability of the biosphere. Given the shift from the status of biological to geological agency implicit in the notion of the Anthropocene, the burden of ethical accountability is even greater. This accountability can only become operational, however, if we have a translation practice grounded in the different domains of ecosemiotics that make up what we consider to be an intelligible world.

When Arran Stibbe argues that 'Ecology [...] consists of the life-sustaining relationships of humans with other humans, other organisms and the physical environment' (Stibbe 2015: 181), it is difficult to see how these relationships can be sustained without a theory of effective and ethically grounded translation which would allow these relationships to form and root themselves in human con- sciousness. If we do not pay more attention to how we translate the different elements of the Great Story into 'our language', it will hardly be surprising that people will remain deaf to the needs and plight of other species and the state of the physical environment. Empathy demands the solicitude of understanding. It is arguably because we currently lack such a theory that we are witnessing species destruction on an unprecedented scale and that the future of the planet itself is in doubt. However, the type of theory that we have in mind is driven by the shift of perspective outlined by McKenzie Wark:

> *from high theory to low theory.* Rather than imagining theory as a policing faculty flying high as a drone over all the others, a low theory is interstitial, its labor communicative rather than controlling. Its method is some species of détournement, such as tektology or the factory of literature or dada. It refracts effects, perceptions and concepts from one domain to another using whatever apparatus is at hand. The verification of whether a concept holds, or a story applies, is specific to each labour process.
>
> (McKenzie Wark 2015: 218; his emphasis)

The 'low' theory in question here is how to account for inter-species communication in an enlarged or expanded notion of what we currently understand translation to be (Tymoczko 2007). Examining the field of animal communication and human-animal communication we will argue that the concept of translation has been remarkably absent from reflections on animal communication just as animal and human-animal communication have been signally missing from debates around translation. This dual absence needs to be remedied if we are to have a viable theory of translation for the coming times.

Communication

Stephen Hart in *The Language of Animals* offers a summary of the debates that have raged over the centuries as to whether the forms of communication used by animals, their own particular biosemiotics, are in any way comparable to human language:

> Historically, philosophers have contended that language sets humankind apart from the simple beasts. Although all modern scientists fully accept Darwin's assertion that most traits blend from simple to complex, they fall into two camps when it comes to language. One group insists human language bears little resemblance to animal communication, and resists the use of the word 'language' to describe animal communication. These scholars – including many linguists – define 'language' using features of human languages such as creativity, rules and meaning. Another group counters that animal communication grades from simple to very complex – human languages – just like any other trait. They point to monkey and chimpanzee behavior in the wild and to experiments in which great apes have learned to some extent to communicate with humans as evidence that the differences between human and animal languages are differences of degree and smaller than some would like to believe.
>
> (Hart 1996: 7)

For many thinkers and writers, from Descartes to Chomsky (Descartes 1959; Chomsky 1965) the stakes are high. Language is what defines humans, what makes them unique. If in monotheistic religious settings, human uniqueness lay in humans being made in the image of the divinity, in the secular moment it is language that takes on the burden of differentiation. Arguably, in the post-Darwinian world, where human inclusion in the animal kingdom is a matter as much of origin as definition, the pressure on language as a marker of species' difference becomes even more pressing (Beer 2009). Part of this investment in language as human essence is bound up with a lingering nervousness around treating the human as 'animal'. The imperial designation of subject peoples as 'barbarous' or 'savage' is borne out by their alleged animality. As Gerald of Wales, a thirteenth-century propagandist for the Anglo-Norman invasion of Ireland puts it in describing the nomadic native Irish, they 'live on beasts only, and live like beasts' (Gerald of Wales 1982: 93). When Richard Bailey charts the emergence of US English, the catalogue of early colonial dispossession locates the indigenous people firmly in the realm of the plant and animal kingdom:

> English adventurers had penetrated the mystery of the North American continent and had brought back wonders – animals and plants unknown in England, and even people, Manteo and Wanchese, Amerindians brought back to Elizabeth's court as part of the bounty of Walter Raleigh's 1585 voyage to Ronoake Island in present-day Carolina.
>
> (Bailey 2004: 4)

Treating the other as animal means that 'human' rights have no purchase. Hence, many of the energies of political enlightenment and progressive politics were directed towards restoring 'humanity' to subjects and peoples who were subject to brutal, 'inhuman' and degrading treatment. As we have argued in an earlier work, an important element in that effort was translation itself where the dominated subject could through the medium of the translator or the interpreter begin to express their own worldview. Allowing the other to be heard meant moving from the positivist object of colonial experiment to the hermeneutic subject of post-colonial expression (Cronin 2006: 77–78). No longer the mute animal, immured in 'savagery', but the articulate human, voicing her translated anguish.

From the rodent metaphors of anti-Semitism to the cockroach images of the Rwandan genocide, there is a long and toxic history of the invocation of the animal as a prelude to intra-human slaughter. In more recent times, it is fears around what is seen as the neo-Malthusian pathology of deep ecology that prompts a reticence around stressing the animal nature of humans. In this reading of ecology, treating humans as one species among others leads inevitably to the conclusion that the only way to deal with human overpopulation is through the mass elimination of humans. As they would not enjoy higher ontological status than other species, such genocidal practices could be justified by the overall flourishing of species on the planet (Ferry 1992). An antipathy to what are seen as the murderous outcomes of radical ecology is shadowed by a similar scepticism as to the biological determinism of sociobiology, a discipline most notably brought to the fore in the work of Edward O. Wilson, *Socio-biology: The New Synthesis* (1975). The notion that social behaviour can be explained by evolutionary pressures over time with genetic selection of the most successful or viable forms of human behaviour in everything from aggression to mating firmly situated humans in the biological realm of the animal kingdom. For the critics of sociobiology, nature and genome almost invariably took precedence over culture and context (Rose and Rose 2014). History becomes subsumed to biology and the selfish neo-liberalism of genes trumps any notion of human autonomy. All of these tainted histories and currents of critique point to a deep concern with language as a marker of radical species' difference. Translation studies shares this commitment to human exceptionalism as the unique focus of its attention to date has been different forms of human communication.

As we make our way through what has been called in Elizabeth Kolbert's book, the 'sixth extinction' (Kolbert 2014), and consider the question of inter-species relationship in an era of anthropogenic climate change, then the question of language and humans' relationship to other species takes on a new urgency. Christine Kenneally in her exploration of the search for the origins of human languages notes that animals cannot be so readily dismissed as different:

> Many of the animals that demonstrate complicated thinking turn out to have a fair bit in common with one another and with us. Even though

many of them are not that closely related to humans, they share many traits that seem as important as DNA. Hyenas, whales, elephants, humans, baboons, crows and parrots all have long lives, extended periods of childhood, complicated systems of communication, and their societies are made up of individuals with distinct roles and relationships.

(Kenneally 2008: 100–101)

One of the recurrent features of studies on animal cognition is that attributes that are seen as uniquely human are constantly being redefined. Humans play but so do animals. Humans have culture and so do animals. Human make tools but in a study on crows published in *Science* in 2002 it was shown that crows could design tools for specific purposes. Two crows, Betty and Abel, were tested to see if they would choose a hooked or a straight wire to get some food out of a tube. During one of the sessions Abel snatched away the hooked wire from Betty, leaving her only with a piece of straight wire. Betty bent the wire into a hook when she realised the straight wire would not work. She repeated the task nine different times using nine different techniques, trying to ensure that she got the angle just right (Weir et al. 2002: 981).

When it comes to language, as Kenneally notes about researchers in Ape Language Research (ALR), 'you won't find anyone playing down the enormous differences between humans and other animals, despite the fact that they happen to be interested in the commonalities' (Kenneally 2008: 49). By focusing on the 'commonalities', rather than being perpetually preoccupied by locating an absolute watershed of difference, it becomes possible to think about another possible role for translation studies in the age of Anthropocene. Thinking about what our relationship might be to 'complicated systems of communication' we might move beyond the either/or alarmism of certain forms of deep ecology and sociobiology critique to consider how inter-species relatedness could be a form of liberation rather than a discourse of debasement. In particular, we might reflect on how the lessons of translation studies which have focused exclusively on human translation up until now might nonetheless have much to offer in the context of an evaluation of the tradosphere.

If classic Chomskyean theory argued that human language was entirely distinct from the communication that takes place between animals, other linguists are less sure. Philip Lieberman argues that to discount the communicative abilities of other animals is wholly unscientific as trying to decide what are necessary and what are contingent traits for human language is only possible if all forms of communication between species are studied (Lieberman 2006). Border collies, African grey parrots and bonobos have some capacity, for example, for perceiving and understanding words within a semi-continuous speech stream (Kenneally 2008: 152). The voluntary production of sounds which are meaningful to other creatures is not a skill that is confined to humans. Klaus Zuberbühler and Katie Slocombe in an experiment on chimpanzees in Edinburgh Zoo demonstrated that they emitted very different cries depending on the type of food that they found. If they found food they valued highly like bread, they uttered high-pitched grunts;

if the food was less appealing, like apples, they made low-pitched grunts. When recordings of the grunts were played to the chimpanzees, they would spend more time and effort trying to find a given food, particularly if the grunt indicated a type of food that was highly prized (Slocombe and Zuberbühler 2005: 1779–1784). In effect, they were using a sound-referent connection to make and communicate distinctions which is not wholly dissimilar to what humans do when they communicate.

Dolphins use what are known as 'signature whistles' to identify themselves to other dolphins. In their first year, they produce an unique sound that is different from other dolphin whistles and which can allow them to be individually recognised (Janik et al. 2006: 8293–8297). Researchers on the Elephant Listening Project at Cornell University's Bioacoustics Research Program are compiling an elephant dictionary compiled of the distinct sounds produced by individual elephants for different purposes (Poole et al. 2005: 455–456). In all three cases, socially complex species have come up with similar tactics to communicate. Though the vocalisations occur in different social and biophysical contexts (air, water, extended atmospheric and ground pitch range), there is clearly a form of structured and intelligible communication taking place between members of the same species. Animals of different species have also been known to understand the cries that other species make. If a predator hears the alarm call of its prey, it often gives up. They know they have been seen. There is no point continuing the hunt (Seyfarth and Cheney 2003: 145–173).

Underlying discussions around animal communication are various understandings of what constitutes animal cognition. Marian Stamp Dawkins argues that true cognition is not hardwired instinctual behaviour nor learning a simple rule of thumb. Rather it can be said to take place when an animal solves a problem under novel conditions (Dawkins 1998). Guide dogs for visually impaired people can be said to exhibit a form of true cognition in that they learn to respond appropriately in new situations. If they did not they would be of little use to their owners. Elizabeth Marshall Thomas in *The Hidden Life of Dogs* describes how the urban dogs she observed learned that crossing at intersections was dangerous. They could get hit by turning cars. The dogs learned that crossing in the middle of the street gave them a view both ways which was appreciably safer (Marshall Thomas 1996). What the existence of animal cognition and complex forms of communication point to is both the socialised nature of the communication observed to date and the varying capacities of animals to understand and implement new learning strategies. The fact that animals do not appear to have the same productive capacity as humans (dogs may learn new tricks but they do not invent new barks) does not take away from the fact that forms of communication are vital to the functioning and survival of a multiplicity of species. It is in this context that we might ask what would be a proper or effective role for translation as a research paradigm. One could argue that there are three elements to the translational exploration of human-animal communication: the rehabilitation of the animal subject; engaging difference; cross-species agency.

The rehabilitation of the animal subject: As we noted earlier, a standard trope of a particular form of imperial discourse was the silencing of the native subject. By refusing to translate what the native had to say into the language of the master, it was assumed that the native had nothing to say. Refusing the subjects communicative capacity was a way of denying them political agency. A move towards liberation was to give language back to the enslaved, the colonised, the downtrodden. Almost always this involved the move of translation as the subject had to articulate their grievances or their oppression in the language of the master so as to get access to resources or to potential allies or to a wider audience. Words falling on ears deafened by linguistic incomprehension were of little consequence. They require the ally of translation whether through direct textual translation or through the agency of language mediators who brought the news of injustice to a wider or more effective stage.

A condition of empathy was often the making manifest or vocal forms of oppression that were often obscured by language difference, an ignorance often knowingly engineered by imperial overlords or slave masters. Roberto A. Valdéon in his *Translation and the Spanish Empire in the Americas* documents the ways in which the 'individual narratives' of particular translators in the period of the conquest expressed a 'form of resistance against the established order' and goes on to note that 'mediators struggled against the invaders in different ways and for different reasons' (Valdéon 2014: 39). When we look not only at the mass extinction of animals on the planet but also at animal welfare we might ask where are the current 'mediators' who will organise a 'form of resistance' against the established anthropocentric order? In the United States the American Society for the Prevention of Cruelty to Animals reports that close on 99 per cent of all farm animals are raised on factory farms. These farms are focused primarily on profit and efficiency rather than on animal welfare:

> Factory farms pack animals into spaces so tight that most can barely move. Many have no access to the outdoors, spending their lives on open warehouse floors, or housed in cages or pens. Without the room to engage in natural behaviors, confined animals experience severe physical and mental distress. Daily life in a factory farm is one of pain, frustration and misery.
>
> (ASPCA 2015)

One of the challenges in the age of mass extinction and industrialised food production and anthropogenic climate change is the mobilisation of translation to construct a notion of animal subjectivity. That is to say, the exploration of different forms of animal communication with a view to the possibility of inter-species communication must be accounted an urgent task in terms of according other sentient beings not only the dignity of just or equal treatment but of developing a sense of post-anthropocentric relatedness. Just as globalisation presupposed translation as part of its *modus operandi* (Cronin 2003) so it is inconceivable that any viable politics in the Anthropocene can forego a theory and a practice of translation as a working premise if we are to move beyond the lethal objectification of other living beings with whom we share the planet.

Engaging difference: Translation may not be enough. Or rather, translation of a certain kind may intensify not lessen oppression. Eric Cheyfitz captures the slippery duality of translation in the colonial encounter:

> In the beginning, as preamble to and constitution of the act of dispossession, we find the activity of colonization as translation, both in the sense of conversion from one language into another and in a metaphorical and transferred sense. In this case, however, translation means precisely not to understand others who are the original (inhabitants) or to understand those others all too easily – as if there were no questions of translation – solely in terms of one's own language, where these others become a usable fiction: the fiction of the Other.
>
> (Cheyfitz 1997: 105)

As far as animals are concerned this fiction of the Other is deeply rooted in human popular culture. From *Black Beauty* to *The Wind in the Willows* and *Winnie the Pooh* and from Mickey Mouse to Peter Rabbit and Peppa Pig, anthropomorphism has been a constant feature of writing and cultural production, particularly for children (Markowsky 1975: 460–466). Animal speech is routinely translated into human speech. We understand these others 'all too easily' as we relentlessly domesticate animals for a variety of political, educational and narrative reasons. The figure of anthropomorphism is so widespread in writing for children that it is rarely an occasion for comment that such a degree of radical translation should be so widely accepted.

More attention has been paid in recent years to the translation of children's literature into other languages (Lathey 2010) but there has been strikingly little commentary in translation studies on the centrality of the trope of translation to the very operation of the anthropomorphic in children's writing. At one level, it is argued that what this form of translation does is to develop a sense of compassionate kinship between young humans and other creatures. The strange or the alien or the unfamiliar is reassuringly domesticated and initial forms of rejection give way to expressions of sympathy and understanding (Markowsky 1975: 460). Indeed, it has been argued that the spectacular growth in anthropomorphism in children's literature in the second half of the nineteenth century was a consequence of the spread of Darwinian ideas about the animal origins of the human species (Magee 1969). Getting to know one's biological neighbours appeared more pressing as the evolutionary evidence pointed in particular directions. Therefore, the fiction of translation in the form of talking beasts makes the changed circumstances more tolerable.

The faultlines of this translational domestication of the other are cruelly exposed in Werner Herzog's documentary film *Grizzly Man* (2005), which chronicles the life and death of Timothy Treadwell. Treadwell, through his video work and public engagements, had made much of his special relationship with the wild bears in Katmai National Park and Reserve, Alaska. Over the 13 summers he spent there he claimed to have developed a special relationship of trust with the bears to the extent that he could approach and touch them. On camera, he is often shown speaking to the bears and he went on to found an organisation called Grizzly People to protect the rights of bears in US national parks. In October 2003, on his thirteenth visit to Katmai National Park and Reserve in Alaska, Treadwell and his girlfriend Amie Huguenard were attacked, killed and partially eaten by a grizzly bear (Sanders 2008). Herzog's film details the tragic outcome of a fiction of the other that founders on the unexpected turn of the sentimentalised and anthropomorphised other, the grizzly bear, who is later tracked down and killed. Underlying the fate of Treadwell is a cautionary tale about the need for any post-anthropocentric ethics of translation to engage properly with difference.

Eduardo Viveiros de Castro and Déborah Danowski from Brazil explore what it might mean to conceive of the relationship of humans with other species and the physical environment. The anthropologist and philosopher are particularly interested in the manner in which the relationship between humans and non-humans is conceptualised in Amerindian cosmologies. In the worldview of the Amazonian peoples they find an anthropomorphism at work but an anthropomorphism that is radically different from the comforting fictions of Mickey and his corporate menagerie. For many of the Amazonian peoples, the primal substance of the world is human or humanoid and this substance gradually develops into different forms, animal, plant, human. The 'spirits' are those who retain the ontological instability of primordial humanity and can shift between animal, human or plant manifestations. Viewing everything as originally stemming from the human means that humans are not in any sense a species apart. They are not superior to 'nature' because in the Amerinidian worldview the notion of humans as separate from nature is meaningless. This does not result, however, in a joss-stick infused nirvana of cosmic fusion. On the contrary, the humanoid monism of the animist Amazonian peoples means that difference matters. It cannot be assimilated to the delusional superiority of the Human Herrenvolk. A conventional critique of animist beliefs is that they engage in a narcissistic projection of the ego on to the surrounding world but Viveiros de Castro and Danowski argue that it is the 'Moderns' who feed off dangerous illusions of instrumental mastery:

> According to those we call animists, it is, on the contrary, we, the Moderns, who in penetrating into the external space of truth – the dream – only see reflections and simulacra of ourselves, instead of opening ourselves to the unsettling strangeness of relations with an infinite number of agencies, both intelligible and radically other, who are distributed everywhere throughout the cosmos.
>
> (Danowski and Viveiros de Castro 2014: 285)[2]

The dream which is critiqued here is the dream of material well-being, the enchantment of consumption. The external world becomes a mere resource or tool for the fantasmatic projection of human desires. In stressing the distinctness of the 'infinity of agencies' Amerindian cosmologies draw attention to the inescapable negotiation of difference. In the words of Danowski and Viveiros de Castro, for Amerinidian peoples, other animals and entities in the world are 'political entities' (*entités politiques*). What we call the environment is for them 'a society of societies, an international arena, a *cosmopoliteia*' (279).[3] Ecological crisis calls for 'a broad openness to dialogue, a *literally* diplomatic conversation with human peoples and non humans who anxiously observe the beginning of the consequences of the irresponsibility of the moderns' (335; their emphasis).[4]

Translation has always shadowed the activity of diplomacy and the notion of an international or foreign policy in human affairs has implied the training, presence and activity of translators and interpreters (Lung 2011; Baigorri-Jalón 2014). Implicit in Amerindian perspectivism – the notion that the world is inhabited by different sorts of subjects or persons, human and non-human, which apprehend reality from distinct points of view – is *relationship as translation*. Taking seriously the multi-perspectives of lived reality means that a relationship in such a context can only make sense in a translational frame. It is only by recognising the defining difference of the other 'political entities', trying to understand their background, culture, forms of communication that we can begin to engage in the diplomatic dialogue on which the future of the planet rests. It is arguably the refusal of translation, the idea that there is one universal model of economic progress – extractivism – predicated on the *Weltsprache* of GNP and needing no negotiation with differing perspectives, which precipitated the current crisis of the Anthropocene. Accepting that translation is like any diplomatic negotiation – open-ended, unpredictable, subject to change, never complete as circumstances alter and protagonists change in profile and importance – means acknowledging that otherness cannot be wished away in a fantasy of identity or assimilation. One potential danger of the notion of the Anthropocene is that the shift in status from biological to geological agency could perversely feed a particular kind of hubris. *Anthropos* as the Angel of Destiny could once again forget a necessary humility in face of a planet and other non-human entities that remain resolutely other and that have their own perspectives on and investment in planetary survival.

Temple Grandin, a specialist in animal science, who has spent over four decades working with animals claims that 'although in many ways animals are similar to us, in other ways they may be totally alien' (Grandin and Johnson 2005: 248). She mentions the case of a person who had a pet lion that was shipped on a plane. It was thought that for the sake of comfort the lion would like a pillow for the flight, in the way a human might. The lion ate the pillow, choked on it and died. For Grandin the point of the story is 'don't be anthropomorphic. It's dangerous to the animal' (15). Hostility to the assimilationist thrust of anthropomorphism does not mean, however, that relationality is excluded. Rather, human-animal relationships must be understood as reciprocal and symmetrical rather than as non-reciprocal and asymmetrical. The example Grandin gives is of horse riding:

riding a horse isn't what it looks like: it isn't a person sitting in a saddle telling the person what to do by yanking on the reins. Real riding is a lot like ballroom dancing or maybe figure skating in pairs. It's a relationship.

(5)

In the case of horses used in riding schools, she points out that 'learning to ride a horse is completely different from learning to ride a bicycle. The horses make sure nobody gets hurt' (6). If they do get hurt, it is because the relationship has, for whatever reason, either momentarily or permanently, broken down.

In terms of what might constitute the basis for relations, it is useful to bear in mind the structural constraints operative in human-animal encounters. Paul MacLean, in his triune brain theory of the make-up of the human, makes a distinction between the reptilian brain which is similar to that found in lizards and which looks after basic functions like breathing, the paleomammalian brain that handles emotions and corresponds to what is found in other mammals and the neomammalian brain which is found in primates – principally humans – and which handles reason and language (MacLean 1990). Though much is made of the neomammalian brain which is seen as a distinguishing feature of higher primates, both MacLean and Grandin point to the importance of what Grandin (2005: 57) calls the 'animal brain' in humans, namely, the reptilian and paleomammalian. What this means, in effect, is considering what brain structure might tell us about shared animality and how this might influence or shape our potential for understanding other species. On the other hand, animals have sensory capacities that humans do not have: 'Dogs can hear dog whistles; bats and dolphins can use sonars to "see" a moving object at a distance (a flying bat can actually spot and classify a flying beetle from thirty feet away)' (59). Humans, by contrast, have highly developed colour vision which most animals do not possess. The reason for this superior colour vision is to do with the large number of cones in the human retina for the perception of colour. This is a sensory receptor that is possessed by humans but not by other animals.

The different sensory receptors possessed by different species of animals means that some forms of communication are available to them that are not available to other species. Caitlin O'Connell-Rodwell, a research biologist, studying elephants in the Etosha National Park in Namibia noticed that before another herd of elephants arrived they would start to pay a lot of attention to the ground with their feet. The elephants would shift their weight or lift their foot or lean forward. The pads of the elephant feet contain Pascinian and Meissner corpuscles which are special sensors for detecting vibrations. In other words, these sensors allow for the reception and interpretation of what is termed 'seismic communication', where the ground is made to rumble by stomping on it. This form of communication where elephants can communicate with other elephants over large distances (infrasonic sound waves are used for shorter distances) is predicated on the possession of a particular kind of sensory receptor (O'Connell-Rodwell 2007: 287–294). The radical difference in sensory receptors, their possession or absence ruling in or out particular forms of communication, might appear to spell the end of any feasible form of translation. How is it possible to translate what you cannot perceive let alone understand?

What studies in ethology and animal behaviour and zoology point to, however, is that communication is never a given and that the understanding of different forms of non-human communication keeps evolving. As part of this evolving research, the role of sensory receptors has to be accounted for in arriving at any understanding of what is being communicated or how it is being communicated. In developing a theory of translation for inter-species communication the role played by discrete sensory receptors must be factored in so that we enlarge our sense of what it means to communicate and, by extension, what it means to translate. Again, what is apparent is that translation studies must engage with difference to produce difference. Differentiated theories of what translation implies in the age of the Anthropocene must naturally look to the physiological structures of perception and cognition in humans and non-humans.

Part of the difficulty in understanding how an enlarged translation studies might deal with new forms of intersemiotic translation may lie in a problem familiar to researchers working in the field of robotics. One of the common misconceptions around robots is that they should ideally resemble humans in order to be deemed successful. Staccato speech and shambling gait are trademark features of failure, the robots doomed to a life of parodic incapacity. However, as researchers such as Kevin Warwick have pointed out, intelligent machines do not have to look like humans to carry out complex mathematical operations in micro-seconds or to move at very high speed or to do any number of things that are outside the range of normal human ability (Warwick 2011). Similarity to humans is not an optimal condition. These robots are defined by their distinctiveness and it is on the grounds of this distinctiveness that we do (or do not) interact with them. The communication involves the use of different signifying systems whether this be sets of mutually intelligible protocols or programming languages. In a similar vein, Christine Kenneally notes that many different kinds of muscular manoeuvres make human speech possible and these are strictly controlled so that the air pressure created by the lungs stays at a steady level as we speak. The range of extension of the human tongue from the larynx, deep in the throat, to behind the teeth, means that it has many possibilities for changing shape. Every time it changes shape, the vocal tract is altered and the new configuration results in a different sound. Most animals do not possess these physiological attributes with the result that 'if you could transplant a human brain into, say, a horse's head, it would not be able to speak human language, because its mouth and tongue would never make the sounds we do' (Kenneally 2008: 71). If Ed the talking horse is a physiological non-runner, this does not mean that Ed the communicative creature is not at the translation races. Human verisimilitude does not have to be the benchmark of intelligibility. An anthropocentric fixation on human language and those who produce it should not be allowed to prevent scholars from pursuing intersemiotic translation between radically different forms of species communication.

Cross-species agency: If ethical discussions around translation to date have dwelt on the ethical dimension to translation among humans (Inghilleri 2012), it is time we extended this ethical remit to other species. Yuval Noah Harari has argued that some of the most momentous journeys in the history of the planet were the first boat journeys made by humans from Indonesia to Australia around 45,000 years ago. On the continent they encountered an astonishing variety of mega-fauna from a two hundred kilogram, two-metre kangaroo to the giant diprotodon, a two and a half ton wombat. Within a few thousand years of human arrival, these giant creatures were no more: 'Of the twenty-four Australian animal species weighing fifty kilograms or more, twenty-three became extinct' (Harari 2011: 72). The Americas which were a spectacular testing ground for evolutionary possibility were to become in time another graveyard of ecocidal practice. Scarcely two millienia after the arrival of *Homo sapiens*,

> North America lost thirty-four out of its forty-seven genera of large animals. South America lost fifty of sixty. The sabre-tooth cats, after flourishing for more than 30 million years, disappeared, and so did the giant ground sloths, the oversized lions, native American horses, native American camels, the giant rodents and the mammoths.
>
> (79)

In the wake of these mega-fauna followed thousands of smaller mammals, reptiles, birds and insects rendered extinct by their ecological vulnerability. *Homo sapiens* in Harari's words is an 'ecological serial killer' and he notes that half of the planet's large beasts were driven to extinction 'long before humans invented the wheel, writing or iron tools' (80). Clearly, human ecological destructiveness has a long history that predates the rise of what McKenzie Wark (2015: xiv) dubs the 'Carbon Liberation Front'. In face of the overwhelming evidence of species destruction and the reckless use of fire agriculture to clear thickets and dense forest in order to produce open grasslands (Miller et al. 2005: 287–290) with devastating ecological consequences, it is not possible in the deeper history of humanity to idealise the practices of hunter-gatherer cultures. Since humans have been around, the world has never been a safe place for animals. The ethical trace of the failure of communicative engagement with other species, the repudiation of the eco-translator's task, goes far back into human time.

Alongside the large-scale annihilation of species, the agricultural revolution brought the domestication and regular incarceration of a select number of species whose numbers have greatly expanded over time. Ten thousand years ago there were only a few million sheep, cattle, goats, bears and chickens living in restricted Afro-Asian niches. Nowadays, the planet is home to a billion sheep, a billion pigs, over a billion cattle, and more than 25 billion chickens, and they can be found everywhere on the globe (Harari 2011: 104). After humans, domesticated cattle, pigs and sheep are the second, third and fourth most widespread population of large mammals in the world. Domesticated animals have supplied and continue to supply food (meat, milk, eggs), raw materials (skins, wool) and muscle power or energy. In the case of energy, turning bulls, horses, donkeys and camels into pliable draught animals means their social ties and natural instincts have to be broken, their sexuality and aggression restrained and their movement limited. The routine castration of male animals, locking animals in pens and cages, the use of whips and cattle prods and the bridling of animals in harnesses and leashes are among the techniques deployed over time to contain and domesticate animals. On industrial meat farms, calves are separated from their mothers at birth and locked inside a cage not much larger than the calf's body. The calf is not allowed to leave the cage, go for a walk or play with other calves as this would strengthen its muscles and soft, juicy steaks are much prized in many cultures. The calf's first walk after four months is its last, to the slaughterhouse (Humane Society of the United States 2015).

What emerges from the human treatment of animals in the aftermath of the first agricultural revolution over ten thousand years ago is a less than edifying tale of subjection and exploitation. The four other large populations of mammals inhabiting the planet are regularly at the mercy of attitudes and practices that are clearly inhumane, particularly, as we noted above, on industrialised factory farms. A dimension to inter-species translation then is the ethical responsibility implicit in caring about and responding to the conditions of treatment of other large animal populations on the planet.

There is a sense, of course, in which translation is already being used not so much to give voice to as to silence the suffering of animals. This is notably through a form of intralingual translation where the reality of the treatment of animals is mediated through a highly abstract, instrumentalised, technocratic language. A particularly telling example is provided by Stibbe where he cites two sources, the first a Walls Meat company manager and the second, a document from the US Department of Agriculture. Both describe the role of the sow in agribusiness:

> The breeding sow should be thought of as, and treated as, a valuable piece of machinery whose function is to pump out baby pigs like a sausage machine.
>
> (cited in Stibbe 2015: 153)

> If the sow is considered a pig manufacturing unit then improved management at farrowing on through weaning will result in more pigs weaned.
>
> (cited in Stibbe 2015: 153)

What is notable about the first description is the brutal, metaphorical reduction of the breeding sow to a reproductive sausage machine whereas the second description uses the abstracted language of techno-economic utilitarianism to capture the position of the sow in the chain of production. Though both mask the reality of the plight of a living animal, it is the intralingual translation of language to a higher register and more formal expression in the Department of Agriculture document which is arguably more damaging. By creating an even greater distance from the experience and conditions of animals in the agribusiness the danger of ethical disengagement is increased. The all-pervasive use of a form of intralingual translation to conceal or minimise animal suffering is hardly surprising in that it is part of a more general move in contemporary societies that we have noted in chapter one to promote ends (food on your table) over means (how it actually gets there). Cultivating sensitivity to these intralingual moves, unmasking the euphemising translation procedures, is a way of opening the 'black box' not only of food production but of inter-species relatedness. This is a prerequisite of any attempt to cultivate a cross-species ethical or political agency which would appear crucial to the notion of collective ecological survival.

This sense of cross-species agency cannot be separated from the embedding of translation in the digital universe that will be explored in the next chapter. How does this manifest itself? One example is provided by the work of Con Slobodchikoff, a US researcher in animal behaviour, author of *Chasing Doctor Dolittle: Learning the Languages of Animals* (2012) who has spent over thirty years decoding animal communication. In one study Slobodchikoff had initially wanted to look at the social behaviour of Gunnison prairie dogs but soon became aware of the translational possibilities of the dogs' alarm calls: 'the alarm calls turned out to be a Rosetta stone for me, in the sense that I could actually decode what information was contained within the calls' (Garber 2013). He made extensive recordings and carried out a statistical analysis on the alarm calls of around 100 of these dogs and cross-referenced the acoustic qualities of the animal cries with the circumstances in which they were uttered. The natural contexts would help provide clues as to the meanings of the different sounds. Slobdod-chikoff discovered that the prairie dogs have word-like phonemes that they combine into sentence-like calls. They have what appears to be social chatter but which he was unable to decipher or translate due to inadequate context and they use vocalisations to distinguish between different kinds of predators based on species, size and colour. The next stage for Slobodchikoff was to cooperate with a colleague in computer science to make a computer record of the different calls, analyse them with AI techniques and then have them rendered into English. The process could then be reversed to produce a call comprehensible to the dog. For Slobodchikoff this research could open up a new future for ubiquitous translation technology. It would be possible to develop devices the size of a mobile phone:

> that would allow us to talk to our dogs and cats. So the dog says 'bark!' and the device analyzes it and says, 'I want to eat chicken tonight.' Or the cat can say 'meow,' and it can say, 'You haven't cleaned my litterbox recently.'
> (Garber 2013)

The animal communication specialist is suitably humble about the complexities of the underlying research claiming that a decade's more research might be necessary to allow translation back and forth between 'basic animal languages'. Working in a country where 40 per cent of households have dogs and

33 per cent have cats, he sees the implications of animal translation research as 'world-changing':

> What I'm hoping, actually, is that down the road, we will be forming partnerships with animals, rather than exploiting animals. A lot of people either exploit animals, or they're afraid of animals, or they have nothing to do with animals because they don't think that animals have anything to contribute to their lives. And once people get to the point where they can start talking to animals, I think they'll realize that animals are living, breathing, thinking beings, and that they have a lot to contribute to people's lives.
>
> (Garber 2013)

Citing a figure of four million dogs that are euthanised each year because of 'behavioral problems', he claims that 'most problems are because of the lack of communication between animal and human'. Implicit in the development of the translation technology envisaged here is the creation of a sense of cross-species solidarity, a new kind of transversal subjectivity, that would contribute to a sense of transformative planetary agency. The difficulty with a brand of cyber-utopianism in translation is of course that it can ignore or minimise notions of cultural difference, intentionality, semantic mapping, consciousness, ambiguity or connotation, the often intractable problems posed by does the other mean what I think they mean or are they saying what I think they are saying? Maria Tymoczko notes that difficulties relating to underdetermination of meaning are particularly acute in the case of texts from very different cultures, texts from the past and texts in dead languages:

> Often most difficult to construe are texts that are radically decontextualized in some way, for instance, by having uncertain authorship, provenance or dating. Scholars of antiquity, medievalists and translators of the Bible and other scriptures struggle with underdetermination of meaning all the time, but translators who work with any textual material from a culture that is significantly different from their own are likely to face similar questions.
>
> (Tymoczko 2007: 301)

The problem of underdetermination of meaning would appear to be even more problematic when we consider translation between different species. But the problems of underdetermination have not prevented scholars of antiquity, Bible translators and medievalists from doing their work. If the perception of the difficulty was to lead to the cessation of all translation of scriptures, medieval texts, or texts from dead or remote languages, the historical and cultural loss would be immense. It is precisely because the history of translation theory and practice has involved an extended reflection on dealing with and conceptualising the difficulties of underdetermination of meaning that translation has much to offer to any attempts to construct a paradigm for inter-species translation. More particularly, scholars in translation studies have centuries of expertise in the area of translation that is at present wholly unknown or unrecognised in the field of the life sciences and which could arguably make a significant contribution to broadening understanding in a wide range of disciplines from biology to zoology. The notion of cross-species agency is not simply to forge a new understanding between different species but also to favour a new dialogue between different disciplines.

Disciplines

Climate change is unintelligible without a range of analytic categories. Biochemistry, DNA, evolutionary developments, the formation of rocks, the construction and deconstruction of ecosystems, land use patterns, plant, animal and human migration, demography, economic equality, food science, political organisation, are just some of the perspectives that have been brought to bear on efforts to account for the origins and consequence of changes to climate across the globe (Edwards 2010). The age of the Anthropocene is rendering increasingly obsolete the disciplinary divisions of high modernity with the 'soft' social and human sciences on the one side and the 'hard' life and physical sciences on the other. The antagonisms of the Holocene need to be reassessed. The notion of the social construction of nature becomes highly problematic when the planet is the site of a whole series of profound changes that have literally brought humans back down to the earth. There is the realisation that there is much that they do not control or understand no matter how persuasive the constructions they have developed. On the other hand, the idea that a natural science can 'naturalise' humanity by reducing the human agent to a set of natural causes becomes more and more difficult as the 'natural' world proves to be saturated by the presence of the human in the form of anthropogenic climate influence. The twin poles of social constructivism and material reductionism prove to be as unhelpful as the founding fiction of modernity, the deep division between Human and Nature. For Bruno Latour, the anthropos that the geologists have pushed centre stage is not the passive entity which used to be found in older narratives full of 'natural' causal agents. It is a being that is inevitably endowed with a moral and political history:

> To the great surprise of those who had tried to paint the human agent as a bag of proteins, computerized neurons and selfish calculations, it is as a *moral* character that human agency is entering the geostory of the Anthropocene.
> (Latour 2014; his emphasis)

The strict delimitation of what is the realm of 'nature' and what is the realm of the 'human' no longer holds. The human, for example, has become a 'natural' force capable of effecting geological change but there is nothing 'natural' about this development. It is the result of a history and a history where there is not one undifferentiated 'human' but a multiplicity of humans with very different degrees of responsibility for climate outcomes. Not only are the divisions inherited from modernity not particularly relevant anymore but the change in the perception of where we find ourselves lends a new relevance and urgency to what we do. Latour argues that one of the consequences of the collapse of the old distinctions is that, 'It is all the disciplines that are now fighting with the urgent mission of assembling humans on newly defined territories' (Latour 2014). In other words, from soil chemists to urban geographers to media studies theorists, the scale and calendar of projected climate change lends an urgency and a renewed relevance to a plethora of different disciplines which must be mobilised transversally to cope with the demands of the new age. Translation studies, in this respect, is no different from any other discipline. However, there is one difference that does make a difference.

Translation studies, like the discipline of anthropology that is a primary concern of Latour, is centrally focused on what might be 'common to all humans and what is specific' to different groups of humans (Latour 2014). The question of what is 'common to all humans' in translation studies is situated at two levels: one, is there a level of universal meaning or intelligibility that allows texts or spoken language to circulate from one language to another in a way that makes sense? Second, are there universals in the practice of translation itself so that irrespective of the language pair certain patterns intrinsic to the act of translation itself become apparent (Susam-Sarajeva et al. 2014: 335–352)? What is 'specific' is equally a matter of pressing concern as translators have to negotiate the specificities of languages, cultures, text types, institutional arrangements, historical legacies, political pressures, faith systems and technical infrastructures. In effect, every translation undertaken involves a continuous dialogue between the 'common' and the 'specific'.

Just as the relationship between 'human' and 'nature' needs to be reconceptualised in the Anthropocene so also does this relationship between the common and the specific, between the general and the particular or between the global and the local. Translation like anthropology takes seriously the ontological dimension to human existence, that is, the specifics of where people find themselves as a constituent element of their being. What this entails is what Latour terms a shift from the utopia (no-place) of modernity to the 'relocalization of all the places and sites':

> By this I mean that everywhere the notion of territory is back, and even, that of the soil. And in the same way as becoming a contemporary is not a return to the past of modernity, this relocalization has nothing to do with attachment to the 'terroir'. What is to be reoccupied is not the post Renaissance idea of a territory, that is, a bounded piece of land viewed and ruled from a centre, but very much a new definition of an unbounded network of attachments and connections. It means that the search for *where* we are in space is just as complicated as to find *when* we are in time.
>
> (Latour 2014)

The dual translation fiction of *terra nullius* that translated colonists in large numbers to 'new worlds' and renamed them using the toponymy of the old allowed the utopia of an infinite frontier to be sustained for a number of centuries. Latour argues that 'a completely new definition of "otherness" will come from this other "great discovery" not, to be sure, of a new continent to be grabbed, but of another way for every piece of land' to reside under the feet of those who live there. We shall see in more detail in chapter five how exactly a 'network of attachments and connections' feed into specific places through translation practice but what is of import here is what is implied by the collapse of the infinitely receding frontier of modernity.

What the shift in focus from no-placedness to relocalisation implies is a move from *plus ultra*, more beyond, to *plus intra*, more inward (Danowski and Viveiros de Castro 2014: 312). In other words, a renewed preoccupation with place in the contexts of the limits to carbon growth has major implications not only for the political imaginary but also arguably for the translation imaginary. Perhaps inevitably we tend to think of translation as part of a modernist logic of *plus ultra*. It is the logic that underlies the comments of Alexander Clapp, a freelance journalist, writing about the Anthony Frost English Language Bookshop in Bucharest. Clapp notes that for many years Romania's best known literary figures were either non-ethnic Romanians writing in German or Romanian intellectuals writing in French. He regrets the blindness that this entails: 'there's a group of Romanians today, writing in Romanian, who are worth reading not least for their ability to treat their national catastrophes in the language of under-statement and black humour' (Clapp 2015: 18). Vlad Niculescu, the owner of the Anthony Frost bookshop, argues that the 'problem with contemporary Romanian literature is that far too little gets translated'. Clapp's closing comment is that since he moved to Bucharest he was resolved to remedy this situation. Seeing transla-tion as a way of bringing a literature or a body of ideas or a belief system beyond the boundaries of a language or a nation or a culture is so integrally a part of how we conceive of translation that we rarely give thought to other complementary (not mutually exclusive) ways of viewing the translator's task.

Staying with the notion of *plus intra*, we might ask what would a 'more inward' kind of translation look like. Part of the difficulty in doing this is that the very word itself 'inward' aided and abetted by the intensifier 'more' suggests bleak withdrawal, a shrinkage, a retreat to the bounded and the narrow. However, if we look at the relocalisation or *plus intra* logic in light of the topic of this chapter, we might arrive at a different appreciation of what is possible in the realm of translation. As we noted above the planet is home to very large populations of different species from tens of millions of dogs to billions of chickens. These species are present in human lifeworlds across the planet and frequently live in close proximity to humans. Ecologically, they are part of that 'unbounded network of attachments and connections' that situate us where we are, in relation to ourselves and other species. In this respect, the drive towards inter-species translation is partly informed by this *plus intra* logic, by a desire to give the other beings that constitute place with us an identifiable habitation and agency. The 'inward' concentration on the beings that make up the local place is an opening up not a shutting down, a form of liberation not incarceration.

Ethically, a new awareness of lines of co-dependency, crucial to multi-species survival and local resilience, can potentially follow on from the commitment to local sites of inter-species translation.

Geontology

It is not only living beings, however, that need to be considered in a logic of relocalisation or the development of a *plus intra* translation practice. In the opening pages of this chapter we advanced the term tradosphere as the sum of all translation systems on the planet which includes translation between living and non-living organisms. The concept of deep history by folding history into geology and geology into history means that the physical world, the world of seemingly inert matter is, in fact, deeply animated with narrativity. When the geologist Jan Zalasiewicz writes an entire book about one Welsh pebble, his history ranges from the Big Bang to now (Zalasiewicz 2012). The 'geostory' is not something that is added to a brute, physical reality. The pebble is the accumulated story of its coming into being over time. This sense of what Latour calls 'animation' to capture key qualities of non-human entities on the planet is clearly behind the notion developed by Elizabeth Povinelli of 'geontology'.

The concept stems from Povinelli's experience of working with indigenous communities in Australia where there was no clear distinction between biography and geography, no sense in which one was clearly inside and the other clearly outside. Aware of the fact that the Anthropocene has opened up channels of communication across disciplines and encouraged a new dialogue between the natural sciences, social sciences, philosophies, humanities and the arts, she nonetheless remains concerned that:

> once we begin doing so we find that two presuppositions have been conserved across these severed branches of knowledge, first, the *distinction* between life and nonlife and second *a collapse* of our understanding of being (entities) into our understanding of a particular kind of being, a life being.
> (cited in Coleman and Yusoff 2014; her emphasis)

The disciplinary inclusiveness may generate other forms of exclusion, notably entities that are not 'life beings'. The consequences of this omission are clear in the extractive industries which dramatically alter physical landscapes through the reckless removal of fossil fuels. In this respect, Povinelli argues for a 'geontology' or 'geontopower' rather than 'biontology' or 'biopower' that would be properly inclusive of all elements that make up the planet and would not unduly privilege living organisms. This geontological perspective means that translation needs to be thought of not only in terms of inter-species communication but of forms or modes of communication between all entities on the planet.

The construction of new forms of transversal subjectivity or the development of a *plus intra* translation practice must look to the ways in which entities, living and non-living, enter into contact with and communication with each other and what are the translation practices used in the world of matter. That is to say, that the research findings of materials sciences, physics, chemistry, engineering, geology, to name but a select number of disciplines, in their investigations of the properties and forms of development and communication of non-living entities would become a standard part of the exploration of the tradosphere. Such an expanded research repertoire would mean that for the purposes of eco-translation, 'scientific' and 'technical translation' would acquire different or enlarged meanings. These domains would not only cover the translation of materials normally classified under the broad headings of 'science and technology' but would also investigate the forms of encounter and exchange between different signifying systems in the material world. When C.W. Spinks writes about Charles Sanders Pierce's interest in 'the whole range of signing activity by all living matter, and perhaps even in non-living matter' (Spinks 1991: 170) he is anticipating the challenge of ecosemiotics and the need to develop a form of inquiry into translation which is equal to this challenge. Povinelli believes that a geonotological awareness means accepting 'The human can no longer matter so much' (Coleman and Yusoff 2014). This is not an argument that humans do not matter. They matter hugely. There is no future for the planet unless significant sections of them do not change their ways. It is rather that any notion of the 'humanities' must take account of the 'inhumanities', all those entitites, living and non-living that have been absent from forms and practices of anthropocentric scholarship, including translation.

The necessity for a renewed humility is captured by Latour's notion of the 'Earthling' or the Earthbound of the Anthropocene which is contrasted with the free-floating Human of the Holocene (Latour 2015). Whereas the Human could aspire to the View from Nowhere – the notion of a distant, de-contextualised, 'objective' viewpoint in a world of abstracted, infinite possibility – the Earthbound are coming to the painful realisation that they do not have several Earths to live on but only one. Part of the strategy of survival for Earthlings is restoring ruptured communications with other entities on the planet. The fatal delusion of human independence of the Holocene must give way to the inter-entity inter-dependency of the Anthropocene.

On a march for climate justice in 2015 on the day the historic agreement on climate change was signed in Paris, a young Scottish activist, Laurie King, expressed her belief in the importance of the global movement to halt environmental destruction, '"This is the most important movement of our time [...] The global environmental movement unites everyone across the globe, because the climate has no borders"' (Marlowe 2015: 5). The activist's credo points up the paradox of the moment. On the one hand, climate change is a perfect illustration of the *plus ultra* form of translation that knows 'no borders', whose effects circulate freely around the planet (though, of course, likely to affect some parts more severely than others). The 'global environmental' movement again partakes of the *plus ultra* translation logic bringing together activists from many different countries, speaking many different languages, united by the common language of opposition to perilous forms of anthropogenic climate change. However, translation is not just about ignoring borders, it is also about negotiating them. Not taking 'borders' between species seriously means that they become blank screens for anthropocentric projection and subjection. Not taking 'borders' between living and non-living matter seriously means the relentless pillaging of extractive industries where physical environments are degraded and/or destroyed. Not taking 'borders' between humans seriously means that humans who have contributed only minimally to the current crisis are obliged to bear the same burden as humans who bear an overwhelming responsibility for climate change. Hence, the necessity for a *plus intra* translation logic to accompany the traditional utopian promise of the *plus ultra*. It is in this sense that translation studies with millennia of practice in engaging with borders is a crucial discipline for our times.

A pressing question for Bruno Latour is how to redistribute human agency in the Anthropocene:

> Where is the politics of assembling a character which is pushed to the center but which simultaneously loses its boundary, consistence and definition because it is tied – morally tied – to all of which in earlier times would have been, to use a now famous subtitle, 'beyond the human'?
>
> (Latour 2014)

One answer to Latour's question is translation. Thinking about translation is an essential part of that 'politics of assembling a character' who is centre stage for all the wrong reasons and needs to revisit a large number of fundamental assumptions about what it is to be human and what it is to live in and be part of the world. If part of the language of borders is to do with spatial arrangements the very notion of the Anthropocene reminds us that time too has its own arrangements and that change takes place in and is constituent of time (a before and after the onset of massive carbon emissions). The change is in the direction of change. If before, time was directed by a motion from the present towards the future, now, momentous decisions must be taken in the present in view of potential future consequences. In other words, the reversal of the flow of time means that futurity is not so much a horizon as a precondition of possibility. Translation studies has to engage with planetary futurity as a guide to the priorities of the present. Like Kay taking that fateful course in Animal Behaviour, it needs to be 'amazingly altered' in terms of current orientations but there is, as the old dictum put it, a world to gain. That world to be regained, however, as virtual as it is real, will be the subject of the next chapter.

Notes

1 Être affirmationiste, c'est aussi passer outre les manoeuvres d'intimidation menées autour de la 'nature'. Il faut affirmer nettement que l'humanité est une espèce animale qui tente de surmonter son animalité, un ensemble naturel qui tente de se dé-naturaliser.

2 D'après ceux que nous appelons animistes, c'est au contraire, nous, les Modernes qui, en pénétrant dans l'espace de l'extériorité et de la vérité – le rêve – ne voyons que les reflets et les simulacres de nous-mêmes, au lieu de nous ouvrir à l'inquiétante

étrangeté des relations avec l'infinité d'agences, à la fois intelligibles et radicalement autres, qui sont disséminées partout dans le cosmos.

3 'une société de sociétés, une arène internationale, une *cosmopoliteia*.'

4 'une ample ouverture dialogique, une conversation *littéralement* diplomatique avec les peuples humains et non humains qui témoignent avec anxiété l'arrivée des conséquences de l'irresponsabilité des modernes.'

4   The Great Transition

Gustav Hackendahl, known to himself and others as 'Iron Gustav', cannot get to sleep. In the troubled wakefulness of the early hours he broods over a life gone wrong and concludes, 'The whole disaster began with the grey, with that race. Everything went wrong from that moment' (Fallada 2014: 268). In Hans Fallada's novel *Iron Gustav* the 'race' in question took place when Hackendahl picked up one of his clients, the Geheimrat Buchbinder, in his horse-drawn cab while Buchbinder's son was taken by chauffeur-driven car. Hackendahl wanted to arrive at his destination before the car (both father and son worked in the same hospital in Berlin) but the 'grey' took fright at the noise of the car, bolted and his severely shaken client vowed he would never again travel with Hackendahl. What Hackendahl refers to contemptuously as 'benzine-stinkers' that in ten years would be 'out of fashion' (31) prove on this occasion to be his nemesis. The Berlin race is a micro-parable of motorised modernity, the rapid victory of fossil-fuel technology over the halting susceptibilities of animal traction. In this chapter we will be asking, however, whether indeed 'everything went wrong' on that fateful day in the German capital, whether the success of the car was not so much a rebuke to the cussed conservatism of 'Iron Gustav' as an eerie reminder of the dependency of the modernist romance with technology on the 'benzine stinkers'.

Hackendahl had to contend with the emergence of a new, physical mode of circulation, the automobile. In the late twentieth and twenty-first centuries, the emergent modes are predominantly virtual. It is currently estimated that there are over three billion people connected to the internet. In 2000, around 740 million people owned mobile phones, now six billion people have access to mobile phones, which means 85 phones for every 100 people on the planet (International Telecommunications Union 2015). In the United States, in 1970, an international phone call cost $2.40. The expansion of carrying capacity through the replacement of copper by fibreoptics networks and competition between telecommunications providers meant that by 2004, the cost per minute had dropped to $0.14. In that period the volume of international telephone traffic rose from 100 million minutes to 63.6 billion (Federal Communications Commission 2004). Vastly increased access (though significant digital divides still remain) and reduced cost have made virtual modes of circulation a real presence in the lives of large numbers of people on the planet. The notion of global connectivity is no longer a utopian ideal but a telecommunications fact. In the context of a necessary planetary mobilisation around ecological vulnerability, the digital would appear to provide a seductive template for the possibility of connection and collaboration. As Langdon Winner points out, 'The arrival of any new technology that has significant power and practical potential always brings with it a wave of visionary enthusiasm that anticipates the rise of a new social order' (Winner 2004: 34). In the age of the telegraph when the submarine cable linking the US and the UK was completed the historians Charles Briggs and Augustus Maverick were moved to declare that 'It is impossible that old prejudices and hostilities should longer exist, while such an instrument has been created for the exchange of thought between all the nations of the earth' (cited in Standage 1999: 83).

There is no connectivity, however, without connection. The digital may deliver information to the other side of the planet in seconds but if the language is different, the virtual letters are dead letters. In a multilingual world, translation is the necessary companion for the global outreach of the virtual. For this reason, Ethan Zuckerman, the media scholar and director of the MIT Center for Civic Media, sees translation as an essential feature of a new 'digital cosmopolitanism'. Zuckerman claims, 'It is not enough to be enthusiastic about the possibility of connection across cultures, by digital or other means. Digital cosmopolitanism, as distinguished from cyberutopianism, requires us to take responsibility for making these connections real' (Zuckerman 2013: 30). Part of this responsibility involves a responsibility to language:

> A connected world is a polyglot world. As we gain access to the thoughts, feelings, and opinions of people around the world, our potential for knowledge and understanding expands. But so does our capacity to misunderstand. As we become more connected, we're able to comprehend a smaller and smaller fraction of the conversations we encounter without help and interpretation.
>
> (134)

As more and more material becomes available in languages other than English, Anglophones, in Zuckerman's view, find themselves increasingly provincialised by their linguistic ignorance. Only foreign language acquisition or translation can make the 'connections real'. Translation as a medium of circulation is aligned with the circulatory possibilities of the internet, part of a programme of cultivation and understanding of the multiple perspectives of others. Anijali Joshi, director of product management at Google, offers Zuckerman her own vision of the cosmopolitan possibilities of a translatable internet, '"Once you can search in every language, and you have perfect translation, you have the best content for everyone on the web. That would be Nirvana"' (166). Information, connectedness, globality, these would, indeed, seem to be part of a re-orientation of knowledge and the economy towards the mobile, the supra-national, the immaterial. However, if we bear in mind Pascal Chabot's contention (see chapter one) that part of the task of transitional thought is to highlight what is obscured and understand what we consume so as not to become victims of what we consume, then we need to attend to the very real material consequences of the immaterial. If digital cosmopolitanism dwells on the baleful gap between the digital promise of connectedness and the parochial reality of internet usage (the overwhelming majority of news sites consulted are hosted in the users' own country and language), it has nothing to say about the consequences for connectedness and understanding of the gap between a virtual ideology of immateriality and the concrete, extractivist practices of information and communications technology (ICT) manufacture and usage.

Impact

There is nothing virtual about the ecological impact of the virtual. It is damagingly real. Telephones, servers, computers, all contain metals that are difficult to extract and difficult to recycle. In the average desktop tower computer and cathode tube monitor, the following valuable and hazardous metals can be found: Aluminium, Antimony (hazardous), Arsenic (hazardous), Bismuth, Cadmium (hazardous), Chromium, Copper, Ferrite, Gold, Indium, Lead (hazardous), Nickel, Platinum, Steel, Silver, Tin and Zinc (Williams 2011: 356). Transmission equipment, aerials, and transoceanic cables expand in number and energy consumption to meet the exponential needs of information-hungry applications. Fibre optic cables may have reduced the mining for copper but they contain boron and rare metals such as Germanium which increase the refraction index and help to retain the light within the fibre. Between 30 per cent and 50 per cent of the world production of Germanium is used in the manufacture of fibre optic cables (Bihouix 2014: 223–224). The toxicity of ICT is particularly to be found in the externalisation of pollution which is a recurrent feature of the global economic system, the tendency to move highly polluting activities to parts of the planet where there are laxer forms of environmental regulation or more authoritarian forms of governance. As Eric Williams observed in an assessment of the environmental impacts of ICT, many of the hazardous environmental emissions emerge during the recycling process:

> A great deal of ICT equipment is not recycled in proper facilities, however, but is processed by an informal (or backyard) industry in the developing world. With low labour cost and no environmental controls, recycling valuable metals from ICT devices in this way generates a profit, rather than incurring a net cost when faced with expensive labour and strict environmental controls. This economic situation drives the growth of an informal electronics industry in many parts of the developing world, such as China, India and Africa. Copper is often recovered from wires by open burning of the insulation, which is usually made from polyvinyl chloride, so combustion releases dioxins, furans and other toxic chemicals. Gold in printed circuit boards is recovered by hydro-metallurgical treatment using cyanide and acid without

environmental controls. There is mounting evidence that informal recycling in the developing world is causing serious environmental pollution

(Williams 2011: 355).

Central to ICT manufacturing as it is currently practised is the extraction of a finite resource (precious metals) and the generation of hazardous emissions that are hidden from view in the sites of consumption by the delocalisation of the recycling of ICT hardware. These emissions have direct consequences for the environments and the communities whose livelihood depends on these activities (Basel Action Network 2005).

The exponential increase in the number of IT devices, the privatisation of usage, the continuous growth in data centres which generate so much heat that it is necessary to systematically cool them down, are continuous and growing consumers of energy resources whose exploitation is a major contributory factor to climate change. The combination of end-use devices (desktops, laptops and smartphones), the network infrastructure (which sends digital information between servers and clients) and the manufacturing process of servers, end-use devices and networking devices means that ICT energy use is increasing apace. The global communications network consumed 1,815 TWh of electricity in 2012 and this corresponded to 8 per cent of global electricity production in the same year (22,740 TWh) (de Decker 2015a). To put this into perspective, if one was to use pedal-power generators each generating 70 watts of electric power, one would need 8.2 billion humans each pedalling in three shifts of eight hours 365 days a year to meet this energy demand. The global electric consumption of ICT was three times greater than the combined energy outputs of all the wind and solar power produced on the planet (Observ'ER 2013). One of the difficulties is that as ICT becomes more energy efficient, overall energy use increases rather than decreases. This is primarily due not to a growth in the number of users (although these are increasing continuously) but to the intensity of energy usage by users. Two factors that have a significant influence here are the increase in mobile wireless computing and the endless growth in the bit rate of content.

Smartphones use less energy than desktops during both their operation and manufacture but their apparent energy efficiency conceals other more onerous forms of energy dependency. As Kris de Decker notes, smartphones move:

> much of the computational effort (and thus the energy use) from the end-device to the data center: the rapid adoption of smartphones is coupled with the equally rapid growth in cloud-based computer services, which allow users to overcome the memory capacity and processing power limitations of mobile devices.
>
> (de Decker 2015a)

However, because the data that is to be processed and the resulting outcome must be transmitted from the end-use device to the data centre and back again, the energy use of the network infrastructure also rises.

The problem of energy use is compounded by the changing nature of the networks themselves. The most energy-efficient way of connecting to a network is through a wired connection, whether Digital Subscriber Line (DSL), cable or fibre. WiFi uses somewhat more energy. Connection through a wireless cellular network tower, however, leads to a dramatic rise in energy consumption. In the case of 3G, energy use compared to a wired connection is 15 times greater and in the case of 4G, 23 times greater (Huang et al. 2012). The rolling out of a 5G network will lead to further multiples of increase in energy usage. In addition, the wide coverage of cellular networks leads to further expansion in mobile computing with the dual effects of increased energy use and increased intensity of energy consumption. Though laptops were initially presented as less energy intensive than desktops, their convenience and portability meant that users spent more and more time online. The spread of the smartphone means that any perceived 'dead time' (commuting, coffee breaks) can be filled with more connectivity. The more energy you save, the more you end up spending.

It is not only how we access the internet that has resource consequences, it is also what we want to access. In the early days of the internet, the network was used exclusively for the transmission of text. Successive improvements led to transmission of images, music and videos. The multi-modal nature of the internet adds further to its attractiveness as a medium of communication. The difficulty lies in the significant differences in the bit rate of content between text and video. The entire content of the English-language version of Wikipedia amounts to nine giga-octets of content. This is the equivalent of two film DVDs (Bihouix 2014: 233). Video content of internet traffic was 57 per cent in 2012 and is expected to rise to 69 per cent in 2017. According to *Cisco Visual Networking Index* 72 per cent of internet traffic in 2019 will consist of the most energy-hungry content of all, mobile wireless video:

> When device capabilities are combined with faster, higher bandwidth, it leads to wide adoption of video applications that contribute to increased data traffic over the network. As mobile network connection speeds increase, the average bit rate of content accessed through the mobile network will increase.
> (Cisco 2015)

High-definition video will be more common and the proportion of streamed content is also expected to increase. The shift towards on-demand video will affect mobile networks as much as it will affect fixed networks.

Power consumption is also determined not only by data rates but also by expectations as to service. In the case of real-time services such as videoconferencing, audio and video streaming, delays are not tolerated. If your favourite YouTube video staggers and starts, frustration quickly sets in. The onus on the service provider is to provide a more effective network but the more performance, the greater the energy consumption.

In addition to the energy consumed in the operation of ICT devices, there are energy resources used in the production of the ICT goods themselves. At the level of components, an assessment of the resource flows and emissions plus environmental impact of a product shows that at least 1.2 kg of fossil fuel is needed to manufacture a 2-g dynamic random access memory (DRAM) chip. This is a ratio of 600:1 compared with a 1:1 or 2:1 ratio for most other manufactured goods (Williams et al. 2002). This is largely due to the stringent purity standards required in semiconductor processing materials and environments. In a car, 88 per cent of the energy required is to drive it, the rest relates to the manufacture of the vehicle. The converse is true for ICT devices:

> For a typical laptop computer [...] 64% of the lifetime energy is used during manufacturing, with just 36% in operation. This is partly because manufacturing computers is energy intensive, and partly because rapid obsolescence leads to computers being purchased more often than many other products with a plug.
>
> (Williams 2011: 356)

The figures for operation have increased since Williams made his observation for the reasons outlined above and are likely to increase further but he does draw our attention to the energy-intensive nature of ICT device production. The point is all the more important in view of the pressures on users to regularly change models, for example, through the subsidisation of new mobile phone purchases by way of minimum contract periods. The rapid turnover in devices is partly linked to what are often known as 'rebound effects'. This occurs when adopting a technology such as fuel-efficient car or a new practice (teleworking) may have unexpected or unintended consequences. An economic rebound would involve using the car more often because it is cheaper to run (you can drive more miles with the same amount of petrol) or spending the money on other goods and services that are environmentally intensive (a large steak or a new mobile phone). A social rebound occurs when saving time leads to a behavioural change that has further impacts, for example, increased non-work driving by teleworkers.

As computers and phones became cheaper, more portable, powerful and user-friendly, users bought (or were encouraged to buy) even more portable, powerful and user-friendly devices. As computers saved time doing repetitive, routine tasks, more and more time was spent on ICT devices doing other things (e-mail, social media, texting). The energy consumed in the making of microprocessors dropped from 0.028 kWh per MHz in 1995 to 0.001 kWh per MHz in 2006 (355). This development did not, however, lead to a drop in energy use in microprocessors. All the gains were cancelled out by the fact that as the microprocessors increased in speed and functionality, they needed more energy. The seemingly relentless expansion in processing capacity that this entails (Moore's Law) and the exponential growth in software development are predictable drivers of the insatiable logic of ICT development. This logic is bound up with a model of economic growth that sees an infinite expansion of goods and services as the horizon of expectation of economic prosperity. Indeed, it is the limitless promise of the virtual that makes the dream of unfettered globalisation seem both desirable and possible. The internet not only facilitates, it induces:

> [The internet] entails a progressive globalisation of the economy that has thus far caused increasing transportation of material products and people [...] The induction effect arising from the globalisation of markets and distributed forms of production due to telecommunication networks clearly leads away from the path of sustainability.
>
> (Hilty 2008: 22)

Another consequence of the information society is the acceleration of innovation processes, and thus the increasingly rapid devaluation of the existing by the new, whether this be in hardware or software, technical products or human skills and knowledge. There are no obvious internal constraints that will stop the internet from further expanding. Size or speed are not problematic. Bit rates continue to expand. Blu-Ray movies give you a better viewing experience but the average Blu-Ray movie contains between 25–50 GB of data which is 5–10 times the size of a HD video. Television viewers are already being promised the possibility of watching 3D movies at home which average at 150 GB in size and the future promises holographic movies at around 1,000 GB (Seetharam et al. 2010). As the ICT industry prepares to launch 5G, the number and intensity of internet connections will further increase. If we take a mode of circulation that put an end to Iron Gustav's flourishing business in Berlin, the motor car, they are, at least, constrained by size and speed. Making heavier, larger or wider cars is not feasible because this would involve the complete reconstruction of road networks and car parks. There is no point in making cars go faster as most nations have imposed mandatory speed limits to protect the safety of other road users. No such limits apply in the case of the internet. The only constraint is energy. The promise of the 'internet of things' where all things will ultimately be connected to the internet through a Radio Frequency Identification Device (RFID) sets up an almost infinite horizon of ICT energy usage (Bihouix 2014: 223). It is precisely this model of indefinite growth that has become deeply problematic in the era of anthropogenic climate change. As resources reveal themselves to be increasingly scarce or to require increasingly unsustainable amounts of energy to extract, how do we rethink the ecological context of ICT? More particularly, in the case of translation, whose fortunes have for millennia been bound up with technologies of knowledge, communication and transmission (Cronin 2013), how are we to think through the carbon consequences of ICT for a sustainable model of translation in the age of the Anthropocene?

A predictable response to the ecological havoc wrought by extractivism is nostalgia. Before was better. If only the Faustian pact had not been entered into with capitalist technological development, the planet would be safe and species, including our own, would survive. This is a version of what McKenzie Wark has called 'capitalist romance', the notion of a harmonious, closed, self-regulating world that has evacuated the murder machines of technological modernity.

However, as he notes, 'There is no real traction to be gained from trying to base a critique on nature versus culture, or the human versus the machine' (McKenzie Wark 2015: 147). The hopelessness of this antithesis had been anticipated by Donna Haraway in her *Cyborg Manifesto* where she argued that 'By the late twentieth century, our time, we are all chimeras, theorized and fabricated hybrids of machine and organism; in short we are cyborgs' (Haraway 1991: 150). What the translation cyborg might resemble is described by Douglas Robinson in somewhat less than dramatic terms:

> Do you instinctively resist the notion that when you translate you too are a cyborg? You sit at the computer, yes. You value the many support functions the computer offers you, not just in typing (no need to retype when you make a mistake!) but in spell-checking, global search-and-replace functions, term-management functions, and formatting.
>
> (Robinson 2016)

Once the computer is connected to the internet, there is access to web resources (online terminological databases, contextualised term searches) and to other translators and experts worldwide. This is a very different scenario from typing translations on a typewriter, relying on print dictionaries and making occasional phone calls to experts. In terms of the progression from the phone to the online query, of course, there is no fundamental change in cyborg ontology. The phone is just as much of an electronic networking prosthetic as the internet-enabled computer, both allow humans to engage in forms of connectivity that would not normally be possible given human physical limitations. Tranquilisers, contraceptive devices, telescopes, binoculars, microscopes, heating and cooling systems, lighting, the ways in which technology or machines are enfolded into our lives are multiple and inescapable. The centrality of tool use to the emergence and development of the human species in its current form has been detailed by paleo-anthropologists (Taylor 2010), even if humans do not have a monopoly of tool use in the animal kingdom. The sense of a return to any notion of pre-technical purity is, in a properly human sense, inconceivable as our humanity is inseparable from our exosomatic development (Bourg 1996). Furthermore, one of the paradoxes of the wholesale rejection of techno-modernity is that it becomes complicit in forms of climate denial, 'That the Carbon Liberation Front is changing the climate is a knowledge that can only be created via a techno-scientific apparatus so extensive that it is now an entire planetary infrastructure' (McKenzie Wark 2015: 180). Abandoning techno-science entails abandoning any hope of tracking the enormity and complexity of global climate change. We would end up powerless in face of something we could no longer understand.

As we saw in chapter two, the demand for translation continues to grow worldwide. Indeed, this growth is both a driver of and is facilitated by expanding ICT capacity on the planet. The very rationale for translation investment is bound up with an ideal of endlessly expanding markets for goods and services. A typical pitch in the localisation industry can be found on the

Lionbridge website where it is claimed that the optimal way to cater to global markets and customers is to offer an app in the native language of the customer. A survey by :

> Common Sense Advisory found that more than half of global consumers only buy products from websites that provide information in their own language. And more than half of the countries on the top 10 list for application downloads and revenue are non-English speaking countries from Europe and East Asia.
>
> (Lionbridge 2016)

Production, consumption, translation and technology are carefully combined in the commercial blandishment of a major global purveyor of translation services and technologies. Political ecology draws attention, however, to the infrastructural unconscious of societies, the resource base that allows activities to happen. A political ecology of translation technology must critically evaluate the resource implications of current uses of technology and advance alternative scenarios for the development of the translation cyborg in the age of the Anthropocene.

Low-tech

Michael Hahn in his *A Basis for Scientific and Engineering Translation: German-English-German* describes the emergence of new courses in database management, translation memory, web searching and so on which allow students to make the 'transition from *low-tech* to *high-tech* translation' (Hahn 2004: 244; his emphasis). In a period of resource scarcity and global warming, we arguably need to make the reverse transition, to go from 'high-tech' to 'low-tech' translation. There are a number of ways in which we can conceive of this transition. Firstly, in the design of the tools that translators use. How can ICT devices be redesigned to radically reduce the consumption of scarce or hazardous materials? How can the devices be produced to optimise their capacity for recycling and put an end to recycling practices that endanger the lives of men, women and children in developing countries? How can 'modular' practices be adopted in the manufacture of machines that would allow for easier repairs and the re-usage of different component parts? How can compatibility be increased or made mandatory not just in the area of chargers but for screens, batteries, processors, ports? In other words, the ecological imperative to reduce, reuse, recycle, must be imbedded in the very tools that translators use if there is to be a proper realignment of our cyborg identities with the radically altered circumstances of our resource environment.

The second dimension to a low-tech transition is the need to revisit the nature of users' relationship with the internet. As Kris de Decker claims, the internet as we know it in the industrialised world:

> is a product of an abundant energy supply, a robust electricity infrastructure, and sustained economic growth. This 'high-tech' internet might

offer some fancy-advantages over low-tech networks, but it cannot survive if these conditions change. This makes it extremely vulnerable.

(de Decker 2015b)

An example of a low-tech network is the Akshaya network in India which covers the entire Kerala State and is one of the largest wireless networks in the world. It uses Long Range WiFi which offers high bandwidth combined with low capital costs. The networks are inexpensive to assemble with the possibility of sourcing components from discarded materials such as old routers, satellite dish antennas and laptops. The WiFi nodes are lightweight and there is no need to build expensive towers, which minimises the impact of any structures that are built. Examples of these networks can also be found in the remoter regions of European countries such as the Catalan Pyrenees in Spain (Vega et al. 2013). Crucially, these networks have a much reduced energy consumption compared to their high-tech counterparts and a much reduced environmental impact in the stages of construction and operation.

Another instance of a low-tech network is the use of 'data mules'. DakNet and KioskNet use buses as data mules. In areas with no conventional internet connectivity the rural bus service is used as a way of carrying data from one point to another. Each vehicle is fitted with a computer, a storage device and a mobile WiFi-node. The installation of a stationary WiFi-node in each village means that the local transport infrastructure can function as a wireless internet link:

Outgoing data (such as sent emails or requests for webpages) is stored on local computers in the village until the bus comes within range. At this point, the fixed WiFi-node of the local computer automatically transmits the data to the mobile Wi-Fi node of the bus.

(de Decker 2015b)

Later on in the day, when the bus arrives at the hub and is connected to the internet, the outgoing data is sent from the mobile WiFi-node to the gateway node and then to the internet. In order to send data to the village the opposite route is taken. The building of delay-tolerant networks moves away from the energy-hungry model of always-on traditional networks and concentrates instead on designing networks based on asynchronous communication and intermittent connectivity. This allows these networks to work well with renewable energy. Data is transferred from node to node and if the next node is unavailable, the data is stored on a hard disk. A node would become active, for example, when the sun shone or the wind blew, eliminating the onerous need for energy storage. While the technical solutions proposed will evolve over time, the notion of a low-tech as opposed to a high-tech internet will become increasingly necessary as societies need to move towards significant reductions in fossil-fuel based carbon emissions.

There is a further geopolitical dimension to the question of the low-tech internet with the dramatic digital divide on the planet where more than four billion people do not have access to the world wide web (World Bank 2016: xiv). Low population density, high infrastructure costs, low income levels (and therefore reduced ability to pay) and an unreliable or non-existent electricity infrastructure means that many telecommunications firms are unwilling to provide digital access to large swathes of the Earth's population. Climate justice has an inescapable technological dimension as evidenced by the digital apartheid of energy-intensive high-tech connectivity. No progressive politics in an era of global warming can afford to ignore these forms of exclusion.

The third dimension to a low-tech transition in translation lies in the human entanglement of cyborg identities. In other words, if we need to look at the technologies and see how they might need to change to allow for sustainable societies, what is the future of human translators' interactions with technologies from an ecological perspective? For Ethan Zuckerman, the practice of translation is central to the rewiring of the internet. If 'we want a world that values diversity of perspective over the certainty of singular belief, a world where many voices balance the privileged few' (Zuckerman 2013: 272), then translators must be part of the dialogue. There are two ways in which this is to be achieved. Firstly, there is the use of volunteer translators to translate content from different languages. Zuckerman cites, among others, the example of Zhang Lei who in 2006 began the group translation website, Yeeyan, to translate key English-language media into Chinese. The site eventually built up a group of 210,000 registered volunteer translators. Another example of volunteer translation are the translations of the TED talks where the average talk is translated into 24 languages within a few weeks (153–158). The second tactic is the use of machine translation and he gives much space to the progress realised by statistical machine translation and the activities of Google in this area. Work in statistical machine translation can eventually be complemented by advances in 'human computation'. Zuckerman refers in particular to the research projects of Luis von Ahn who is best known for 'reCAPTCHA'. The reCAPTCHA is familiar to internet users who are often asked on sites to transcribe two words to show that they are human beings and not computer programs. Users are not usually aware of this but they are helping to transcribe scanned book pages and already by 2008 reCAPTCHAs were transcribing the equivalent of 160 books per day. Von Ahn wants to harness this collective computing power for translation by encouraging users to learn a second language through Duolingo. As learners progress, they will be invited to translate simple sentences at first before eventually being asked to translate sentences from live web pages. The harnessing of this collective translational power through advanced technology is Von Ahn's answer to his initial question: 'How can we get 100 million people translating the Web into every major language for free?' (Von Ahn 2011)

In the digital utopia of cosmopolitan connectedness, no one gets paid. When Zuckerman argues that 'What we really want are translations that are as nuanced and accurate as those produced by TED or Global Voices and as fast as Google Translate' (Zuckerman 2013: 158), he might equally have added that what 'we' really want are translations for which no money changes hands. This demonetisation of translation, stripping it of its value as an economic activity, makes the activity and its practitioners particularly vulnerable in a world where cash rather than compassion is generally needed to put food on the table. More broadly, as we saw in chapter two with the advent of the second machine age, translation becomes one of those higher-level cognitive activities which is the target of advanced automation. In the dematerialised abstraction of high-tech digital cosmopolitanism, the resources consumed are not only scarce metals and energy but also the human resources of translators who become part of that infrastructural unconscious hidden from view by high-tech hyperbole. This is, in effect, a dual form of extractivism where both human and non-human resources are extracted with little concern for those who find themselves in the 'sacrifice zones' of depletion. The cyber-cosmopolitan vision is one which suffers from the inevitable consumption bias of much commentary on technical innovation. More, faster and for free, this is the dream of the flattered consumer. But what about the consequences for the producer? If everything is free, who pays the supplier? Who bears the cost, if not the translators who work for no pay or whose work is appropriated by the owners of services who ultimately find ways to monetise them? It is in this context that we might attend to what McKenzie Wark has called the 'labor point of view'. The Australian theorist argues that there is a tendency for commentators to dwell on what he calls the 'language of molar drama', the large-scale stories of 'Man against Nature' or 'Man against the Gods'. There is less interest in the 'molecular', the view from below, on the ground:

> For it is the molecular scale which corresponds best to the labor point of view. If nature is that which resists labor, it does so in a granular way. The molar is the language of management. It's the dialogue of ideas, in which the experience of those who organize labor substitutes for the experience of those whose labor organizes the world directly.
>
> (McKenzie Wark 2015: 219)

The transition to 'low-tech' as it relates to cyborg labour is the challenge to an economic model that pursues infinite material growth at the expense of sustainable and meaningful employment. Seeing translation from the 'labor point of view' is to consider the ways technology is used to disempower and impoverish translators and how 'high-tech' is wasteful both of human and material 'resources'. Philippe Bihouix in his seven low-tech commandments includes 'Démachiner les services' or 'de-mechanize services' (Bihouix 2014: 167). This injunction is based on the notion that each time humans are replaced by energy-intensive machines which consume precious resources, the loss in human contact and conviviality in many instances is compounded by the increased pressure on the carrying capacity of the planet. In this sense, the move away from the fetishisation of high-tech towards an engagement with low-tech is part of a move towards employment-rich rather than employment-poor economies and societies. The founding figure of cosmopolitanism, Diogenes, may have practised poverty as a virtue but this does not make poverty virtuous. Re-engaging with the molecular perspective of the translator making a living wage is about using sustainable forms of computer use to increase human involvement in cyborg labour, not lessen it. From the perspective of climate justice, it entails the move to low-tech translation in the interests of better conditions of employment and remuneration.

Data

Luis Von Ahn's stated ambition was to find a way to get the entire web translated into every major language for free. The ambition is wholly consonant with the culture of maximisation mentioned in chapter one where more is always more. What gets forgotten in the fetishisation of infinite growth is the finitude of means. The question that might be asked in terms of a political ecology of translation is whether a form of *translation maximisation* is in fact desirable. Is it necessary or indeed advisable that we get Von Ahn's one hundred million subjects translating the entire web? We have already seen the dramatic expansion in the bit rate of content and the data sizes of what is being transmitted on the internet with clear consequences for energy consumption. There is, however, the further issue of storage. Data may appear virtual but its forms of storage are strikingly material. In the case of the United States, it took the equivalent of 34 power plants, each capable of generating 500 megawatts of electricity, to power all the data centres in operation in 2014. By 2020, it is estimated that the US would need another 17 similarly sized power plants to meet projected data centre energy demands with the shift of economic activity to digital platforms. In 2013, US data centres used 91 billion kilowatt-hours of electricity, which would be enough to provide power to all of New York City's households twice over. By 2020, annual data centre energy consumption is expected to reach 140 billion kilowatt-hours (Thibodeau 2014). There have, of course, been numerous calls for greater efficiency in the energy use of data centres (US Environmental Protection Agency 2007) but here one encounters the same troubling paradox found in personal computing noted above. The more energy saved, the greater the demand for energy, 'the energy intensity of the internet (energy used per unit of information sent) is decreasing while total energy use of the internet is increasing' (de Decker 2015a). Increased storage capacity on ICT devices, the offer of 'unlimited storage' on mail accounts, the continuous incentives to move users to cloud computing, repeated initiatives by governments and security agencies to compel telecoms providers to store data on their users, the vogue for the use of 'big data', among other developments, all point to the ever increasing amounts of data requiring storage. Energy may be saved but the amount of data that needs to be stored generates even more energy requirements. In addition, land is needed for the construction of the data centres and valuable metals and materials are used in their fabrication. Albert Pimentel, President of Global Markets and Customers for the data storage company Seagate, outlined the scale of data expansion:

Market research firm IDC predicts that digital data will grow at a compound annual growth rate (CAGR) of 42 percent through 2020, thanks to the proliferation of cellphones, digital entertainment and new technologies like Big Data and the Internet of Things that tend to generate vast amounts of files.

(Pimentel 2014)

The total amount of digital data generated in 2013 came to 3.5 zettabytes. A zettabyte is 1 with 21 zeros after it and is equivalent to the storage of about one trillion USB keys. The 3.5 zettabytes generated in 2013 was triple the amount of data created in 2010. By 2020, the world is expected to generate 40 zettabytes of data annually, which represents more than 5,200 gigabytes of data for every person on the planet (Pimentel 2014). The surge in global demand for translation that we noted in chapter two is part of this overall expansion in data storage requirements and indeed the efficiency and increased performativity of statistical machine translation or Von Ahn's 'human computing' is predicated on having larger and larger corpora of stored translations from which to work.

High-tech translation is data hungry. In a world of constrained resources, however, is less not more for translation? In other words, as part of a 'low-tech' approach to translation, should the emphasis not be on a more strategic approach as to what should be translated? Is it really necessary to translate the entire web with all the environmental consequences of the storage requirements that would ensue? In this context, it might be useful to advance or promote the notion of *digital connoisseurship* as a form of curatorial practice in translation. What this implies is that not all that can be translated would be translated. Mindful of the environmental impact of data expansion and storage, decisions would have be made as to what would generate significant added value as a result of its translation. Translators in the move away from the pumping iron productivism of high-tech translation, characteristic of the age of maximisation and extractivism, would be called upon, in conjunction with others, to consider the most effective or beneficial form of the use of the resources for a translation project. As connoisseurs of language, culture and/or different specialisms, they would assist in the evaluation of the likely impacts or benefits of the translation of particular texts. In an era of anthropogenic climate change, it is no longer possible to abstract the 'externalities' of environment from the cost of engaging in or pursuing a particular activity and this includes translation.

Demand-side ecology

Central to the notion of digital connoisseurship is the need in the context of low-tech translation to balance supply-side and demand-side ecology (Bihouix 2014: 114–115). Supply-side ecology stresses the potential of a green translation technology. This might include promoting the design and construction of computers based on the reduce, reuse, recycle principles mentioned above or the shift to a resilient, low-tech internet. The ever-present danger is 'greenwash'.

Promoting products as 'organic', 'environmentally friendly' or 'kind to the planet' can simply become another tagline to fuel the endless consumption of new goods and services. It is business as usual but through green-tinted glasses. Demand-side ecology, on the other hand, sees the primary challenge as one of reducing the level of demand for goods and services to environmentally sustainable levels. Demand in this scenario involves choice and discernment. Less is more. The task becomes an ethical one of allocating scarce translation resources – scarce because they are dependent on the infrastructural unconscious of a material economy – to the development of a just, sustainable and resilient society, ensuring the survival of the planet and the species that dwell on the planet with us. In the next chapter we will consider in more detail the question of translation and context-sensitive communication but here it may be useful to consider the question of what might determine the values of a demand-side translation ecology and how these relate to a version of supply-side ecology.

Donna Haraway has argued that information is not simply a convenient metaphor for describing forms of causality in the world, it also becomes a powerful means of organising worlds:

> Communications science and modern biologies are constructed by a common move – the translation of the world into a problem of coding, a search for a common language in which all resistance to instrumental control disappears and all heterogeneity can be submitted to disassembly, reassembly, investment and exchange.
>
> (Haraway 1991: 164)

In Haraway's vision of techno-science in a commodity economy, 'translation' becomes the instrument of the destruction not the promotion of heterogeneity. Translation underpins the move towards the construction of a 'common language' that spells the end of resistance, the surrender to the command and control mode of instrumental reason. The sense in which the pressures to embrace a 'common language' are already present is borne out by global developments in different fields of knowledge.

The sociologist Boaventura de Sousa Santos coined the term 'epistemicide' to describe the manner in which Western science marginalised or eradicated the knowledge systems of non-Western countries. These knowledges included, among others, traditional medicines, community justice systems and local lore relating to the natural world (Sousa Santos 2001: 251–279). Karen Bennett has explored this notion of epistemicide in the context of the expansion and hegemony of English Academic Discourse (EAD). The internationalisation or globalisation of the university system in the past three decades has seen a commensurate rise in quantitative comparability. The QS World University Rankings, the THE World University Rankings, the Centre for World University Rankings, the Academic Ranking of World Universities, all purport to rank the quality of universities worldwide on the basis of largely quantitative data. This move towards international comparability feeds into national research exercises that in turn privilege quantitative outputs to determine who or what should get funding. The difficulty is that the language or, more particularly, a single language, English, becomes the medium of comparison. In other words, for an article or a journal or a book to be deemed 'international', it must almost invariably be published in English. Non-native speakers of English who wish to access funding and promotional opportunities have either to write directly in English or to have recourse to translation into English. This obligation is not epistemically innocent. As Chip Bruce and Maureen Hogan point out, tools that are habitually used become invisible, 'We might say, "I talked to my friend today," without feeling any need to mention that the telephone was a necessary tool for that conversation to occur' (Bruce and Hogan 1998: 272). This makes tools convenient, we no longer have to think about them but because we no longer have to think about them, we forget about their inbuilt biases, how they structure our lives and our environment. Language, of course, is one of the tools we use to understand and organise our world: 'As one of the most pervasive and powerful tools we use, language biases what we encounter and what we fail to encounter, every day' (Zuckerman 2013: 141).

Bennett argues that EAD is heavily embedded in a world view which is bound up with the emergence of a scientific discourse in England in the seventeenth century that resolutely rejected the text-based knowledge of the Medieval scholastics and Renaissance humanists. Thus, a faultline emerges between Anglo-Saxon empiricism on the one hand and so-called 'Continental philosophy' on the other which could be said to include hermeneutics, German idealism, phenomenology, existentialism, structuralism and post-structuralism:

> in the first case, 'reality' is believed to precede language, which means that it is perceived in much the same way by everyone, irrespective of linguistic or cultural background; hence, language serves merely to name things that have an objective existence in some extralinguistic domain (a philosophy known as *linguistic realism*). The second, on the other hand, holds that humans learn about external reality through the categories set up by their mother tongue; thus our entire experience of the extralinguistic world is not only mediated but actively constructed by culture (a philosophy known today as *constructivism*).
>
> (Bennett 2015: 12)

Not surprisingly, these two opposing paradigms have radically different forms of expression. The empiricist paradigm with its commitment to a pre-existing 'reality' wants the minimum amount of authorial intrusion so that this reality can be concisely and transparently articulated. In this paradigm, 'short simple sentences are valued, as is clearly defined vocabulary, a hierarchical text structure, impartial style and structured rational style supported by evidence' (12). In the 'constructivist' or 'hermeneutic' paradigm, by contrast, the aesthetic, emotive and ethical dimensions of language are valued. Following in the tradition of Classical Rhetoric more attention is paid to the figurative and connotative resources of language and there is an overt concern with the artistic construction of a phrase or argument. The prose is more akin to literary writing than technical discourse, 'as meanings are not fixed and immutable, but rather open-ended, shifting and susceptible to multiple interpretations' (13). The dark side of the internationalisation of third-level education is the overwhelming emphasis on the English language and its dominant empiricist paradigm as the gateway to global recognition. 'Excellence' is based on what can be assimilated into one language and one paradigm. This assimilation can either occur through non-native speakers of English writing directly in English and conforming to the empiricist paradigm or through the domestication of texts in English-translation to the dominant model. Resistance 'to instrumental control disappears' as a rejection of this hegemony, the 'common language' of global comparison, means no career, no promotion, no funding. In Bennett's words, this is a kind of epistemicide, 'which, if left unchecked, may ultimately result in the elimination of epistemological diversity and its replacement by a monoculture of global proportions' (11).

If monocultures – agricultural, industrial, political, economic – are the precondition for extractvism and ecological vulnerability, any meaningful transition to a sustainable planet must entail a systematic challenge to these monocultures, whatever their origin. In this respect, translators both as connoisseurs of epistemological diversity, through in-depth study of cultures and languages, and as potential brokers in making others aware of difference in translation, are central to the construction of resilient knowledge spaces. In looking to the operations of a demand-side ecology and what might be the values determining the choices to be made, both in terms of what is to be translated and how it is to be translated, a paramount value must be the preservation of epistemological and ontological diversity in global cultures. The danger is that in thinking about translation there can often be a fatal confusion between *translation as infrastructure* and *translation as flow*.

There are two potential ways to map a city. The classic city map gives you the layout of the streets, the location of key transport hubs, sites of cultural and historical interests and major public utilities (government buildings, hospitals). This is a map of the city's infrastructure. It will indicate all the possible ways that you might travel through the city and the different routes you might take to get from the station to the national gallery. You might want to draw another kind of map, however, which is based not on what routes people might take through a city but what routes they actually do. This is a flow map (Zuckerman 2013: 61–62). An infrastructure map like a city map or a conventional road map offers a Platonic idea of circulation. It is a dream of mobile possibility. It does not, however, indicate roadworks, or tell you when traffic is particularly heavy, or what sections are particularly prone to black ice or subsidence. You can, in principle, walk anywhere in a city (infrastructure) but as many examples show, the vast majority of city dwellers have a very restricted range of movement between places of study, work and play (flow) (Biermann 2011). We can say then when we consider the number of languages spoken in the world, the numbers of speakers of different languages, the number of languages taught in different translator training institutions, the processing capacities of new technology, the potential of translation itself to handle a very wide range of tasks from sign language interpreting to game localisation, the infrastructural possibilities of translation are immense. The difficulty is the reality of the flows.

If only 2–3 per cent of the world's literature finds its way into English or if English becomes the effective lingua franca of the European Union despite an extensive translation infrastructure (van Parijs 2011) or if a study of public health research in Europe that covered 210,433 publications found in the Science Citation Index (SCI) and the Social Science Citation Index (SSCI) (with exclusions of overlap) indicated that 96.5 per cent of publications were published in English with only 3.5 per cent in a non-English language (Larsen and von Ins 2010: 575–603), then translation flows indicate the potential drift towards monolingual, epistemic monocultures. Situating translation in a demand-side ecology means placing the emphasis on altering the nature of flows. An excessive concentration on supply-side cyberutopianism by hyping the infrastructural possibilities of technology to deliver translation for all neglects not only the hidden environmental costs but also the geopolitics of wealth and influence that determine translation choices in the world today. It is the flows after all that dictate whether translation is to be the nemesis or the guardian of epistemic uniformity.

In the age of the 'knowledge economy', the 'smart society', attending to the possibilities of low-tech or the willed asceticism of demand-side ecology, can seem disturbingly retrograde. The project smacks of neo-Luddism, a nostalgic hankering after an obscurantist past. More worryingly, for knowledge workers, like translators, academics and students, eco-translation could suggest a hostility or antipathy to research, innovation and, indeed, knowledge itself (Phillips 2015). This is manifestly not the case if only because the 'production and reproduction of our species-being, whatever it may be, has to be a central concern of any critical knowledge' (McKenzie Wark 2015: 134). The challenge of the Anthropocene is precisely the need to question deeply-help assumptions, to think the unthinkable and to develop new forms of knowledge that are responsive not just to our current predicament but to the planet that will be inherited by those who come after us. The need to orient knowledge to different ends by taking means seriously (see chapter one) requires among other things that we reconsider the infrastructures of knowledge, in particular those whose avowed aim is the support and promotion of research, universities. It might be asked, however, whether universities as they are currently constituted are capable of the development of a critical knowledge that meets the current and future needs of the 'production and reproduction of our species-being'. In other words, does the practice of eco-translation not only change how we might approach the translator's task but also challenge conventional assumptions about the organisation of knowledge?

Organisation of knowledge

If one examines the evolution of the European university, it is possible to posit three stages of development. The first stage is the emergence of what might be termed the *monarchical university*. The universities which emerge from the eleventh century onwards largely depended on royal patronage, not least in allowing for a degree of autonomy from church authorities. The second stage is the emergence of the *national university* notably in the early nineteenth century where the primary duty of the university was to prepare the future citizens of the nation-state (Readings 1997). The third stage is the emergence of the *corporate university* in the latter half of the twentieth century where the relative loss of economic sovereignty by individual nation-states, the rise of supra-national governance, the deregulation of markets and the global connectivity of ICT meant that universities conceived of themselves less as national public bodies and increasingly as transnational, corporate entities committed to maximising the financial resources of the institution through competition in an international educational market (Collini 2012). The proliferation of rankings and quantitative comparators noted above is an intrinsic part of the marketisation of education in a globalised world. If we are not to experience a dramatic depletion of the resources of the planet it would seem necessary that we develop alternative ways of thinking which challenge the core tenets of a shareholder-driven model of maximalist growth and financialised models of economic practice. The financial crisis of 2008 did not fundamentally alter this model and indeed the rationale of austerity was employed to restore the growth orthodoxy as a core value of economic and political activity (Lanchester 2010).

The difficulty is that the employment needs, the nutritional needs, the educational needs of the planet's inhabitants cannot be met by a growth model which is predicated on the unsustainable and destructive use of increasingly scarce resources whether this be water, land, food or knowledge itself, corralled off in the auction rooms of the patents market. This is where we might speculate on the emergence of the *transitional university*, a form of knowledge organisation that is directed to the creation of a carbon-neutral, sustainable and resilient economy and society. The transitional university is more ambitious in its conception than the 'green campus' model, which, however laudable, confines itself to minimising the carbon footprint of individual institutions. The transitional university is a form that responds to the radically changed circumstances of the Anthropocene by developing forms of knowledge covering every domain of human activity as they interact with the human and non-human world. The transitional university should not be conceived of as a return to an idealised past of cloistered privilege but it is of necessity future-focused: 'There's no going back. There's only forward. It's a question of struggling to open another future besides this one which [...] has no future at all' (McKenzie Wark 2013). It is not our purpose here to establish a detailed template for this new or potentially emergent form but to mention briefly four areas – technology, the natural and physical sciences, political economy and comparative literature – where eco-translation might fit into an altered infrastructure of knowledge communication and transmission.

Technology: If information is the most valuable commodity of the information economy, then developers, suppliers and repositories of information such as universities are called on to play a significant role. The role of ICT hardware and software in networked societies and economies is inescapable: 'Building better futures will take all the technical infrastructure we can get. But it's not as simple as repurposing existing infrastructures, all of which are based on ever-expanding resource use and labor exploitation as design givens' (McKenzie Wark 2013). A technology, of course, is not simply what it does, it is what it might do. From the standpoint of the translation cyborg, the task of computer science departments in conjunction with translation studies is to develop an 'open-ended experimental approach, a critical design approach' (McKenzie Wark 2013) to the development of a green translation technology. Such a technology would involve, as we have seen, everything from a fundamental redesign of ICT devices to the construction of a low-tech internet. However, it is not only hardware that matters here. It is also where and how eco-translation would figure in a revitalised digital cosmopolitanism. That is to say, in terms of the 'ecology of attention' we mentioned in chapter one, how do we best use digital translation resources to construct a viable sense of planetary solidarity? We are unlikely to save the planet if we, literally, do not know what we are talking about to whom.

Natural and Physical Sciences: The natural and physical sciences have a long relationship with translation (Montgomery 2000). When translators discuss biology or physics and translation it is usually in terms of scientific or technical translation. In the age of the Anthropocene, where the fate of all species are bound with each other and where anthropogenic climate change has fundamentally altered human relationships to the physical world, human/nature, (active) sub-ject, (passive) object distinctions are no longer tenable. These distinctions which have featured so prominently in the different parables of Western modernity (Latour 2013) are no longer adequate to the task of either accounting for what is happening or of planning for what might happen. It is in this context that we might want to broaden the conception of translation studies to cover the different forms of communication and signifying systems in the natural and physical world. We will consider this issue in much greater detail in the next chapter but suffice it for now to suggest that translation's role in the disciplines of physics, chem-istry and biology in the emergent transitional university would arguably be as much one of commenting on and analysing processes as of translating outputs.

Political Economy: Translation is critically bound up with the market economy. As we noted in an earlier work (Cronin 2003), the very notion of globalisation would have been a dead letter if it were not for the activities of translators whose activities accompanied the movements of goods and services across the languages of the world. Localisation companies routinely sell translation services and products on the basis that their clients will access previously untapped markets. Translation can, therefore, be said to be part of the infrastructural unconscious of the global economy. What this means, by implication, is that if the economy needs to change so too does translation. An emerging current of critical thought is 'environmental economics' or 'green economics' which sees the economy as subordinate to the ecosystem in which it finds itself rather than treating the ecosystem as an invisible, non-valued externality (Cato 2008). Different crises – climate, biodiversity, fuel, food, water, the global financial system – have led to pressures on political economists to rethink their discipline. In the United Nations Environment Programme (UNEP) Report on the Green Economy the tension between forms of growth and the possibilities of sustainability are made explicit:

> Most economic development and growth strategies encouraged rapid accumulation of physical, financial and human capital, but at the expense of excessive depletion and degradation of natural capital, which includes the endowment of natural resources and ecosystems.
>
> (UNEP 2011)

Depleting the world's stock of natural wealth – often irreversibly – this pattern of development and growth has had negative impacts on the well-being of current generations and carries with it tremendous risks and challenges for the future. If certain kinds of growth are harmful, if particular forms of energy use are unsustainable, if specific types of investment are damaging, if named modes of transportation are toxic, it follows that the core value of deregulated market growth on which a dominant conception of capitalist realism is based needs to change. But what would a changed political economy mean for translation? Here again, thinking about translation and political economy in the context of the transitional university means asking whether translation would be treated as a scarce resource like any other, so that it would only be used to support economic activities that were not harmful to overall ecosystemic well-being. Indeed, one of the consequences of this coupling of translation and political economy is to shift a concern with translation ethics from exclusively political settings to a concern with economic ones. If there is a campaign for disinvestment in fossil fuel companies, should there similarly be a campaign to stop translating for them? What is important here is less the ability of translators to carry out this threat than raising the issue in the first place. Bruno Latour has claimed that with the advent of the Anthropocene 'all disciplines [...] are now seized by the same feeling of urgency' (Latour 2014) and this disciplinary uncertainty must make for a porosity that will change the orientation and emphases of translation studies.

Comparative literature: What about the role of eco-translation as a human science in the transitional university? The discussion around travel writing in chapter five will attempt to suggest some answers to this question but here we want simply to mention just one aspect by way of illustration of the potential forms of dialogue. Kato and Allen in proposing an 'eco-critical approach to translation' speak of the potential in comparative literature to explore what they refer to as the 'environmental imaginary':

> The term was coined by historian Diana K. Davis to describe "the constellation of ideas that groups of humans develop about a given landscape," and which are commonly mediated through stories or narratives "about that environment as well as how it came to be in its current state."
>
> (Kato and Allen 2014)

In imperial and colonial settings, the control of these environmental representations and their meanings can determine who wins and who loses out when this imaginary is translated into concrete environmental policies and practices. Translation as part of the apparatus of empire and colonial domination (as well as, of course, of resistance) can be co-opted into the project of representing particular landscapes to the readers of translations that can either create afresh or reinforce imaginary constructions of political lands. Presenting the subject land (Ireland, Algeria, India, Brazil) to readers in translation as in some way alien or exotic or fantastic or abnormal or degraded invites justifications for projects of restoration or normalisation or 'improvement'. In other words, whether discussing the Age of Empires or contemporary 'World Literature' it is possible to explore the overlap between translation, comparative literature and other humanities disciplines such as geography and history in the elaboration of environmental imaginaries in different settings. The consequences of these imaginaries are all too real as a common characteristic of 'sacrifice zones' (see chapter five) in extractivism is that they are often to be found in places that are deemed 'wild', 'barren' or 'remote'. This way of approaching texts, the move towards an eco-critical framework, suggests as with the example of translation and political economy above that the transitional university, the institutionalisation of a form of organisation of knowledge in the age of the Anthropocene, must be defined not so much by its disciplines as by its concerns. That is to say, taking the example of what was discussed in chapter two, one might have rather than a traditional Faculty of Science or Faculty of Humanities, a Faculty of Food where agricultural scientists, biochemists, political economists, comparative literature specialists, computer scientists, anthropologists and translation scholars would come together united by a common concern to develop local and global food cultures that are resilient and sustainable. Again, the concern is with critical knowledge informed by ecological issues arising from the 'production and reproduction of our species-being'.

The Great Transition

Paul D. Raskin in his *The Great Transition Today: A Report from the Future* (2006) tries to imagine a world that has taken seriously the dire predicament of our species-being. The imagined place of writing is 'Mandela City' and the year is 2084. A new set of values underpins the entire edifice of society, 'Consumerism, individualism, and domination of nature – the dominant values of yesteryear – have given way to a new triad: quality of life, human solidarity, and ecological sensibility' (Raskin 2006: 1). Issues of governance and new forms of geopolitical organisation loom large in his utopian blueprint. Organisation on the basis of nations has given way to the primacy of regions and these regions tend to cluster around three types, 'Agoria', 'Ecodemia' and 'Arcadia'. Agoria represents a type of advanced social democracy, Ecodemia is akin to a radical socialism with an emphasis on collective ownership and participation and Arcadia is the expression of an essentially left libertarian outlook with the emphasis on self-reliant communities, face-to-face democracy and community engagement (4–5). Raskin is mindful also of the pressing questions of wealth creation and income redistribution. He imagines the answers to these questions as taking two forms, changing enterprise organisation and a difference in the nature of demand. With respect to the first, he argues:

> The forms of economic enterprise are much more varied than they were when large corporations dominated the economic landscape. First, the number and significance of non-profit entities continues to surge (particularly in *Ecodemia* and *Arcadia*, but in *Agoria*, as well) as people find it increasingly appealing to frame their work and 'corporate culture' in terms of a 'social mission'. Second, businesses take diverse forms, including the large corporations of *Arcadia* (long ago re-chartered to ensure social purpose and worker participation in governance), the worker-owned cooperatives of *Ecodemia*, and the small private operations typical of *Arcadia*. Third, a labor-intensive secondary economy, expanding alongside the high-technology base, produces a breathtaking array of esthetic goods and skilled services, giving producers an outlet for creative expression, a sense of purpose, and a supplementary income. This 'people's economy' is encouraged by shorter work weeks (see Time Affluence indicator), material security, and enabling policies.
>
> (9)

All of these forms of economic enterprise currently exist. The difference between then and now is distribution. In Raskin's vision of the Great Transition political and economic dominance would no longer be exercised by large, transnational corporations (TNCs) working primarily for the benefit of non-worker shareholders. For example, in 2011, a group of mathematicians from the Swiss Federal Institute of Technology in Zurich found that a small minority (1,318) of the 43,000 TNCs currently in existence controlled over 80 per cent of the world economy (Coghlan and MacKenzie 2011). The usefulness of Raskin's utopian projections is that they suggest alternative models of development for translation rather than automatic incorporation into ever-larger transnational language services and localisation corporations. Social enterprises (in the area of community interpreting, for example), workers' co-operatives, low-scale artisanal translation workshops (containing small groups of two or three highly specialised translators in literature, art history, music), are possible models of economic organisation that need to be considered as core rather than peripheral if we are to deal with 'the terrible bequest of degraded ecosystems, threatened species, and a destabilized climate' (Raskin 2006: 11). A broader and more imaginative conception of the enterprise landscape also means that a sense of ethical investment, collective ownership and a much greater sensitivity to the social and environmental consequences of the economic activity of translation needs to feature in translator education. Cynicism about the present should not foreclose possibilities for the future.

The changing nature of enterprise is in part a response to the changing nature of demand. In this chapter we have emphasised the values underlying a demand-side ecology and Raskin tries to express the emergence of a new demand culture and a shrinking human ecological footprint: 'Changing consumption patterns have decreased the share of tangible goods in the world economy in favor of dematerialized sectors such as services, arts, knowledge, and crafts production' (11). What Raskin is advocating in the Great Transition is the shift from a society largely preoccupied with wealth in the form of the acquisition of material goods to one that is primarily focused on the notion of fulfilment through the enjoyment of intangibles. This raises the possibility for an enhanced role for translation as translation can either become the auxiliary of material goods based on wealth creation (product documentation, advertising literature, website localisation) or it can be part of a new economy of intangible demand centred on fulfilment where its energies are focused on translation for artistic performance, literary enjoyment, intellectual stimulation, spiritual development and creative practice. The potential role for translation in this new economy is closely bound up with one of the triad of values that Raskin sees as underpinning the Great Transition, human solidarity:

> The second value – 'human solidarity' – expresses a sense of connectedness with people who live in distant places and with the unborn who will live in a distant future. It is a manifestation of the capacity for reciprocity and empathy that lies deep in the human spirit and psyche, the 'golden rule' that is a common thread across many of the world's great religious traditions. As a secular doctrine, it is the basis for the democratic ideal and the great social struggles for tolerance, respect, equality, and rights.
>
> (1)

It is difficult to see how such a notion of human solidarity could be realised if translators are not central to the Great Transition. Not only because what is translated connects us with people who 'live in distant places' (translation as communication) but because translations are also read (and reworked) by those who come after us (translation as transmission).

Enthusiasm for the 'dematerialised' needs, of course, to be tempered by the ecological realism we have been advocating as to the material consequences of the 'virtual'. Caution is also needed in privileging intangible fulfilment over material wealth on a planet of gross inequality and shocking disparities in income. However, in this case, it is worth bringing to mind once more that ecological sustainability is bound up with social justice. The forces that fuel environmental destruction are also those driving income inequality. As John Bellamy Foster notes, 'a shift away from capital accumulation and towards a system of meeting collective needs based on the principle of enough is obviously impossible in any meaningful sense under the regime of capital accumulation' (Foster 2015). Only when the regime of capital accumulation changes can there be a new form of development, 'qualitative, collective and cultural'. In thinking through this development, it is important to be aware of how the '[n]eglect of natural-scientific developments and a strong anti-technology bent' (Foster 2015) has limited the contribution of progressive thinkers to the ecological dialogue in the past. Part of the 'anti-technology bent' John Bellamy Foster refers to may stem from a false opposition.

Spinning wheels and spinning jennies are both forms of technology, the differences lying in the scale of operation and the degree of human intervention. Bearing this commonality in mind, it is possible to envisage two 'technical' futures for translation. One is the future that has been discussed in this chapter with the valorisation of particular forms of 'low-tech' and the development of a demand-side ecology. Translation for reasons of scale, effectiveness and connectivity is seen as a central part of a reconfigured ICT. Another future is alluded to in Raskin's evocation of 'craft production'. The words evoke cabinet makers and knitters and potters but it should not be forgotten that a frequent way of describing translation over the centuries has been to describe it as a 'craft'. In 1958, when Eric Jacobsen publishes his monograph on the translation background to the composition of Christopher Marlowe's *Elegies* he calls his volume, *Translation a traditional craft* (Jacobsen 1958). In 1961, Roger Shattuck and William Arrowsmith publish the proceedings of a critical symposium under the heading *The Craft and Context of Translation* (Shattuck and Arrowsmith 1961). When John Biguenet and Rainer Schulte in 1989 publish a selection of essays from leading literary translators, it is entitled simply *The Craft of Translation* (Biguenet and Schulte 1989). Translation as a 'craft' activity has been a standard trope over the centuries to describe what translators do. In this respect, translation could be seen as one of those activities that would fall easily under the homely rubric of 'craft production'. It might be useful in a conclusion to this chapter to pursue briefly this notion of 'craft' more closely less as metaphor and more as activity or process to illuminate the different ways in which the technical might shape or be shaped by our ecological future.

Richard Sennett in *The Craftsman* argues that 'craftsmanship' is not a lost skill but a permanent human trait:

> 'Craftsmanship' may suggest a way of life that waned with the advent of industrial society – but this is misleading. Craftsmanship names an enduring basic human impulse, the desire to do a job well for its own sake. Craftsmanship cuts a far wider swath than skilled manual labor; it serves the computer programmer, the doctor and the artist; parenting improves when it is practised as a skilled craft, as does citizenship.
>
> (Sennett 2009: 15)

Making music, cooking, bringing up children, these are all activities where the desire to do them well can be frustrated by obstacles such as the lack of time or forced inattention or the inability to make a long-term commitment. The rise of subcontracting, 'flexible' working practices, zero-hour contracts and the disappearance of long-term job security in the extractivist economy makes the necessary investment of time and attention in craft more problematic. For Sennett, the best craftsmanship involves continuing involvement over many years so that the complex skills required by, say, glass blowing, ballet dancing or writing become deeply engrained and become readily available to those who practise the craft almost without their being aware of them.

Translation falls into this category of craft where years of practice lead to the development of an almost instinctive feel for how texts might or might not be translated. Doug Robinson, for example, has argued that 'translation is an intelligent activity involving complex processes of conscious and unconscious learning' and that it demands 'creative problem-solving in novel, textual, social, and cultural conditions' (Robinson 1997: 51). The difficulty is, of course, when this 'craft' dimension to translation is implicitly devalued whether through the imposition of impossible time constraints that prevent proper attention to the task at hand or through the mechanisation of the translator's task. For Sennett the Enlightenment response of thinkers like Diderot to the arrival of the machine was not rejection but accommodation: 'The enlightened way to use a machine is to judge its powers, fashion its uses, in light of our own limits rather than the machine's potential. We should not compete against the machine' (145). One could argue that events have both overtaken and confirmed Sennett's diagnosis. On the one hand, our attitude to the machine is not simply to be judged in terms of 'our own limits' but in terms of resource limits and the finitude of particular climactic conditions. On the other, the need for long-term, resilient, sustainable forms of activity that are not invested in the infinite accumulation of material goods means a shift to a human-machine, human-tool interaction that incorporates Sennett's notion of craftsmanship. Implicit in the development of the craft is what for Sennett are the lost spaces of freedom, the possibility of making mistakes, trying out new techniques, new ideas, of losing oneself in a piece of work to find oneself. The possibility of trial and error for translators, the creative learning of the blind alley, the preservation of these endangered spaces, are crucial to any concept of a green translation technology. In a political ecology of translation, the machine must be crafted so as to allow for the flourishing of a digital connoisseurship that will make for the most transformative and least harmful use of human and non-human resources in translation. Iron Gustav may have lost the race but the race that now needs to be won is not so much the race against the machine as against the time of resource exhaustion and cultural depletion. Otherwise, things will indeed go terribly wrong. In the next chapter we will consider how particular writing practices in relation to translation can point up more hopeful scenarios for the future.

5   Language worlds

Arran Stibbe, towards the end of his work on the emerging discipline of ecolinguistics, makes the following observation:

> There is, however, a shortage of voices, in this book and in ecolinguistics in general, from traditional and indigenous cultures around the world. Within these cultures are a great multitude of stories, some of which may be invaluable in the reinvention of self and society in the transition to new ways of living and being.
>
> (Stibbe 2015: 193)

The importance of 'traditional and indigenous cultures' is not simply to do with past stories as a source of future change but with present stories as a pointer to imminent survival. Naomi Klein notes that running economies on energy sources that release poisons into the atmosphere as an inescapable part of their extraction and refining has always necessitated the existence of 'sacrifice zones'. These zones have a number of features in common:

> They were poor places. Out-of-the-way places. Places where residents lacked political power, usually having to do with some combination of race, language, and class. And the people who lived in these condemned places knew they had been written off.
>
> (Klein 2014: 310).

It is often the poorest people on the planet speaking lesser-used languages in more remote parts of the world that find themselves at the frontline of the race to extract as much fossil fuel resources as possible from the earth. Describing how the Beaver Lake Cree Nation took on oil and gas companies over tar sands oil extraction, Klein claims that 'some of the most marginalized people in my country are [...] taking on some of the most wealthiest and most powerful people on the planet' (379). The move to a carbon credits system, a market solution that allows wealthier countries and corporations to offset carbon emissions by buying carbon 'credits' from countries with low emissions, has made the situation of indigenous peoples even more precarious. Bram Brüscher, a geographer, has coined the term 'liquid nature' to describe the way in which fields, forests and mountains lose their intrinsic, place-based meaning and become deracinated, abstract commodities in a global trading system (Brüscher 2013: 20–36). In the Bajo Aguán region of Honduras, owners of palm oil plantations have been able to register a carbon offset project that they claim captures methane. Encouraged by the promise of financial gain from captured gas, huge tree farms have disrupted and displaced local agriculture. A resulting violent cycle of evictions and land occupations had by 2013 led to the deaths of up to a hundred local farmers and their advocates (Wong 2013). As Klein remarks, 'it's easier to cordon off a forest inhabited by politically weak people in a poor country than to stop politically powerful corporate emitters in rich countries' (Klein 2014: 223). An additional irony is that it is indigenous peoples practising some of the most sustainable, low-carbon lifestyles on the planet who are being sacrificed for the carbon market. In this chapter we want to explore how various indigenous peoples and their languages are represented in a number of contemporary travel accounts. Our purpose is to situate these representations within the context not so much of ecolingusitics as eco-translation. A central concern here is how writing travel can both complicate and transform the demands of biocultural diversity.

Travelling through language

John Steinbeck knows that companionship demands speech. Even when the companion is his dog Charley, the question of human speech seems inescapable. What is also inescapable is that human speech is plural and in the case of Charley, Steinbeck's travel mate on his odyssey through the United States, this plurality makes a difference:

> He [Charley] was born in Bercy on the outskirts of Paris and trained in France, and while he knows a little poodle-English, he responds quickly only to commands in French. Otherwise, he has to translate and that slows him down.
>
> (Steinbeck 1997: 7)

In a multilingual world language and language difference is an inevitable feature of travel (Cronin 2000; Di Biase 2006; Polezzi 2006). How travellers deal with the fact of languages other than their own, or radically distinct varieties of their own language, has clear implications for their capacity to engage with or interpret the realities they encounter. From an ecological standpoint, it is no less apparent that language contact has two distinct impacts, one representational, the other instrumental. The representational impact relates to the ability of the travel writer to represent the thoughts, values and experiences of others, who do not speak his or her language, in the language of the writer. Pronouncements about the lives and habitats of others, however strong or tenuous the truth claims, do suppose an access to knowing that must, however, take account of post-Babelian realities, the existence of a multilingual world. The instrumental impact relates to the influence of travel itself on language communities. In other words, if the travel writer is the practitioner of a major world language, to what extent are they as travellers complicit in the major ecological problem of global linguicide that may see up to 90 per cent of the world's 6,000 plus languages disappear by the end of the century (Crystal 2000: 35)? Mass travel has long been acknowledged as a significant pull factor in language shift and language death (Nettle and Romaine 2000: 82–90) so how do major world-language travellers face up to the sociolinguistic consequences of their own travelling practices?

In this section we will explore contemporary travel accounts, written in a major world language, English, which seek to engage with language difference, not as a by-product, but as an object of travel. That is to say, the accounts take language itself, or rather languages, as the primary motive for travelling. Inevitably, ecological and ethical concerns, which range from species destruction to the legitimacy of political violence, are a recurrent feature of the narratives as they probe the current state and future prospects of the world's languages and this feature will emerge from the analysis of the accounts. The inevitability is partly a function of how the language variousness of the world is constructed. Published within six years of each other by major English-language publishers, Pamela Petro, *Travels in an Old Tongue: Touring the World Speaking Welsh* (1997), Helena Drysdale, *Mother Tongues: Travels through Tribal Europe* (2001) and Mark Abley, *Spoken Here: Travels Among Threatened Languages* (2003), all take minority languages as the structural theme of their travels. The accounts become part travelogue, part crusade, as the travellers try to come to terms with the unpalatable realities of language decline.

Place

In describing her rationale for visiting some countries and not others, Helena Drysdale explains her exclusions. Shortage of space prevented her from including the Irish, Welsh, Scots, Luxembourgois, Sorbs and Galicians, 'I also had to cut out Romanies and Jews, on the grounds that I was investigating speakers of language that were rooted to a place, and the relationships between them and that place' (Drysdale 2001: xiii). For her part, Pamela Petro, an American Welsh-language learner, wonders how Welshness or Welsh identity might be defined and she concludes:

> Truth is, there's no formula in the world for gauging Welshness, no recipe that calls for three stereotypes mixed with five pints of beer that will cook up a Welsh person. Except [...] except perhaps enthusiasm for the place, and a simple wanting to be there. The only reason I say I felt 'more Welsh' is that on the basis of an evening's talk (pretty paltry evidence, I admit), I seem to like Wales better. I miss the salty dampness and the bumpy landscape and the fruity smell of life lived near big, mature-manufacturing animals.
>
> (Petro 1997: 192)

Mark Abley considers wrangling over orthography in Mohawk communities in Canada and claims, 'Mohawks feel an intense loyalty to their own place. But the rivalries between those places stands in the way of a united language. Nobody wants to feel that his or her own speech, so jealously guarded against the encroachments of the outside world, is being shoved aside in favour of somebody else's dialect' (Abley 2003: 174).

Language is seen to define place and places are inextricably linked to forms of speech. The placedness of language is however variously expressed. For Drysdale, it reveals itself in the many Sami words for lichen or a list of Sardinian foodstuffs in Sard. For Abley, it is the plethora of words for flora and fauna in the Australian aboriginal language Wangkajunga for which there are no English equivalents. But of course, the places are not just any kind of place, they are particular kinds of places. They are generally peripheral, remote or marginal so that frequently in these accounts the endangered state of the languages becomes conflated with the physical peripherality of the speakers. The landscape and the tongue become one in a topography of possession and dispossession.

Pure movement is not likely to endear readers if there are no moments to punctuate kinesis. Travel demands the immobility of place if only to make sense of mobility itself. Language in the interaction between movement and place can, of course, occupy two positions. On the one hand, it is language that allows meanings to circulate in a place between speakers, within a community, and beyond that to other speakers and other places. The very act of writing a travel account partakes of the circulatory capacity of language. Other speakers, at other times and in other places, can read the words, the text of what you have to say. On the other, language becomes the quintessential expression of a specific group of speakers in a specific place. It is precisely the non-circulatory nature of language that defines its socio-cultural *raison d'être*. Helena Drysdale's assertion that, although she did not speak Breton, 'I would have thought it was the language of the fields and fishing boats' (Drysdale 2001: 382) captures what she sees as the inevitable fit between territory and utterance. The dual nature of language, the two positions it can occupy in the dialectic between movement and place, sets up a fundamental ethical tension in the language-centred accounts which is never fully resolved.

Abley, Petro and Drysdale are all animated by a concern for the loss of language diversity. In travelling the world (Petro, Abley) or Europe (Drysdale), they repeatedly insist on the irrevocable loss to world culture which would be represented by disappearance of the planet's many languages. Speaking of the Kimberly region in Western Australia, Abley notes of the 30 different languages that only three are spoken by children, 'It's as though twenty-seven sphinxes are crumbling away before our eyes' (Abley 2003: 35). Travelling is testimonial, a bearing witness to the fragility of the human constructions that are languages. These verbal edifices are just as complex and worthy of attention as their monumental counterparts. The difficulty is that the very process which allows the reportage of loss, seemingly unfettered mobility, is also the process which construes minority languages in a particular way and ultimately imprisons their speakers in a teleology of extinction.

The Swiss travel writer, Nicolas Bouvier, commenting on the nature of travel, argued that it rested on the fundamental dyad, 's'attacher, s'arracher' [to become attached/to become uprooted](Bouvier 1992: 136). The travel writer moves on but the travelees stay put. It is indeed this basic urge to keep on moving that brings writers to the genre in the first place as Helena Drysdale, author of *Alone Through China and Tibet* (1986), *Dancing with the Dead* (1991) and *Looking for George* (1996) makes clear in her utopian vision of a restless world as articulated in *Mother Tongues*:

> I wanted our restless life to last for ever. I would lean back and envisage a future in which everyone lived on the road – the ultimate in the free move-ment of peoples. Cities would be deserted; our descendants would hardly believe that there was once an era of static living, in which people were shackled to one place, often for their entire lives.
>
> (Drysdale 2001: 80)

If 'being shackled to one place' is seen as a precondition for linguistic survival, then a profound ambivalence will dog any attempt to enthuse over the linguistic benefits of place, whether the benefits are construed as access to a lesser-used language or the necessary splendour of physical isolation. So when Drysdale meets Tiziana, a speaker of Sard, she feels that the young woman has one overriding desire, to leave the island as soon as possible. The writer herself gives expression to this desire by admitting that, after listening to polyphonic singing in a church and coming close to the cultural and linguistic 'epicentre of the island', 'she couldn't wait to escape' (291). Similarly, when she meets Kamberi, an Albanian doctor from Macedonia in the village of Vranjovce, she feels that he 'faced being stuck here for ever' (326). The movement which brings the writer to celebrate and validate language diversity *in situ*, the championing of various forms of 's'attacher', provokes an equally resistant strong desire to 's'arracher', to give voice to a deep suspicion about all forms of 's'attacher'. In order to understand the origins and the consequences of this ambivalence as they relate to travel and language, it is worth considering language and travel in a broader framework of cultural analysis.

One of the most common icons of the global age is, not surprisingly, the globe itself. From the shots of the blue planet suspended over abyssal darkness courtesy of the Apollo space missions to the sketchy outline of earth on notices encouraging hotel customers to re-use their towels, images of the planet are increasingly common in the contemporary imaginary. But seeing things from a distance is as much a matter of subjection as observation. That is to say, it is not just a matter of looking (observation), seeing also begs the question as to who is doing the seeing and who is being observed (subjection).Occupying a superior vantage point from which one can look down on a subject people or a conquered land is indeed a staple of colonial travel narratives (Pratt 1992: 216). There is a further dimension to the question of distance described by Tim Ingold where he draws a distinction between perceiving the environment as a 'sphere' or as a 'globe'. For centuries, the classic description of the heavens was of the earth as a sphere with lines running from the human observer to the cosmos above. As geocentric cosmology was gradually discredited and helio-centric cosmology came into the ascendant, the image of the sphere gave way to that of the globe. If the sphere presupposed a world experienced and engaged with from within, the globe represented a world perceived from without. Thus, in Ingold's words, 'the movement from spherical to global imagery is also one in which "the world", as we are taught it exists, is drawn ever further from the matrix of our lived experience' (Ingold 2000: 211). In the movement towards the modern, a practical sensory engagement with the world underpinned by the spherical paradigm is supplanted by a regimen of detachment and control. As the images of the globe proliferate, often ironically to mobilise ecological awareness, the danger is that these images themselves distort our relationship to our physical and cultural environment by continually situating us at a distance, by abstracting and subtracting us from our local attachments and responsibilities. However, it is precisely such an ability which is often construed as a basic requirement for both national and, more latterly, global citizenship.

It is the capacity to look beyond the immediate interests of the clan or village or ethnic grouping which creates the conditions for a broader definition of belonging at a national or indeed global level. Szerszynski and Urry argue, for example, that 'banal globalism', the almost unnoticed symbols of globality that crowd our daily lives, might 'be helping to create a sensibility conducive to the cosmopolitan rights and duties of being a "global citizen", by generating a greater sense of both global diversity and global interconnectedness and belonging' (Szerszynski and Urry 2006: 122). But Szerszynski and Urry ask the following questions,

> is this abstraction from the local and particular fully compatible with dwelling in a locality? Could it be that the development of a more cosmopolitan, citizenly perception of place is at the expense of other modes of appreciating and caring for local environments and contexts?
>
> (123)

In opposition to the figure of the citizen we find the notion of the 'denizen', propagated notably by the non-governmental organisation Common Ground. A denizen is deemed to be a person who dwells in a particular place and who can move through and knowingly inhabit that place. The word originates in the Latin *dē intus* (from within) which mutates into Old French *deinzein-deinz* (modern French *dans*). What is compelling about the term is that it both espouses a relationship to place (a knowing from within) and a flexibility in terms of adoption and adaptability as among the dictionary definitions listed for 'denizen' are 'one admitted to the rights of a citizen: a wild plant, probably for-eign, that keeps its footing: a naturalised foreign word' (Kirkpatrick 1983: 332). Therefore, Common Ground dedicates itself to encouraging the proliferation of vernacular, ideographic and connotative descriptions of local places which can take the form of place myths, stories, personal associations and celebrations of various kinds and these descriptions are widely varied in origin (www.comm onground.org.uk). In a sense, what travels in and through a world of languages does is to bring into sharp relief the tension between the traveller as citizen speaking a global language and the inhabitant as denizen speaking a local language. Pamela Petro expresses the attendant doubts when she claims that: 'I feel we English-speakers are weightless and language is our wings. We circle the globe in a tail-wind of convenience, but from our bird's eye viewpoints can't tell our destinations from our points of departures' (Petro 1997: 166).

Decline

Self doubt aside, what the dovetailing of physical and linguistic mobility results in is a careful scaling of social development and historical sensibility. Minority language speakers are not only stuck in a particular place, but they are also stuck in a particular mode of development and in a particular relationship towards time itself. When Drysdale, for example, arrives in Corti on the island of Corsica, her comment is 'Corti was astonishingly rundown. Yellow stucco façades on the main street were crumbling; their back regions were little more than stacks of stones with plumbing tacked on. Many shops were boarded up' (Drysdale 2001: 260). Stand still long enough and everything begins to decay and rot. The decline of language is mirrored in the decrepitude of its speakers and their environments.

When a region, Catalonia, offers evidence of a contrary development the occasion is one not of celebration but of disappointment for Drysdale. Noting the spread of high-rise residential developments throughout the region, she claims, 'It was happening throughout Catalonia. I was beginning to look at everything with a premature nostalgia. Catalonia was a victim of its success. I couldn't warm to it' (222). The traveller as global citizen is implicated in the 'denial of coevalness' observed by Johannes Fabian (1986: 35) where at one end of the scale we find the advanced late modern Western traveller and at the other the pre-modern or lapsed modern denizen. It is because of their position on this scale that the minority language speakers have a sense of long-range historical memory which appears touchingly anomalous to the schismatic time traveller of late modernity. Encountering a Breton-language enthusiast, Drysdale points out that 'He referred to events of the ninth century as if they happened last week' (383). The important qualification in these English-language accounts, however, is that they speak to an internally differentiated West. That is to say, it is not simply a question of Westerners stereotyping non-Westerners but of the use of language in motion to position other Westerners differently.

The recurrent ethical dilemma for the travel writers is that they want through their testimonies to make an eloquent plea for the value of linguistic diversity. In order to articulate their case and stress the uniqueness of the languages observed, they have to argue for a close correlation between language and place, which also has the added structural and narrative advantage of allowing writers to go and describe these places. However, the placedness of the speakers puts them beyond the pale of schismatic modernity and global mobility. Their defining attribute becomes a mark of their belatedness. Time stands still and minority language speakers become the prisoners of the picturesque landscapes lovingly articulated in their disappearing languages. As the travellers (with the exception of Petro in Wales) do not spend radically extended periods of time in any of the places they describe or at least nothing like the time necessary to learn any of the minority languages they encounter, the world becomes once again a picture or a set of pictures, as time cedes place to space, and diversity alliteratively echoes decline.

In his analysis of French travel literature in the twentieth century, Charles Forsdick notes that the perceived decline of diversity is one of the most common preoccupations of the literature. Travellers go to far-off places, tell their readers that the 'exotic' is an illusion, that everywhere has now become much the same and the writers themselves are the last witnesses of differences which are about to disappear forever:

> The implicit sense of erosion [of diversity] that characterizes certain nineteenth-century and earlier twentieth-century attitudes to the distinctiveness of individual cultures may, in its more extreme manifestations, have bordered on apocalypticism; but the transfer from generation to generation of such renewed prophecies of entropic decline uncovers the pervasive and conservative tendency according to which transformation is cast as death and loss.
>
> (Forsdick 2005: 3)

Forsdick draws a comparison with Raymond Williams' analysis of the trope of the decline of rural England, which Williams saw less as a precise event happening at a specific moment in time than as a 'structure of feeling' running through English writing for centuries (16). In other words, though the notion of the decline of diversity may be differently accented depending on whether the context is the triumph of the Fordist factory or the predatory designs of globalising Goliaths, there is a sense in which the theme of the imminent demise of diversity is akin to a recurrent structure of feeling as proposed by Williams (1979: 156–165).

Things are always getting worse and the cultural critic, like the despairing travel writer, can only report on a world that is about to lose its distinctiveness and leave us adrift in a 'standardised world'. As Chris Bongie observes when discussing the terminal pessimism of Claude Lévi-Strauss's *Tristes Tropiques* on the future of diversity:

> Dire visions such as these however, most often resemble each other not only in their pessimism but also in their propensity for deferring the very thing that is being affirmed: although humanity is settling into a 'monoculture', it is at the same time still only *in the process of*, or *on the point* of, producing a 'beat-like' mass society.
>
> (Bongie 1991: 4; his emphasis)

There is no time like the present to tell us about all that is soon to be past. The attraction of the entropic, of course, is that it does away with the historic. Indeed, Thomas Richards sees the scientific origins of the concept of entropy as a convenient means of ensuring the end of history: 'As a myth of knowledge, entropy, like evolution, would seem to place history outside the domain of human activity. Because it transfers agency from human beings to physical principles, it ostensibly represents a pessimistic relinquishing of all possibilities of social control' (Richards 1993: 103). Are late modern English-language travel accounts on minority languages similarly obsessed with threnodies of loss? Is the entropic the default condition for a politics of cultural despair?

When Mark Abley goes in search of the Native American language Yuchi he is taken by his informants Richard and Henry to the house of Josephine Keith, the youngest fluent speaker of Yuchi:

> Yuchis, as ever, are harder to find. At last we crossed a bridge over Polecat Creek and turned hard right onto a gravel road that swung past farmland and juvenile woodland. Richard leaned forward and said, 'We're arriving at the last household in the world where Yuchi is spoken every day.'
>
> (Abley 2003: 80).

Here as in Lévi-Strauss's sad tropics, we find a vanishing community, a last clutch of speakers, in the process of terminal decline. A historical analogue is provided by a story of Alexander von Humboldt being presented in Brazil with a parrot whose language no one could understand. The reason for this was simple. The bird spoke the language of the Atures people: 'The Atures language had died out among humans. It was last heard coming from a bird's beak' (200). Australia, in Abley's account, is peopled by speakers of language, who in certain cases find that their only remaining interlocutor is a sibling living many miles away. Petro, meanwhile, is frequently frustrated in her global attempts to find communities of Welsh speakers and Drysdale's most common complaint is about the vanishing traces of the languages she has come to observe. It is indeed the parlous state of minority languages that provides an ethical justification for travel as the writers repeatedly invoke the decline of diversity trope.

Abley quotes a remark by MIT linguist Ken Hale, 'Losing any one of them [languages] is like dropping a bomb on the Louvre' (126), to convey a sense of the scale of cultural loss as the result of worldwide language attrition. Travels into languages become a form of salvage archaeology, last dispatches from the frontiers of monolingualism. There are cases mentioned which frustrate the entropic momentum, for example – Welsh, Catalan, Faroese and Manx. Abley claims that in the case of Manx, '[t]he purists, the visiting linguists, the reference books: all of them are wrong. On a global level the triumph of English may seem unstoppable, but on a local level you can find innumerable tales of a refusal to submit' (Abley 2003: 99). There may not be many speakers of Manx but they are bringing the language back from the grave and succeeding despite what their more skeptical critics might say. Catalan is even more anomalous in its rude good health. As Drysdale notes, 'Catalan is not a marginalised folkloric language, but normal, confident, mainstream' (Drysdale 2001: 217). However, the exceptions serve mainly to highlight the hopeless plight of the great majority of speakers of lesser-used languages. The overwhelming evidence points to imminent extinction.

Politics and culture

If the role of the travel writer is to report on the scale of the catastrophe, at what point does description cede to explanation or interpretation sideline dismay? Petro, Drysdale and Abley all advance explanations as to why many languages are in an endangered state, which involves everything from the impact of the logging industry to the social niceties of exogamous marriages. However, the accounts share a collective antipathy to forms of the political which eventually places history outside the domain of human activity in keeping with the entropic paradigm. In other words, if the entropic paradigm looks to physical principles rather than human agency as a source of explanation, then inquiring into the influence of social control is superfluous. Abley, for example, notes that, 'I didn't go looking for politics. I didn't want to write about politics' (2003: 182) but confesses that in the presence of Canadian Mohawks the subject was hard to avoid. Helena Drysdale discussing one of her informants, Madame Herault, claims, 'Madame Herault was passionately Provençal, but it was culture, not politics' (Drysdale 2001: 20). Pamela Petro observes that in Lampeter in Wales, 'To become a "learner", I grasped early on, was to take a political stand. If you're Welsh, that is; I'm still not sure what it implies for Americans' (Petro 1997: 95). The reluctance to engage with the political is expressed in a canon of distaste where activism is duly lauded but militancy is always suspect. The difficulty is that the two activities are not always easily distinguishable, particularly for the traveller passing through, so that one community's activist quickly becomes another's fanatic. That is to say, that even when the writers feel that language maintenance is on the whole a good thing, they rest uneasy at the thought that conviction may shade into more extreme forms of action.

When Helena Drysdale finally crosses over the border from the Spanish Basque Country into France, the relief is palpable, 'I felt lighter myself, happy to leave a somber, oppressive culture for something more frivolous, more chatty' (Drysdale 2001: 201). No part of the community is immune from Drysdale's suspicions of violent intent. In a beach near Bilbao as she takes her daughter for a walk, 'I glanced up to see a man alone on the cliff. He stood, silhouetted against the shale, a malevolent presence. He stared down at me, then pointed his stick at a pigeon, and I saw it was a gun' (Drysdale 2001: 163). Just as hunters may turn out to be not what they seem so too with taxi ranks which are scanned for ETA anagrams. As with a later trip to Corisca, the environment is uniquely foreboding, the sense of imagined violence darkening the perception of the people and the place. In Brittany, links are discovered between Basque separatists and Breton autonomists. Mark Abley appeals to his experience as an

Anglophone living in Quebec to state that 'nationalist movements often draw their most potent energy from fears of language loss and cultural unease' (Abley 2003: 123). So the Boro language of north-eastern India offers fascinating examples of verbal expression but '[a]dvocates of Boro who found the students and the politicians too mild-mannered have formed a guerilla army, the Bodo Liberation Tigers' (123). Languages have their lovingly documented charms although the lines between cultural defence and political offence are notoriously unstable. Pamela Petro, for her part, is ever watchful for an unwelcome political edge to her engagement with Welsh speakers abroad. In her encounter with Keith, a Welsh-speaker in Singapore, physiognomy is the giveaway, 'Keith's eyes narrow in a dangerous way when he says that England is economically prejudiced against Wales. "Still," he says, "we'll have home rule in ten years, mark my words"' (Petro 1997: 171).

In the absence of the political, the inevitable recourse is to a pseudo-anthro-pology of type, hence the sub-title of Drysdale's account is 'Travels in Tribal Europe'. Moreover, when Drysdale describes the efforts of Corsican women to end political violence, she bemoans the fact that, 'as in Northern Ireland, ancient hatreds would continue to tear the place apart' (Drysdale 2001: 257). Atavism, not circumstance, becomes the driving factor in situations of language conflict. 'Ancient hatreds' firmly situate present-day tensions in the pre-modern and the pre-historic, where neither politics nor reason have a purchase in the maelstrom of emotion which compel the benighted pre-political unit of the tribe to repeat the blood sacrifices of the house gods. So the Corsicans and the Basques like the Northern Irish are governed not by the socio-historical circumstances of sub-national power struggles but are caught up in forms of bloodletting that are pre-modern and belong to the time of myth rather than history.

As politics are explicitly disavowed, situation ethics gives way to a fine-boned morality which prompts the enlightened traveller to condemn rather than explain. The failure is all the more striking in that power is often invoked in historical analyses but is noticeably absent from contemporary descriptions of language tensions; a notable exception is Drysdale's description of present-day Belgium. She describes how the French-speaking Walloons previously wielded considerable economic power in Belgium through their dominance of heavy industry. Flemish speakers were treated as second-class citizens thus generating considerable resentment, exacerbated by the hegemony of the French language in the Belgian army during the First World War. The situation changed with the decline of heavy industry in post Second World War Belgium and the rise of a Flemish-speaking middle class (155). Abley, for his part, details the abuses piled on indigenous peoples in the past in the educational systems of North America and Australia (Abley 2003: 62). However, more generally, hostility between minority and majority language speakers becomes naturalised into an essentialist predisposition, an innate failure on the part of minority language speakers to negotiate modernity rather than analysed in terms of clear dis-crepancies of state power, economic resources and socio-psychological vulnerabilities.

When the reader is reassured that Madame Herault's interest in Provençal is to do with culture not politics, the travel writer reveals a kind of culturalist credo which has become the common currency of many contemporary encounters with the languages and cultures of others. That is to say, culture itself has assumed a foundational role in contemporary society. If, in previous ages, God or Nature was seen as the ground on which all else rested for its meaning, in the post-modern age, it is Culture which is summoned to the basement of epistemic and ontological coherence (Eagleton 2003). The sense that culture goes all the way down satisfies the essentialists, who see culture as a set of immutable attributes passed from one generation to the next. Conversely, the notion that anything can be understood as a cultural construction cheers the relativists, who can disassemble the handiwork of national chauvinists. The primary difficulty is that both camps explicitly or implicitly subscribe to culturalist readings of social and historical phenomena which have the signal disadvantage of marginalising structural questions in political discourse and analysis. In other words, whereas formerly racial or class difference was invoked to justify exclusion and inequality, it is now culture which is being recruited to justify surveillance and marginalisation. 'They' are not like 'Us' not because they eat differently or dress differently or speak differently. The differentialist racism of societies becomes culturalised.

This is one of the reasons why a common response to the highly mediated and mythologised 'crisis' of multiculturalism ('ghettoes' as the sleeper cells of terror) is to focus on the cultural shibboleths of integration, notably language and citizenship tests, designed to elicit appropriate cultural knowledge. Petro, Abley and Drysdale, indeed, all give accounts of the attempts by governments in historically different periods to force language change as a means of shoring up citizenship claims, most notably in the educational systems of France, Britain, Australia and the United States. However, the point about citizenship tests is not that most British or German or Danish or Dutch citizens would fail them. That is not what they are there for. The purpose is explicitly performative. The aim is to subject migrants to the public gaze, where the State can be seen to exact a particular form of linguistic or epistemic tribute. What is crucial to note is that 'integration', which is held up as the telos of the tests, is not a static but a dynamic category that can be indefinitely reframed depending on the exigencies of the moment. That is to say, if the other becomes too well 'integrated', if they enthusiastically embrace the language, institutions, habitus of the host society, they become equally suspect as the 'fifth column', the 'enemy within', who dissimulate treachery through feigned assimilation.

The sense of the labile nature of integration that we have already alluded to in chapter two is inadvertently referred to by one of Pamela Petro's acquaintances, Liz Shepherd, a diplomat working for the British embassy in Thailand. Petro receives a fax message from Shepherd which reads, 'I did try Ambassador Morgan for you, but he's out of the country at the moment. Pity – he's a great character, and nationalistic in the nicest possible way' (Petro 1997: 193). The Ambassador has integrated into mainstream British, English-language culture but 'nationalistic in the nicest possible way' suggests acceptable levels of difference, a line not be crossed that would trouble the always provisional, irenic prospect of integration.

The murderous forensics of anti-semitism in European history fed off precisely the highly volatile reconfiguration of what it meant to be 'integrated.' Therefore, the question which might be asked is whether the 'culturalisation' of difference, deeply seductive to the practitioners of a literary genre like travel writing, is not complicit in a less than ethical de-politicisation of the public sphere. As the social theorist Alana Lentin has noted:

> Many theorists, artists, musicians and writers have emphasised the fluidity of cultural identities. But without challenging the underlying reason for why culture dominates our understandings it is unlikely that this will have a significant impact in the realm of politics and policy making. Thinking culturally about difference is the default for not talking about 'race', thereby avoiding the charge of racism. But the need for such a substitute obscures the fact that the hierarchy put in place by racism has been maintained.
>
> (2004: 99)

In the instances of language suppression, discussed by Abley in his Australian and North American travels, settler racism has clearly affected the fortunes of indigenous languages. However, it is Lentin's broader contention that thinking culturally about difference becomes a way for not thinking about all kinds of other things which is particularly pertinent to travels through the territories of endangered or minority languages. The axiomatic inclusion of language as a feature of culture, comparable to a local cheese or a distinctive wine, means that the speakers are almost invariably deprived of agency. This is because there is no structural analysis in the present moment as to what it is they can do apart from withering away in their picturesque surroundings. In the words of the critic Seamus Deane, they have no option but 'to stay quaint and stay put' (Deane 1987: 47).

Communication

A difficulty faced by the travel writer who explicitly tackles the subject of language difference in travel is how to communicate that difference. The problem is compounded in the case of a dominant global language like English by ethical concerns around the imperialist pretensions of the language. As he moves through the language space of others, Mark Abley is particularly sensitive to the predatory presence of the language of his narrative, English. Comparing English to the Native American language, Yuchi, Abley claims that 'modern English is the Wal-Mart of languages: convenient, huge, hard to avoid, superficially friendly, and devouring all rivals in its eagerness to expand' (Abley 2003: 56). One of his informants in the Yuchi-speaking community, Richard, has an even darker reading of the Wal-Mart metaphor:

'At Wal-Mart', he said, 'you can still buy the stuff that smaller stores used to sell. Languages aren't like that. Languages are unique. English doesn't sell the other merchandise – it eliminates the other merchandise.'

(79)

Tourism, as Abley notes in the case of Welsh, is one of those practices, which puts minority languages under even greater pressure. This makes travelling through the medium of English ethically problematic, as the traveller is less small store owner and more a part of the Wal-Mart salesforce. Petro is particularly sensitive to the impact of her other language, English, as she scours the planet in search of Welsh speakers: 'My native and, until recently, only tongue is spoken as a first or second language by one-third of the earth's population (some two billion people): such universality can't help but corrode the intimate links between language and place' (Petro 1997: 166). Drysdale, for her part, is explicit about the linguistic and ethical dilemma for the travel writer caught between the desire for contact and the reality of difference. In Greece, she wants to speak to a group of women foraging for edible leaves but does not know their language:

> For all my rejoicing in the diversity of Europe's languages, here I was faced with the reality of their exclusiveness. They rendered me frustrated, alienated, confused, physically handicapped. Not that this was the language's fault; it was my own.
>
> (Drysdale 2001: 311)

Language is crucial in establishing the types of contacts that are necessary to provide information and human insight for the travel writers. A global language like English permits global movement but the ethical end stops are the perceived linguistic destructiveness of that global mobility (Abley on English-language tourism) and the real-world limits to the global reach of an international vehicular language (Drysdale in Greece).

It is partially in response to these dilemmas that Pamela Petro conceives of her travel project from a different perspective. Finding that as an American Anglophone learning Welsh in Wales it was very difficult not to slip back into the dominant language, English, she resolves to travel the world to speak Welsh with other Welsh speakers. She chooses destinations where the other language is not English in the hope that Welsh will function as an effective *lingua franca*. In other words, in Petro's case, global travel is not to enhance the position of English but to bolster the status of Welsh. It becomes, in a sense, a search for a global solution to a local problem. The project is rendered problematic by her lack of full proficiency in the Welsh language and by the fact that many of the Welsh people she meets are either fully Anglophone or are bilinguals who know more English than Petro does Welsh. However, even apart from the circumstantial difficulties of specific Welsh-language contact, Petro is forced to reflect on the nature of global language use and her position as a speaker of American

English. She notes that learning Welsh as an outsider, she has no 'birthright antagonisms' and that, 'I am most me, most American – enterprising, optimistic, composite – when I'm trying to anchor myself with words in someone else's home, and in motion all the time' (Petro 1997: 109). Off in search of Welsh, what she frequently finds are particular perspectives on English. She argues that she sometimes feels that to be American 'is to be blank, without a nationality or language' and she wonders, 'Is this because America is such a polyglot culture that it contains pieces of everywhere else, or because American culture in the late twentieth century is so monolithic and transcending that it *is* everywhere else?' (165–166; her emphasis). At one level, what Petro articulates is the Wal-Mart dystopia of Abley, the transcendent, universal language which defines everywhere else. At another, she implies that it is the polyglossic background to American culture and, by extension, the language, that makes it uniquely poised to describe the world.

That this self-perception is not confined to Americans is evident in Drysdale's musings on cultural and linguistic difference where she claims, 'being a typically British hybrid, I could never belong anywhere' and 'perhaps it is that hybrid quality that gives the British – or at least the English – a natural dislike of homogeneity' (Drysdale 2001: 389). What is worthy of note is not the dubious sociolinguistic or socio-cultural truth-value of the claims, but the construction of two major Anglophone cultures as the sites of mixity and openness, a construction precipitated by the conjoined experience of 'motion' and language difference. In a sense, for all the paeans to language diversity, and notwithstanding a nervousness around the omnipresence of English, English emerges as more open house than closed shop. Paradoxically, travels by the English speakers in and among minority languages tend not to diminish the status of majoritarian Anglophone language and culture but serve rather in the case of Petro and Drysdale to enhance it.

One means of capturing minority language difference in major language narrative is lexical exoticism (Cronin 2000: 40–41). The communicative ambition of the major language is tempered by the untranslatable residue of the minor. In North-Eastern India the Boro language provides Abley with a list of words that have no equivalent, which must be paraphrased, in English, '*onguboy*: to love from the heart, *onsay*: to pretend to love, *onsra*: to love for the last time' (Abley 2003: 124). It is the very resistance to translation that constitutes the unique identity of these languages and becomes a further argument for the importance of their retention and development. For Drysdale and Petro it is less the limits to translation that announce difference than the material presence of the other language. So the names of countries visited and sub-headings appear in both English and Welsh in *Travels in an Old Tongue* and Drysdale in *Mother Tongues* regularly includes excerpts from texts or isolated words in the languages of the regions she visits. Indeed, for Drysdale, the phonic substance of language makes it admirably fit for certain purposes. In Brittany, she notes:

I bought a dictionary full of wonderful no-nonsense words like *gwinkal*, 'to kick', *gortoz*, 'to wait for', *didamall*, 'blameless', *trimiziad*, 'quarter'. It looked blunt and humorous. It sounded not sophisticated like French or intellectual like German, but ancient, peasant like. It wore sabots.

(Drysdale 2001: 384–385)

Noteworthy here is not so much the eccentric personification of language as the underlying commitment, present in all three accounts, to versions of linguistic relativism. That is to say, languages are deemed to involve radically different ways of seeing the world, and even if the words have equivalents, the lifeworlds of speakers inhabiting different languages are inescapably various. It is the language itself which shapes the world in which they dwell. Therein lies the problem for the traveller sensitised to language. If languages do hold within them distinct worlds of experience and sensibility, then how much can the traveller be said to understand? Does the championing of language diversity and the celebration of linguistic uniqueness, a comprehensible ethical stance, deftly undermine any representational function for the travel account by suggesting, in fact, that what is essential about these worlds of communication cannot be communicated? It can be argued, therefore, that what the language trails reveal is not the visual transparency of the globe but the linguistic opacity of its denizens. This opacity, paradoxically, reveals as much as it conceals. That is to say, the problematic nature of knowing and ways of knowing about the 'minority' languages and cultures of indigenous peoples does not have to lead to forms of ontological nationalism. In other words, the 'untranslatable' does not have to be sacralised, the minority language seen as the sacred bearer of exalted difference. Language does not have to become the shield of ethnic otherness, a weapon of exclusion with translation forever bound up in a teleology of loss and betrayal. We can explore forms of minority and minoritisation that from an ecological standpoint have more transformative outcomes.

Language worlds

Nobody has eaten yet and tempers are slightly frayed. Some people are out on the floor dancing and, inevitably, there are others who prefer speech to steps. Gabriel Conroy soon finds himself in a heated discussion with his friend Molly Ivors, a member of the Gaelic League:

[Miss Ivors] said suddenly:

– O, Mr Conroy, will you come for an excursion to the Aran Isles this summer? We're going to stay there for a whole month. It will be splendid out on the Atlantic. You ought to come. Mr Clancy is coming, and Mr Kilkelly and Kathleen Kearney. It would be splendid for Gretta too if she'd come. She's from Connacht, isn't she?

– Her people are, said Gabriel shortly.

– But you will come, won't you? said Miss Ivors, laying her warm hand eagerly on his arm.

– The fact is, said Gabriel, I have just arranged to go –

– Go where? asked Miss Ivors.

– Well, you know, every year I go for a cycling tour with some fellows and so –

– But where? asked Miss Ivors.

– Well, we usually go to France or Belgium or perhaps Germany, said Gabriel awkwardly.

– And why do you go to France and Belgium, said Miss Ivors, instead of visiting your own land?

– Well, said Gabriel, it's partly to keep in touch with the languages and partly for a change.

– And haven't you your own language to keep in touch with – Irish? asked Miss Ivors.

– Well, said Gabriel, if it comes to that, Irish is not my language.

(Joyce 1993: 136)

This scene from James Joyce's story 'The Dead' is usually parsed for its language politics. Critics comb through the Conroy-Ivors encounter for clues to Joyce's attitude to language revivalism and his profoundly ambivalent relationship to the Irish language. What we would like to do is to undo a number of the polarities in this exchange and to suggest that the relationship between travel and minority languages opens a multiplicity of perspectives not bound by the necessary pieties of place. In particular, we will examine this relationship within the broader framework of a political ecology of translation. We want to disentangle idiom and destination. For Molly Ivors, travelling to the Aran Islands means travelling into Irish and for Gabriel Conroy, travelling to the European continent means travelling away from Irish. Language overlaps territory in the classic idiom of cultural nationalism. In examining Torlach Mac Con Midhe's *Aistí Eorpacha* (2015), we want to consider what happens when the opposites are scrambled, when the traveller moves through the countries and languages of Europe, thus does not visit his 'own land' but keeps in touch with his 'own language', Irish. Secondly, we would like to stress the relational as opposed to the essentialist nature of what constitutes 'minority'. In other words, in considering the topic of travel and minority languages, it is important to consider how particular forms or ways of travelling in a major language can reveal 'minoritised' dimensions to the language and its culture(s) which are normally occluded. In this context, we will be analysing Robert Macfarlane's *Landmarks* (2015) where Macfarlane's journeys through the 'Word-Hoard' of English illuminate landscapes of dispossession and discovery. Thirdly, we want to draw attention to another language minority in our society – who have their own language within language – children. More specifically, we will attempt to show how the travel trope which is at the heart of so much classic children's literature raises ethico-political considerations about language and culture in the context of a renewed political ecology. Overseeing this trinity of analysis is Gilles Deleuze's and Félix Guattari's contention in *Kafka: Toward a Minor*

Literature that the 'first characteristic of minor literature [...] is that in it language is affected with a high coefficient of deterritorialization' (Deleuze and Guattari 1986: 16). My concern then is with what this deterritorialisation might reveal in terms of a re-centring of minority language as a way of exploring not only the literature and practice of travel but the role of a political ecology of translation in travel settings.

One English translation of the title of Torlach Mac Con Midhe's work might be 'European Essays'. They are, however, essays in the sense of trying or testing out Mac Con Midhe's belief that his Irish readers need to get back in touch with a world that they have lost, the European world, and central to this task is a sensitivity to language:

> Nowadays, Ireland belongs solely to the Anglo-Saxon world – Australia is nearer to Irish people than Germany. But it wasn't always like that. From the missions of the Irish monks in the Middle Ages to the Flight of the Earls and the Wild Geese, the attention of the Irish was on the European continent as they frequently travelled from country to country. Indeed, I wrote this book to re-connect Irish-language readers with Europe and not just with the English-speaking world. To make this connection, the first thing you need is the languages.
>
> (Mac Con Midhe 2015: 7)[1]

If the traces of Irish European connectivity are to be found in their travels, Mac Con Midhe's writings are a set of travelogues which go from Freiburg im Breisgau to St Gallen to Paris to Chur to Vienna to Montagnola, Naples and Serres in Northern Greece. These displacements involve language shifts and it is the shifts themselves that set up an exploratory tension between the language of the narration – Irish – and the different language worlds which are described. As a trained linguist, Mac Con Midhe is at pains in the early part of his work to explain what he means by a language world. It is the stories you hear as a child, the songs you sang, the kind of history you learnt at school, the books you read as a youngster, the films that you know and that shaped you in some way, the writers that you quote when you are writing and so on (19–20). For Mac Con Midhe, major language cultures inhabit discrete language worlds, worlds that are fully capable of an independent, coherent existence. Minority languages, on the other hand, have much greater difficulty in sustaining that sense of substantive separateness and find themselves squatting in the dwellings of others, the Big Houses of the major languages.

Travelling then becomes a way of moving outside habitual languages of reference, the overly familiar worlds of self-definition, to resituate the minority language and culture in an alternative history and an alternative geography. In a chapter entitled 'Gluais imill ar lámhscríbhinn' [Marginal gloss on the manuscript], Mac Con Midhe visits the monastery in St Gallen which was formerly home to Irish monks in the medieval period engaged in the evangelisation of post-Roman Europe. The most famous of the manuscripts associated with the monastery is the Codex Sangallensis 904. The manuscript has a number of interlinear glosses in Old Irish which explain particular terms or passages in Priscian's Latin grammar. The margins also contain poems composed in the vernacular language including one that describes the pleasure of working outside on the manuscript on a bright summer's day surrounded by bird song (St Gallen 2006). At one level, the object of his trip is hardly surprising. As an Irish speaker he can be expected to pick out those traces of Irish-language culture in Europe, his travel account an act of restitution for those major language travel accounts which ignore or minmise the history and influence of his Irish-speaking compatriots on European culture. When Mac Con Midhe goes to Vienna, for example, he is quick to point to the *Schottenstift*, the *Schottentor* and the *Schottenring* as relics of the scholarly preeminence the Irish enjoyed under the reign of the twelfth century Duke Heinrich II and his successors. For Mac Con Midhe, however, what is significant in the visit to the monastic library in St Gallen is not the monastery as site of the birth of Irish as one of Europe's earliest written vernaculars but rather his engagement with the marginal gloss as a kind of template for what it means to be a minority language speaker and traveller.

Contrary to the classic move in language loss where the journey backwards is an act of retrieval, a return to the *aeteas aurea* of plenitude when the language was widely spoken and minority status an unimaginable prospect, Mac Con Midhe focuses in on the marginal practices of the Irish monks as already involving a version of peripherality. Latin was the language of the Church, learning and administration. The monks could toy around on the margins but there was no question of them taking over the page, 'The Irish could only write in the interstices or gaps of that discourse, on the margin of the page or between the lines' (Mac Con Midhe 2015: 52).[2] This position is not perceived by Mac Con Midhe to be an admission of defeat, an acknowledgement of crippling secondarity. Instead, he uses his own interstitial travelling, his travelling through the tourist *interstices* of Europe from Freiburg im Bresgau to St Gallen to Serres as a way of elaborating an alternative *modus operandi* for the minority language.

In the German university town of Freiburg he is quick to home in on the pronouncements of one of the university's most famous sons, Martin Heidegger. Heidegger, professor and later notoriously, rector of the university during the Nazi period, was greatly preoccupied by the relationship between language and being. For Heidegger, a crucial component of any philosophical tradition is listening. Conventionally, philosophical debate is thought of in terms of speech, rhetoric, winning the argument. It is less common to conceive of it as involving particular practices of listening. From E.H. Gombrich to John Berger to Simon Schama we are replete with histories of seeing but histories of listening and, more especially, of philosophical listening are much rarer (Gombrich 2007; Berger 2008; Schama 2014). Heidegger claims in his 1950 essay 'Die Sprache' that 'Die Sprache spricht' and that the role of the human is to answer, respond to this language (*der Mensch ent-spricht*). In this context, one of the most powerful forms of response is listening (*das Entsprechen ist Hören*) (Heidegger 1985: 30). For Mac

Con Midhe, Heidegger's invitation to listen involves a dual engagement with language. On the one hand, if it is language rather than specific individuals who speak then we have to be more attentive to the particularities of that language, we have to listen carefully to what it is that makes it different, and in particular, to the manner in which poets articulate that difference (*Aistí Eorpacha* is punctuated throughout by poetic extracts). On the other, we need to engage with these differences if we are to avoid in the minority language, a culture of 'síoraistriú' (37), perpetual translation. That is to say, for Mac Con Midhe, there is no point in rewriting the 'téacs mór an domhain' [the large text of the world], relentlessly translating what has already been said in English, for example, into Irish. The role of the writer in Irish is more that of a graffiti artist, saying different things, differently, rather than hovering expectantly in the afterglow of repetition. Thus, the minority language should not be engaged in endless terminological catch-up, trying to say what has already been said in the major language, but should express opinions, insights, ideas, that are uniquely its own.

What this notion of scribal peripherality might mean in geopolitical terms becomes apparent when Mac Con Midhe travels to Italy and Greece. Ireland, Italy and Greece were famously or infamously members of the PIGS group (Portugal, Ireland, Greece, Spain), the disparaging moniker used to refer to the more spectacular victims of post-2008 austerity meltdown. Club Med was another hyperborean putdown that enjoyed much tabloid currency in the aftermath of the troika (EU/IMF/ECB) bailouts. In Naples, under the shadow of Vesuvius, Mac Con Midhe travels back in time to his graduate days in Canada and realises that almost all of his friends were from Latin America. Indeed, he claims that the liveliness of the 'Laidnigh', the Latins, made him feel Irish, very Irish, indeed he felt more Irish in their midst than he ever felt in Ireland: 'I was more Irish in their midst than I ever was in Ireland' (187).[3] He concludes that the Irish are basically a community of Southerners stranded in Northern Europe: 'To cut a long story short, we are a southern people in northern Europe'.[4]

Obvious elements of connection are the continued importance of agriculture and a religion, Catholicism, and this is mentioned by Mac Con Midhe. However, as he travels from Rome to Northern Greece, he feels increasingly that religion is problematic as a cypher of shared identity because of the increased secularisation of Irish and other societies and the obvious differences between Roman Catholicism and Greek Orthodoxy. He does draw, however, on the historical unease of the Celtic church with centralised Roman authority to posit a shared hermeneutics of suspicion among cultures that find themselves on the edge towards the politics of the centre. When they get close, as the Irish did to Rome (as seat of the Church) or Brussels (as the seat of patronage) or Washington (as the source of finance), it all ends in tears. In claiming that the Irish have more in common with the Greeks, Italians, Portuguese and Spaniards than with what he calls the 'náisiúin Ghearmánacha' [Germanic nations], Mac Con Midhe is partly retracing the travel destinations of Irish-speaking exiles of the seventeenth and eighteenth century who settled predominantly in Catholic Europe. But he finds a more persuasive explanation for this elective affinity in the motif of travel as it plays out in the respective mythologies of Greece and Ireland. He sees Odysseus and Oisín as figures who are seized by the desire to leave, to explore new territories, to discover new worlds, yet who are at the same time in the grip of a profound nostalgia, a deep, unyielding love of home. Odysseus pleads with Calypso to let him return to Ithaca and Penelope. Oisín pleads with Niamh to let him leave Tír na nÓg, the Land of the Young, and return to Ireland and to his warrior companions in Na Fianna. At one level, as the Swiss writer, Nicolas Bouvier has pointed out, this is the eternal drama of travel, 's'attacher, s'arracher' (Bouvier 1992: 136) but for Mac Con Midhe the fates of the mythological heroes point to mobility as a crucible of definition:

> We recognise something important about Odysseus and Oisín, and about ourselves, Greek and Irish; not only that we are peripheral but that we are centrifugal. The Greeks see Europe but they also see the Middle East on the other side and the historical relationship they have with it. We see Europe too, but we also see the mighty Atlantic on the other side, and this is where the Land of the Young lies, that is, America.
>
> (211)[5]

There is a crucial difference, however, in the destiny of the Greek and Irish heroes. When Ulysses returns, notwithstanding the tests and the minor obstacle of the insistent suitors, he does find Penelope and he is reunited with his community. When Oisín returns, on the other hand, there is no one there to greet him. Hundreds of years have passed. Fionn and the Fianna are long since dead and in their place he finds a new Fionn, Patrick, and a new band, the clergy, for whom he feels limited sympathy. His native land has become foreign to him. This sense of estrangement, the feeling that home can never be taken for granted or is increasingly difficult to define, is for Mac Con Midhe the default condition of the minority language speaker. By way of expressing this, he travels in space and time between the city of Chur, the oldest urban settlement in Switzerland, and the city of Derry, in Northern Ireland, home to relatives who had moved there from rural Donegal. He comments on the religious Protestant/Catholic divide in both cities and in the material expression of divisions in walls, gates, partitions. As Mac Con Midhe travels through both cities he is less concerned, though, with the traces of division in iron and stone and more preoccupied with the perpetually conflicted speaking subject of the colony.

He imagines the walled city of Derry as a 'cathair thoirmiscthe', a forbidden city. The City is raised to the realm of Platonic Idea or psychosocial Metaphor as a way of accounting for the situation in many different times and places where two cultures and language come into contact, often violent, with each other. The result is a hybrid subject, where the former enemy is a troubling unconscious or punitive superego. Identity is no longer unitary and the fantasy of a return to prelapsarian purity is just that, fantasy. The forbidden city is that psychic territory within that contains the dividedness, that bears the traces of multiple belongings. So for English speakers in Ireland, the forbidden city is the Irish language, the fraught legacy of the natives who are translated en masse into the language of the colonisers and for Irish speakers, it is the Saxon within, the hypercritical voice that scorns the hubris of sovereignty: 'Even when he has secured an independent Republic, the Gael hears the English voice in his heart, telling him that he is worthless as an Irishman, that he should be an Englishman' (90).[6] If Mac Con Midhe argues that wherever you travel you find a Derry, he has in mind these skeins of differentiated cultural and linguistic belongings that are the default condition of the nomadic subjects of globalisation and mass migration (145). These subjects can frequently fall foul of monoglot and monocultural populism that wishes to construct other kinds of forbidden cities of exclusion and pauperisation as in famous *banlieue* of the French political imaginary. Derry, of course, during the Troubles, had its famous No-Go areas and what Mac Con Midhe tracks through his interstitial travels are those No-Go areas, those territories which the minority language traveller feels compelled to explore, even if the truths are unpalatable or the conclusions awkward. Like Oisín, he must make his way in a world of new pieties, changed circumstances and a distinctly unheroic vision of language and place.

Language deficit

If Oisín returns from the dreamworld of youth to a landscape of loss, a pre-occupation with language and landscape calls into question the very notion of what we understand by a major language. The botanist Oliver Rackham in *The History of the Countryside* (2000) outlines four ways in which, in his words, the 'landscape is lost' (14), through the loss of beauty, the loss of wildlife and vegetation, and the loss of meaning. For the travel and nature writer Robert Macfarlane, it is the loss of meaning that is particularly troubling. He claims that *Landmarks* is fundamentally, 'a book about the power of language – strong style, single words – to shape our sense of place' (Macfarlane 2015b: 1). As words to describe specific aspects of landscape – land, sea, weather, atmosphere – begin to ebb from a major language like English, then the ability of English speakers to be able to see the world around them becomes fatally compromised. As Macfarlane puts it, 'Language deficit leads to attention deficit' (24). Increasingly, he argues,

> The nuances observed by specialized vocabularies are evaporating from common usage, burnt off by capital, apathy and urbanization. The terrain beyond the city fringe has become progressively more understood in terms of large generic units ('field', 'hill', 'valley', 'wood'). It has become blandscape.
>
> (23)

So Macfarlane sets about compiling a 'Counter-Desecration Phrasebook' with glossaries grouped under the headings of Flatlands, Uplands, Waterlands, Coastlands, Underlands, Northlands, Edgelands, Earthlands, Woodlands and a Glossary left blank for the reader's own use. These glossaries in their coverage of the British landscape draw on 'Norn and Old English, Anglo-Romani, Cornish, Welsh, Irish, Gaelic, the Orcadian, Shetlandic and Doric dialects of Scots, and numerous regional versions of English, through to the last vestiges of living Norman still spoken on the Channel Islands' (1). Each glossary follows a discussion of a nature writer who has travelled through a particular area and where explicitness of naming is concomitant with accuracy of description. Nan Shepherd, Roger Deakin, John Alex Baker, Richard Skelton, Richard Jeffries, Jacquetta Hawkes, John Muir, Barry Lopez are among the writers discussed, their travels through landscape a pilgrimage of poetically precise perception.

What is striking about the glossaries is the extent to which the minority languages of Britain and minoritised varieties of English ('regional versions of English') themselves become central to this process of the recovery of landscape from lexical abandonment. In other words, the loss of meaning Rackham describes and which is repeatedly emphasised by Macfarlane in his own travels in the book and through the travelling of others show how a major language can become in a sense *minoritised* through the shrinkage of its lexical range and semantic reach. In the edition of the *Oxford Junior Dictionary* that came out in 2007, Macfarlane notes words that were deleted included 'acorn, adder, ash, beech, bluebell, buttercup, catkin, conker, cowslip, cygnet, dandelion, fern, hazel, heather, heron, ivy, knigfisher, lark, mistletoe, nectar, newt, otter, pasture and willow' (3). Reversing this loss of description and reference involves admitting two forms of minority to the major language, the word-hoard of Britain's different minority languages, and the multiple dialect forms of English throughout the island. The major language as it excludes language minority becomes increasingly unable to describe the natural and physical world in which its speakers dwell. The opacity of the world reveals the impoverished descriptive hubris of a language that loses more insights as it gains more speakers.

Ignoring the minority reports of English and other languages has implications beyond a poverty of description. A failure to see means a failure to see a great many things and not just the landscape before you. McFarlane describing his reactions to Barry Lopez's travel writings, *Arctic Dreams*, claims that one of the lessons the book taught him was that 'while writing about landscape often begins in the aesthetic it ends in the ethical'. Lopez's intense attentiveness was 'a form of moral gaze born of his belief that if we attend more closely to something then we are less likely to act more selfishly towards it' (211). In other words, attending to lexis is a matter not of nostalgia but of urgency. The American poet and farmer Wendell Berry sees language as a way forward not a step backwards:

> People *exploit* what they have merely concluded to be of value, but they *defend* what they love and to defend what we love we need a particularizing language, for we love what we particularly know.
>
> (Berry 2000: 41)

What this might mean politically is illustrated by the responses to a proposal submitted by an engineering company AMEC supported by British Energy for the development of a wind farm on Brindled Moor on the Isle of Lewis in the Outer Hebrides. The proposal consisted of a wind 'power station' of 234 turbines each 140 metres high with a blade span of 80 metres (the terminology of 'farm' tries to mask the reality: these installations are dispersed power stations). Each turbine required a foundation of 700 cubic metres of concrete and '5 million cubic metres of rock and 2.5 million cubic metres of peat would be excavated and displaced' (Macfarlane 2015b: 28). One response was a collaborative art project *A-mach an Gleann/A Known Wilderness* where the co-authors Anne Campbell and Jon McLeod mapped their moor-walks, describing in great detail features of landscape, wildlife, folk memory that they observed or remembered on the way. The second was the compilation by Anne Campbell and Finlay McLeod of *Some Lewis Moorland Terms: A Peat Glossary*, a glossary of 126 Gaelic terms to describe features of the moorland such as *teine biorach*, 'the flame or the will-o'-the-wisp that runs on the top of heather when the moor is burnt during the summer' or a *rùdhan*, 'set of four peat blocks leaned up against one another such that the wind helps their drying' (Campbell 2013: 18). The terms here are in Scots Gaelic but in the glossary at the end of the second chapter discussing the moorland controversy there are English dialect words from Sussex, Yorkshire, Essex, Exmoor, Northamptonshire, Somerset, Suffolk, Cumbria, East Anglia and the West Country. What the *Peat Glossary* and *A Known Wilderness* are contesting is the notion of the moorland as a *terra nullius*, ripe for development and extraction. When James Carnegy-Arbuthnot, an estate owner in Angus, argued in 2013 that it was right that so few people own most of the land in Scotland because most of it was 'unproductive wilderness', he was readily equating emptiness of landscape and plenitude of possession. What the excluded languages – minority languages outside and within English – do is to restore a sense of history, particularity, complexity and (common) ownership to place. Noteworthy in the responses to the AMEC development is that travel and language – the moor-walks and the glossary – are both intertwined in opposition to the proposed project and detailed and loving description of place becomes inescapably ethical. In a broader sense, what the strategic minoritisation of the major languages of industrial development through travel involves is an overall shift from what Naomi Klein calls an ideology of extractivism (see chapter one) to an ideology of regeneration. A regenerative move challenges through the energies of minority and minoritised major languages the neo-colonial and predatory emptying out of landscape and language.

Many of the journeys described by Macfarlane, the journeying of Nan Shepherd or Richard Jeffries or John Alex Baker are endotic journeys, they are journeys around sharply circumscribed local places, trips to proximate, nearby places. Walter Besant, commenting on Richard Jeffries' naturalist excursions around the edgelands of London, exclaimed, 'here were the most wonderful things possible going on under our very noses, but we saw them not!' (Besant 1905: 167). So whether it is what Macfarlane calls the 'bastard countryside' of the outer limits of the expanding metropolis or the strictly delimited hunting ground of the peregrine falcon in Essex, the travellers in *Landmarks* are not covering large expanses of territory. The local idioms in a sense do justice to the local places. The dialectal minoritisiation of English is, for Richard Skelton, 'a way of looking at the world that is now also lost, an attention to the form of things and a care, a generosity in the bestowing of names' (Skelton 2011: 138–139). In the West Pennine Moors, a *brog* is not simply a branch, but a broken branch. A *lum* is not just a pool but a deep pool. However, this reduction of scale is not commensurate with a withdrawal of ambition. Minoritised language is not the shrivelled parlance of exhaustion, a way of speaking haunted by extinction. On the contrary, what the spatial constriction reveals is the inexhaustible richness of detail that crowds even the most apparently banal or featureless of landscapes. It is through the retrieval of the analytic and poetic resources of local languages that the sightseer becomes a sight-seer, one who is capable of investing the immediate landscape with both detail and larger frames of significance. Macfarlane, for example, describes Aberdeen-born Nan Shepherd, who was born, lived and died there as 'a localist of the best kind: she came to know her chosen place closely, but closeness served to deepen rather than to limit her vision' (56). There are two immediate consequences of what I have described elsewhere as the practice of analytic microspection (Cronin 2012). Analytic microspection is the proper investigation of places and their inhabitants through methods and practices which reveal the full, fractal complexity of human habitation. Operational microspection is the application of forms of social, economic and political organisation to local places in a way that ensures their future sustainability. The vision of economy and society underlying a politics of microspection is one of the basic units of sustainability being the local in a transnational context. As Alastair McIntosh has observed, 'It is only if we can find fulfilment in close proximity to one another and local place that we can hope to stop sucking what we need from all over the world' (McIntosh 2008: 71–72) The local as revealed through analytic microspection is open to not cut off from the world.

The first consequence of analytic microspection is that the teasing out of local, proximate linguistic detail reveals the deeply connected nature of landscape and human dwelling and mobility. When Richard Skelton and his partner Autumn Richardson move to Cumbria, we are told about how they 'learnt to navigate the linguistic-historical complexities of toponymy and language in Cumbria' (187). These range from Gaelic and Old English to the impact of the Scandinavian settlements in the eighth to eleventh centuries. Embedded in the local language and landscape are the trails of influence, 'the impacts of trade, exploration and colonization on the region' (187). The second consequence is the re-enchantment of language and experience which runs counter to the Weberian disenchantment of modernity. In the Weberian account of the rise of the modern, all other forms of knowing are cast aside in favour of the master narrative of rationalism. This single way of knowing promises control over nature and mastery of the emotions. Wonder gives way to will and mystery to mastery. The rationally apprehended and instrumentally organised world is one in which 'there are no mysterious incalculable forces that come into play, but rather that one can, in principle, master all things by calculation' (Weber 1946: 139). Language in this sense is a powerful agent of re-enchantment as in Macfarlane's words, 'it does not just register experience, it produces it' (25), it has a formative as well as an informative impulse. The forgotten, minoritised forms of language can both make us see the world anew – refresh or clarify our vision – but also vivify and reinvigorate the idiom we habitually use to describe, talk about or live in that world.

Children

In biographical as opposed to social terms, banishment from the world of childhood is often seen as the precondition of disenchantment. We leave the playgrounds of wonder for the battlegrounds of performance. In arguing for the place of children's literature in our discussions around minority languages and travel, we want to claim that the enchantments of childhood and childhood language, what Macfarlane calls 'Childish' can be usefully included in extending the remit of what we commonly think of as the relationship between travel, ecology and translation.

It is commonplace in discussions of minority languages to speak of the importance of children's literature for intergenerational language transmission (O'Sullivan 2005; O'Connell 1999: 208–216). If the children do not speak or read the language, it is to all intents and purposes dead. Conscious of this fact, official and non-governmental bodies devote considerable efforts to the translation of children's literature from major to minor languages. We might, however, think not just about children speaking a minority language but of the language of childhood itself as a minority language, spoken by a group in our society who do not, in any real sense, possess full rights as citizens. Loriz Malaguzzi, the teaching pioneer, who developed what was known as the Reggio Emilia approach to the education of children, stressed the need to listen to what children have to say rather than continually tell them what we think they should know. He spoke of the 'hundred languages of children' (Malaguzzi 1993: vi). What Malaguzzi has in mind here is children have ways of naming, ways of describing, ways of situating themselves that are all their own. The extent to which this is true is borne out by an experiment carried out by Deb Wilenski and Caroline Wendling. Each Monday morning, for three months, they brought thirty four- and five-year-old children into Hinchingbrooke Country Park which borders the grounds of their primary school in North Cambridgeshire. In *Fantastical Guides for the Wildly Curious* (Wilenski 2013) made up largely of the children's speech, stories and drawings what is most noticeable is the relentless mapping of place by the children, their penchant for coining new words to describe what they saw ('honeyfurs' for the soft seed-heads they gathered from the grasses) and the collapse of the fantastical into the real ('My name is Kian and I'm going to jump over the whole world' or another girl, 'I was born in the climbing tree'). In other words, through toponyms and neologisms they re-enchant the surrounding reality of the park which appears inexhaustible in its possibilities.

This re-enchantment is crucially bound up not just with the expressive possibilities of their minoritised language, it is also connected to the freedom to roam. The 2012 British 'Natural Childhood' report found that between 1970 and 2010 the area in which British children were allowed to play unsupervised had dropped by 90 per cent (Moss 2012: 5). The proportion of children found to be regularly playing in 'wild' places had dropped from one in two to one in ten. Regular interaction with nature becomes problematic in a world reduced to the policed precincts of house, garden and (possibly) pavement. Therefore, mobility itself or rather the possibility of mobility becomes crucial to the emergence of forms of language practice and forms of engagement with the proximate world which are at the heart of children's literature from *The Lion, the Witch and the Wardrobe* to *Stig of the Dump*. Robert Macfarlane describes how becoming a father had altered his focal length and adjusted his depth of field:

> Children are generally uninterested in grandeur, and rapt by the miniature and the close at hand (a teeming ants' nest, a chalk pit, moss jungles, lichen continents, a low-branched climbing tree). From them I have learned [...] that magnitude of scale is no metric by which to judge natural spectacle, and that wonder, is now, more than ever, an essential survival skill.
>
> (238)

Analytic microspection come easily to that significant minority group, children. Their accounts of their travels and the literature which is directed at children draws extensively on these minority travelling practices. The ecological implications of minority and minoritised travelling practices are immense and much can be learned from them in terms of the defence and transformation of people, habitat and ecosystems.

Resources

It is in the context of the culture of extractivism, sacrifice zones and the liquefaction of nature through the creation of carbon markets that a role for ecotranslation becomes manifest. For indigenous peoples to tell their stories, whether of ancestral lore around place or political narratives around exploitation, it is crucial that they have access to the resources of translation. Without translation, without a way of making their voices heard, they are silenced, potentially forever if the destruction of surrounding ecosystems proceeds apace. If 'language' is in there with 'race' and 'class' as a marker of peripherality and disadvantage, then struggles around language advocacy and translation rights become part of the broader ecological struggle. Russ Rymer, in an article discussing the predicament of endangered languages, argues that small languages often offer particular insights into nature, because their speakers tend to live close to the animals and plants around them. Talk in these languages reflects the distinctions their speakers observe:

When small communities abandon their languages and switch to English or Spanish, there is a massive disruption in the transfer of traditional knowledge across generations – about medicinal plants, food cultivation, irrigation techniques, navigation systems, seasonal calendars.

(Rymer 2012)

It is striking that the 'traditional knowledge' Rymer lists has primarily to do with ecological knowledge, the things that a community needs to know in order to maintain a sustainable lifestyle. Cmiique Iitom is a language spoken by the Seri people of Mexico, traditionally seminomadic hunter gatherers living in the western Sonoran desert near the Gulf of California. Cmiique Iitom has terms for more than three hundred desert plants. The Seri word for harvesting eelgrass offered a clue to scientists about its nutritional merits and it turned out that its protein content was comparable to that of wheat. Seri names for animals reveal behaviours that were treated with initial scepticism by scientists:

The Seris call one sea turtle *moosni hant coit*, or green turtle that descends, for its habit of hibernating on the floor of the sea, where the traditional fishermen used to harpoon it. 'We were sceptical when we first learned from the Seri Indians of Sonora, Mexico, that some Chelonia are partially buried on the sea floor during the colder months', stated a 1976 paper in *Science* documenting the behaviour. 'However, the Seri have proved to be highly reliable informants'.

(Rymer 2012)

The case for the value of Cmiique Iitom is articulated at two levels, both involving translation, one case involving impossibility, the other, possibility. At one level, the language is valuable because it contains words or terms for which there is no equivalent in other, particularly dominant languages, an example being the many unique terms for desert plants. Zero-equivalence here is a version of the 'untranslatable' as there is nothing to translate the terms into (though this does not mean that they cannot be translated), they only exist in the Cmiique Iitom language. Similarly, a lack of a term can point to the specificity of a culture rooted in a particular ecological niche. Rymer claims that in the Aka language, spoken in Palizi in Arunachal Pradesh, India's northeasternmost state, there is no word for a job in the sense of salaried labour. At another level, the value of the language is revealed through the act of translation, translating the term for the sea turtle reveals the depth of indigenous knowledge. The nutritious qualities of eelgrass become apparent in the act of rendering the term for harvesting in another language and thus point to capacity for resilience of local food cultures. The resistance to translation points up the place-based particularities of language expression but it is this very resistance that encourages the translator to articulate a sense of what the language is trying to express or describe for a wider community whose actions as a result of anthropogenic climate change are affecting communities of language speakers the world over, no matter how localised or remote. Global audiences need to understand what they do not understand and what they do not understand may be the key to what they need to understand, namely, the value of biocultural diversity (Maffi and Woodley 2010).

In September 2000, at the Millennium Summit, the 189 member states of the United Nations committed themselves to the eradication of extreme poverty and to improving the health and welfare of the world's poorest people by 2015. The commitment was set forth in the United Nations Millennium Declaration. This vision was expressed in eight time-bound goals, known as the Millennium Development Goals (MDGs). These goals were to eradicate extreme poverty and hunger, achieve universal primary education, promote gender equality and empower women, reduce child mortality, improve maternal health, combat HIV/AIDS, malaria and other diseases, ensure environmental sustainability and develop a global partnership for development. Implicit in these goals is a link between social progress and planetary wellbeing. One of the responses to the formulation of these goals came from the SIL (formerly known as the Summer Institute of Linguistics), a faith-based NGO with a particular interest in the protection and promotion of minority languages. SIL produced a brochure entitled *Why Languages Matter: Meeting Millennium Development Goals through Local Languages* (2014). In the brochure, SIL outline the importance of the use of local languages for the realisation of the MDGs. In the case of Goal 1, for example, the eradication of extreme poverty and hunger, the reader is introduced to Michel, a farmer from the African country of Benin. He completed adult literacy classes in his mother tongue, Waama. Literacy allowed him to access information about improved farming methods and significant agricultural dates. His reading skills also allowed him to learn about the best times and places to sell his produce so he was no longer the unwitting victim of unscrupulous middlemen. Under Goal 6, combatting AIDS/HIV, malaria and other diseases, in the web version, we learn about a Cameroonian who one day in a local church is given a brochure on HIV/AIDS in his mother tongue:

> That day, reading through it, the message was so clear and spoke directly to my heart. I understood that HIV/AIDS was speaking my mother tongue – meaning, it was a member of our community and present in our village.
>
> (SIL 2014a)

He wished that he had read this brochure before because it might have saved at least one of his brothers' lives. We are told that 'similar reports have come from other language communities that have this AIDS brochure' and that the brochure has been translated into and published in 34 languages: Aghem, Bakossi, Bafut, Babanki, Bulu, Bum, Badwe'e, Cuvok, Fang (Equatorial Guinea (EG)), Fulfulde Ajamiya, Fulfulde Romans, Hdi, Gemzek, Kako, Kejom, Kenyang, Kombe (EG), Lamnso', Mbembe, Mékaa, Meta', Moloko, Muyang, Nomaande, Ngomba, Nuasue, Nugunu, Numaala, Pinyin, Spanish (EG), Tuki, Tunen, Yambetta and Yemba.

The provision of translated information in local languages whether relating to health, agriculture or education is obviously crucial to any notion of eco-translation in allowing a community to function in all spheres of life in the language of their choice. If from an ecological point of view there is a clear ethical imperative to have recourse to translation, the translation activity itself is not without its own ethical quandaries, one relating to inputs and the other to consequences. For example, at the level of inputs, in the case of HIV/AIDS, faith and non-faith groups may have different understandings of what constitutes sexually moral behaviour so what gets translated is going to reflect in whole or in part the belief systems of the organisations involved in the dissemination of information on sexual health. In the web version of the SIL response to Goal 6 of the MDGs the reader is told about *Kande's Story*, the true story of a young African girl who has to raise her brothers and sisters after their parents die from AIDS. The reader is informed that '[t]he story not only addresses the problems faced by HIV/AIDS, but it teaches people that they can resist the temptation to participate in extramarital relationships' and that along with translation into Bafut, *Kande's Story* has been translated into fifteen other languages of Cameroon as well as dozens of other languages across Africa and around the world (SIL 2014a). Clearly, the translated content is in part dictated by the value system of the faith-based NGO so that any discussion of translation into or out of indigenous or endangered languages must not only consider the ecological impact of the fact of the translation activity but also of the content of translation (what gets translated by whom for what purposes). With respect to consequences, translation when it takes place becomes part of the cultural ecosystem in which the indigenous language functions. If translation occupies a preponderate place in the life of the language to the detriment of other forms of written and oral production in the language, then concerns can emerge about the viability or sustainability of the indigenous language as a distinct entity. This is the anxiety expressed earlier in this chapter by Torlach Mac Con Midhe around a culture of *síor-aistriú* or perpetual translation. It came to the fore in the 1930s and 1940s in Ireland when a number of writers and commentators felt that the government scheme to fund substantial amounts of literary translation into Irish was undermining the development of indigenous forms of expression in the language. One critic Cathal Mac a'Bhaird claimed that:

> If the Irish language grows at all, it will have to do so naturally, and as I see it, there is nothing at all as unnatural as hearing or reading a story in Irish when that story is set in London, Berlin or the capital city of France.

> (cited in O'Leary 2004: 385)

Tadhg Ó Murchadha, the translator of *Robinson Crusoe* into Irish, first published in 1909 as *Eachtra Robinson Crúsó* saw the specific difficulty of the translator's task lying in the very wide gap between English and Irish languages and cultures:

The thoughts and ideas in 'Robinson Crusoe' are altogether foreign to the thoughts and ideas of the tales I heard told in my youth, a fact which in itself made this translation all the more difficult.

(Ó Murchadha 1915: n.p.)

Whether these criticisms are valid or not, and there are clear traces of a nationalist defensiveness around the notion of the foreign in both comments, it must be acknowledged that in the more fragile biocultural ecosystem of minority or endangered languages, translation can, for reasons of power, prestige or pre-ponderance, become a significant presence with clear consequences for the allocation of expressive resources in the language.

As we observed at the beginning of this chapter, 'minority' is a matter of relationship not essence. In other words, minoritised languages are not only to be found in remote, isolated or peripheral parts of the planet. There are many kinds of 'sacrifice zones' and among these are the zones inhabited by migrant communities living in prosperous, developed countries or in large metropolises who can find themselves working long hours for low pay, without proper legal status, and who do not speak or have limited knowledge of the dominant language of the host community. They too are part of the ecological story of extractivism, the globalised exploitation of finite resources with the increasing mobilisation of a poorly paid migrant underclass (Khalaf et al. 2014). Examples of abuse and ill-treatment were aired on the Australian Broadcasting Corporation's *Four Corners* programme in 2015 where footage from secret cameras was used to show migrants working up to 18 hours a day in harsh conditions for less than the minimum wage. As the promotional material for the programme 'Slaving Away' explained, 'labour hire contractors prey upon highly vulnerable young foreigners, many with very limited English, who have come to Australia with dreams of working in a fair country' (Meldrum-Hanna and Russell 2015). If some of the exploitation was on large, industrialised farms outside of Australia's main urban centres, within the centres themselves there were many instances of exploitation, particularly in the retail sector. What most of the migrants had in common was a limited or non-existent ability to speak English (Coorey 2015). The migrants may be the speakers of a language like Chinese which cannot in any sense be considered 'endangered' but in particular contexts of usage, the speakers of the language have all the disadvantages of speakers of a minority language which has no status or recognition in a community. It is for this reason that a central concern of eco-translation must be community interpreting in all its forms as community interpreters operate at the frontline of language contact with different authorities that impact on the lives and wellbeing of migrant workers everywhere. In other words, eco-translation is not only about voices from 'traditional and indigenous cultures around the world', it is also about the minoritised voices of migrant workers, often speakers of sizeable or major languages, who find their wellbeing seriously compromised by a lack of access to translation resources and the services of community interpreters (see Inghilleri 2012).

In their work on language practices in urban spaces, Alastair Pennycook and Emi Otsuji note the parallels between different sites of multi-language use:

> There are many strong parallels between the multilingual contexts that we focus on in cities and the studies of dynamic change, multivocality and local language practices within a wider focus on globalization in 'peripheral' Sámi, Irish, Corsican and Welsh language contexts.
>
> (Pennycook and Otsuji 2015: 30)

Strangely, translation as a named language practice is notably absent from the book, although the ethnographic research depends in part on the translation skills of the co-researchers to understand and communicate what is going on in the different sites of ethnographic research and there is an acknowledgement that, in the case of migrants, 'linguistic networks may provide work, but one is often dependent on other linguistic mediators' (39). What is significant, however, from the point of view of eco-translation is the stress in Pennycook and Otsuji's work on the quotidian nature of multilingual language practices which are widespread across the planet. In their version of a grassroots globalisation or a globalisation from below cities are the sites of continuous, unceasing 'metrolingualism' which they have defined as 'the ways in which people of different and mixed backgrounds use, play with and negotiate identities through language' (Pennycook and Otsuji 2010: 244). It is, of course, the sights and sounds of this metrolingualism which have mobilised many European populist movements and conservative parties in their repeated calls for stringent language tests and the removal of budgets for the provision of community translation and interpreting services. In the 2015 general election manifesto for the British Conservative Party under the heading 'We will promote integration and the British values', voters are told that:

> Being able to speak English is a fundamental part of integrating into our society. We have introduced tough new language tests for migrants and ensured councils reduce spending on translation services.
>
> (Conservatives 2015: 31)

The 'tough new language tests' and the reduction of 'spending on translation services' make language the litmus test of integration. Assimilation is mastery of the dominant host language and a refusal of the translation process. The language ideology informing these commitments is firmly rooted in a notion of monolingualism that is historically a relatively recent phenomenon in world history. Yasemin Yildiz has argued emerging in the age of nations it is 'monolingualism, not multilingualism, that is the result of a relatively recent, albeit highly successful, development' (Yildiz 2012: 3). Monolingualism becomes much more than a quantitative term to isolate and designate a particular language but emerges as 'a key structuring principle that organises the entire range of modern social life from the construction of individuals and their proper subjectivities to the formation of disciplines and institutions, as well as imagined collectives such as cultures and nations' (3). As we saw earlier in this chapter with Mcfarlane's minoritisation of English, the notion of the monolingual is highly problematic given the wide variety of speech forms and histories that are encompassed in any one language (Busch 2013). These forms and histories become as obvious to the translator when they begin their own endotic journeys through their mother tongue as when they move with texts from one language to another. However, what concerns us here is not the false reality but the genuine political effects of a language ideology of monolingualism which seeks to marginalise translation and limit language difference.

A political ecology of translation views languages in their connectedness not in their isolation. That is to say, a language can be seen as offering its speakers a set of possibilities in terms of understanding or relating to the world, what is often called 'culture', but it cannot be reduced to that. As Heller and Duchêne have pointed out the equation of one language with one culture simply maintains, 'the language-culture-nation ideological nexus' (Heller and Duchêne 2007: 7). Translation historians have shown that languages are endlessly open-ended, repeatedly subject to the influences of other cultures and languages even if translation has also served to define and maintain the contours of language. Therefore, an ecological championing of language diversity cannot be a simple, mimetic reflection of the monolingual language ideology that underpins the defence of 'integration and British values'. Rather, in terms of a globalisation from below, eco-translation must be alert to those practices which engage translation across a wide range of languages and cultures in a plurality of urban and rural settings and where the translational history of languages trouble any easy symmetry between mono-language and mono-culture. García and Li Wei define 'translanguaging' as:

> an approach to the use of language, billingualism and the education of bilinguals, that considers the language practice of bilinguals not as two autonomous language systems as has traditionally been the case, but as one linguistic repertoire that have been societally constructed as belonging to two separate languages.
>
> (García and Wei 2014: 12)

They are clearly unhappy with the ontological fixation we discussed in chapter one which sees language practice as being about one language *or* the other. Notions of translanguaging or metrolingualism are in a sense an attempt to capture that transitional nature of the *inter*, of the silent transformation which characterises translation in the movement between and through language and context. Pennycook and Otsuji, through they largely silence translation in their discussion, are sensitive to the play between fixity and fluidity in language contact and use:

> When considering multilingualism, therefore, we are by no means blind to the fact that people also incorporate fixed modes of identities. Metrolingualism

is not so much convergent diversity (the bleeding of fixed elements) but dynamic emergence in the form of a spiral as people move between fixed and fluid understandings of and uses of languages and identity.

(Pennycook and Otsuji 2015: 100)

Policies on migration can be extractivist in nature, following the well-trodden path of imperial practice, where labour is extracted from a people, who become 'resources' rather than subjects. One consequence of the objectifying move of the resource is to strip the subject of the markers of subjective interiority, one of which is the language of native expression. From the point of view of a political ecology of translation, the 'spiral' or the movement between fixed and fluid understandings is bound up with the active principle of 'regeneration' (Klein 2014: 447). The constant regeneration of materials, peoples, life-forms, ideas, the endless translation, that generates multiple forms of language, textual and cultural practice is the ultimate form of resistance to the extractivist lock-down of toxic uniformity. It is also ultimately the necessary precondition to the transition to 'new ways of living and being'.

Notes

1 Sa lá atá inniu ann, baineann Éire leis an domhan Angla-Shacsanach amháin – tá an Astráil níos gaire do mhuintir na hÉireann ná an Ghearmáin. Ach ní mar sin a bhí tráth. Ó mhisinéireacht na manach Gaelach sa Mheánaois go dtí Imeacht na nIarlaí agus na Géanna Fiáine, bhí aird na nGael riamh ar mhór-roinn na hEorpa agus iad ag taisteal go minic ó thír go tír. Leoga, scríobh mé an leabhar seo mar iarracht lucht léite na Gaeilge a chur i dteagmháil leis an Eoraip arís agus níl le domhan an Bhéarla amháin. Chun an teagmháil sin a bheith ag duine, caithfidh teangacha a bheith aige ar an gcéad dul síos.
2 'Níorbh fhéidir leis na Gaeil ach a gcuid a scríobh in *interstices* nó bearnaí an díoscúrsa sin, ar imeall an leathanaigh nó idir na línte.'
3 'B'Éireannaí mé ina measc siúd ná mar a bhí mé in Éirinn riamh.'
4 'Chun an scéal uile a chur i mbeagán focal, is pobal deisceartach i dtuasiceart na hEorpa sinne.'
5 Aithnímid rud tábhachtach faoi Odaiséas is Oisín, agus fúinn féin, Gréagaigh is Éireannaigh: ní amháin go bhfuilimid forimeallach ach go bhfuilimid lártheifeach. Feiceann na Gréagaigh an Eoraip ach feiceann siad an Meánoirthear freisin ar an taobh eile, agus gaol staire acu leis. Feicimidne an Eoraip freisin, ach feicimid an t-Atlantach ollmhór ar an taobh eile, agus sin an treo a bhfuil Tír na nÓg, is é sin, Meiriceá.
6 'Fiú agus poblacht shaor bainte amach aige, airíonn an Gael guth an tSasanaigh istigh ina chroí, ag rá nach bhfuil aon mhaitheas ann mar Éireannach, gur cheart dó a bheith ina Shasanach.'

Bibliography

Abley, M. (2003) *Spoken Here: Travels Among Threatened Languages*, London: Heinemann.

Allen, B. (2015) *Vanishing into Things: Knowledge in the Chinese Tradition*, Cambridge (MA): Harvard University Press.

Anders, G. (2007) *Le temps de la fin*, Paris: L'Herne.

Anderson, K. (2015) The hidden agenda: how veiled techno-utopias shore up the Paris Agreement. Available online: http://kevinanderson.info/blog/the-hidden-agenda-how-veiled-techno-utopias-shore-up-the-paris-agreement (accessed 26 March 2016).

Apter, E. (2013) *Against World Literature: On the Politics of Untranslatability*, London: Verso.

ASPCA (2015) Factory farms. Available online: www.aspca.org/animal-cruelty/factory-farms (accessed 8 December 2015).

Augustine (2003) *The City of God*, trans. H. Bettenson, London: Penguin,.

Baigorri-Jalón, J. (2014) *From Paris to Nuremberg: The Birth of Conference Interpreting*, Amsterdam: John Benjamins.

Bailey, R.W. (2004) 'American English: its origins and history', 3–17, *Language in the USA: Themes for the Twenty First Century*, Cambridge: Cambridge University Press.

Basel Action Network (2005) *The Digital Dump: Exporting Re-use and Abuse to Africa. Media Release Version*, Basel: Basel Action Network.

Beck, J. and Davenport, T. (2001) *The Attention Economy: Understanding the New Currency of Business*, Cambridge (MA): Harvard Business School.

Beer, G. (2009) *Darwin's Plots: Evolutionary Narrative in Darwin, George Eliot and Nineteenth-Century Fiction*, third edition, Cambridge: Cambridge University Press.

Bennett, K. (2015) Towards an epistemological monoculture: mechanisms of epistemicide in European research publication, 9–35, in R. Plo Alustrué and C. Pérez-Llantada (eds), *English as a Scientific and Research Language*, Berlin: De Gruyter Mouton.

Benveniste, É. (1969) *Le vocabulaire des institutions indo-européennes*, 2 vols, Paris: Les Éditions de Minuit.

Berardi, F. (2010) *Precarious Rhapsody: Semiocapitalism and the Pathologies of the Post-Alpha Generation*, London: Minor Composition.

Berger, J. (2008) *Ways of Seeing*, London: Penguin.

Bergson, H. (1959) *Oeuvres*, Paris: PUF.

Berry, W. (2000) *Life is a Miracle*, Berkeley (CA): Counterpoint Press.

Besant, W. (1905) *The Eulogy of Richard Jefferies*, London: Chatto and Windhus.

Biermann, Kai (2011) Betrayed by our own data, *Zeit Online*. Available online: www. google.ie/?gws_rd=ssl (accessed 20 January 2016).

Biewald, Lukas (2010) How crowdsourcing helped Haiti's relief efforts. Available online: radar.oreilly.com/2010/03/how-crowdsourcing-helped-haiti.html (accessed 12 May 2013).

Biguenet, J. and Schulte, R. (1989) (eds) *The Craft of Translation*, Chicago (IL): University of Chicago Press.

Bihouix, P. (2014) *L'Âge des low tech: vers une civilisation techniquement soutenable*, Paris: Seuil.

Blair, A. (2010) *Too Much to Know: Managing Scholarly Information before the Modern Age*, New Haven (CT): Yale University Press.

Bohm, D. (1981) *Wholeness and the Implicate Order*, London: Routledge and Kegan Paul.

Bongie, C. (1991) *Exotic Memories: Literature, Colonialism and the Fin de Siècle*, Stanford CA: Stanford University Press.

Bonneuil, C. and Fressoz, J.-B. (2013) *L'Événement Anthropocène: La Terre, l'histoire et nous*, Paris: Seuil.

Bonneuil, C. and de Jouvancourt, P. (2014) En finir avec l'épopée récit, géopouvoir et sujets de l'anthropocène, 57–105, in É. Hache (ed.) *De l'univers clos au monde infini*, Bellevaux: Éditions Dehors.

Bourg, D. (1996) *L'homme artifice*, Paris: Gallimard.

Bouvier, N. (1992) *L'Usage du monde*, Paris: Payot.

Bradley, F. and Kennelly, J. (2009) *Capitalising on Culture, Competing on Difference: Innovation, Learning and Sense of Place in Globalising Ireland*, Syracuse (NY): Syracuse University Press.

Braidotti, R. (2013) *The Posthuman*, Cambridge: Polity.

British Council (2015) Our organisation. Available online: www.britishcouncil.org/orga nisation (accessed 18 May 2015).

Brown, J. S. and Weiser, M. (1996) The coming age of calm technology. Available online: www.ubiq.com/hypertext/weiser/acmfuture2endnote.htm (accessed 18 March 2014).

Bruce, B. C. and Hogan, M. P. (1998) The disappearance of technology: toward an ecological model of literacy, 269–281, in D. Reinking, M.C. McKenna, L.D. Labbo and R.D. Kieffer (eds), *Handbook of Literacy and Technology: Transformations in a Post-Typographic World*, London and New York: Routledge.

Brüscher, B. (2013) Nature on the move: the value and circulation of liquid nature and the emergence of fictitious conservation, *New Proposals: Journal of Marxism and Interdisciplinary Inquiry*, 6, 20–36.

Brynjolfsson, E. and McAfee, A. (2011) *The Race Against the Machine*, Lexington: Digital Frontier Press.

Brynjolfsson, E. and McAfee, B. (2014) *The Second Machine Age: Work, Progress and Prosperity in a Time of Brilliant Technologies*, New York (NY): W&W Norton.

Buell, L. (2007) Ecoglobalist affects: the emergence of U.S. environmental imagination on a planetary scale, 227–248, in W.-C. Dimock and L. Buell (eds), *Shades of the Planet: American Literature as World Literature*, Princeton (NJ): Princeton University Press.

Burton, R. (1927) *The Anatomy of Melancholy*, eds. F. Dell and P. Jordan-Smith, New York (NY): Tudor.

Busch, B. (2013) *Mehrsprachigkeit*, Wien: Facultas Verlags.

Business Victoria (2015) Use social media for business. Available online: www.business.vic. gov.au/marketing-sales-and-online/online-business-and-technology/social-media-for-busi ness/using-social-media-to-boost-business (accessed 13 May 2015).

Cabré, J. (2014) *Confessions*, tr. M.F. Lethem, London: Arcadia.

Campbell, A. (2013) *Rathad an Isein: The Bird's Road – a Lewis Moorland Glossary*, Glasgow: Faram.

Carr, H. (2009) *The Verse Revolutionaries: Ezra Pound, H.D. and the Imagists*, London: Cape.

Cassin, B. (ed.) (2014) *Dictionary of Untranslatables: A Philosphical Lexicon*, tr. E. Apter, J. Lezra and M. Wood, Princeton (NJ): Princeton University Press.

Castells, M., Fernandez-Ardevol, M., Qiu, J., Linchuan, P. and Sey, A. (2006) *Mobile Communication and Society: A Global Perspective*, Cambridge (MA): MIT Press.

Cato, M.S. (2008) *Green Economics: An Introduction to Theory, Policy and Practice*, London and New York: Routledge.

Cehan, A. (2004) Sécurité, frontières et surveillance aux États-Unis après le 11 septembre 2001, *Cultures & Conflits*, 53, 113–145.

Center for Biological Diversity (2015) The extinction crisis. Available online: www.bio logicaldiversity.org/programs/biodiversity/elements_of_biodiversity/extinction_crisis (accessed 30 November 2015).

Chabot, P. (2015) *L'Âge des transitions*, Paris: PUF.

Chakrabarty, D. (2009) The climate of history: four theses, *Critical Inquiry*, 35, 207.

Cheyfitz, E. (1997) *The Poetics of Imperialism: Translation and Colonization from the Tempest to Tarzan*, Philadelphia (PA): University of Pennsylvania Press.

Chirac, J. (2014) Discours d'Orleans. Available online: www.scienzepolitiche.uniba.it/area-docenti/documenti_docente/materiali_didattici/244_Annexe–Le_bruit_i_odeur_et_la_misere_du_monde.pdf (accessed 2 July 2014).

Chomsky, N. (1965) *Cartesian Linguistics*, New York (NY): Harper and Row.

Christiansen, M. H. and Kirby, S. (2003) *Language Evolution*, London and New York: Oxford University Press.

Chrostowska, S.D. (2015) *Matches: A Light Book*, New York: Punctum Books.

Cisco (2015) Cisco Visual Networking Index: Global Mobile Data Traffic Forecast Update 2014–2019 White Paper. Available online: www.cisco.com/c/en/us/solutions/collateral/service-provider/visual-networking-index–vni/white_paper_c11–520862.html (accessed 15 January 2016).

Citton, Y. (2014) *Pour une écologie de l'attention*, Paris: Seuil.

Clapp, A. (2015) Freelance, *The Times Literary Supplement*, 5875, 6 November, 18.

Coghlan, A. and MacKenzie, D. (2011) Revealed – the capitalist network that runs the world, *New Scientist*, 19 October. Available online: www.newscientist.com/article/m g21228354.500-revealed–the-capitalist-network-that-runs-the-world (accessed 22 January 2016).

Coleman, M. and Yusoff, K. (2014) Interview with Elizabeth Povinelli, *Society & Space*, March 6. Available online: http://societyandspace.com/2014/03/06/interview-with-eliza beth-povinelli-with-mat-coleman-and-kathryn-yusoff (accessed 14 December 2015).

Collini, S. (2012) *What Are Universities For?* London: Penguin.

Conservatives (2015) The Conservative Party Manifesto 2015. Available online: https://s3-eu-west-1.amazonaws.com/manifesto2015/ConservativeManifesto2015.pdf (accessed 6 November 2015).

Coorey, M. (2015) Australia urged to crack down on the abuse of migrant labour, *Yahoo News*. Available online: http://news.yahoo.com/australia-probe-exploitation-m igrant-labour-041915275.html (accessed 3 November 2015).

Corbey, R. (2005) *The Metaphysics of Apes: Negotiating the Animal-Human Boundary*, Cambridge: Cambridge University Press.

Cronin, M. (1988) Translator training: two cultures reconciled? 325–329, in P. Nekeman (ed.), *Translation, Our Future/La Traduction, notre avenir*, Maastricht: Euroterm.

Cronin, M. (2000) *Across the Lines: Travel, Language, Translation*, Cork: Cork University Press.

Cronin, M. (2003) *Translation and Globalization*, London: Routledge.

Cronin, M. (2006) *Translation and Identity*, New York and London: Routledge.

Cronin, M. (2008) Downsizing the world: translation and the politics of proximity, 265–275, in A. Pym, M. Shlesinger and D. Simeoni (eds), *Beyond Descriptive Translation Studies: Investigations in Homage to Gideon Toury*, Amsterdam: John Benjamins.

Cronin, M. (2012) *The Expanding World: Towards a Politics of Microspection*, Washington: Zero Books.

Cronin, M. (2013) *Translation in the Digital Age*, New York and London: Routledge.

Crosbie, J. (2013) The growth of intolerance, *The Irish Times*, 29 June, 3.

Crosby, A.W. (1995) The past and present of environmental history, *American Historical Review*, 100, October, 1185.

Crutzen, P. and Stoermer, E. (2000), The Anthropocene, International Geosphere-Biosphere Programme, *Global Change Newsletter*, 41, 17.

Crutzen, P. (2002) Geology of mankind, *Nature*, 415, 3 January, 23.

Crystal, D. (2000) *Language Death*, Cambridge: Cambridge University Press.

Danowski, D. and Viveiros de Castro, E. (2014) L'Arrêt du monde, 221–339, in É. Hache, *De l'univers clos au monde infini*, Bellevaux: Éditions Dehors.

Dawkins, M.S. (1998) *Through Our Eyes Only? The Search for Animal Consciousness*, Oxford: Oxford University Press.

De Decker, K. (2015a) Why we need a speed limit for the internet, *Low Tech Magazine*. Available online: www.lowtechmagazine.com/2015/10/can-the-internet-run-on-renewable-energy.html (accessed 15 January 2016).

De Decker, K. (2015b) How to build a low-tech internet, *Low-Tech Magazine*. Available online: www.lowtechmagazine.com/2015/10/how-to-build-a-low-tech-internet.html (accessed 16 January 2016).

de Laet, M. and Mol, A. (2000) The Zimbabwe bush pump: the mechanics of a fluid technology, *Social Studies of Science*, 30, 225–263.

Deane, S. (1987) *Celtic Revivals: Essays in Irish Literature 1880–1980*, Winston-Salem (NC): Wake Forest University Press.

Deleuze, G. and Guattari, F. (1986) *Kafka: Toward a Minor Literature*, Minneapolis (MN): University of Minnesota Press.

Delisle, J. (1999) *Portraits de Traducteurs*, Ottawa: Les Presses de l'Université d'Ottawa.

Delisle, J. (2002) *Portraits de Traductrices*, Ottawa: Les Presses de l'Université d'Ottawa.

Delisle, J. and Woodsworth, J. (2012) *Translators through History*, revised edition, Amsterdam: John Benjamins.

Dennis, K. and Urry, J. (2007) The digital axis of post-automobility, 1–74, Lancaster University: Department of Sociology. Available at: www.kingsleydennis.com/The%20Digital%20Nexus%20of%20Post-Automobility.pdf (accessed 5 March 2014).

Descartes, R. [1637] (1959) *Discours de la méthode*, Colin: Paris.

Di Biase, C.G. (ed.) (2006) *Travel and Translation in the Early Modern Period*, Amsterdam: Rodopi.

Diner, H. R. (2003) *Hungering for America: Italian, Irish and Jewish Foodways in the Age of Migration*, Cambridge (MA): Harvard University Press.

Drysdale, H. (1986) *Alone through China and Tibet*, London: Constable.

Drysdale, H. (1991) *Dancing with the Dead: A Journey to Zanzibar and Madagascar*, London: Hamish Hamilton.

Drysdale, H. (1996) *Looking for George: Love and Death in Romania*, London: Picador.

Drysdale, H. (2001) *Mother Tongues: Travels Through Tribal Europe*, London: Picador.

Dufour, D.-R. (2011) *L'indvidu qui vient ... après le libéalisme*, Paris: Denoël.

Eagleton, T. (2003) *After Theory*, London: Allen Lane.

Edwards, P. (2010) *A Vast Machine: Computer Models, Climate Data and the Politics of Global Warming*, Cambridge MA: MIT Press.

Elkins, J. (2000) *What Painting Is*, London and New York: Routledge.

Elsner, J. and Rubiés, J.-P. (eds) (1999) *Voyages and Visions: Towards a Cultural History of Travel*, London: Reaktion.

Epstein, J.B. (2015) What's cooking? Translating food, *Translation Journal*, 13, 3 July. Available online: http://translationjournal.net/journal/49cooking.htm (accessed 4 June 2015).

Espeland, W. and Stevens, M. (1998) Commensuration as a social process, *Annual Review of Sociology*, 24, 313–343.

Fabian, J. (1986) *Time and the Other: How Anthropology Makes Its Object*, New York: Columbia University Press.

Falkinger, J. (2007) Attention economies, *Journal of Economic Theory*, 133, 266–294.

Fallada, H. (2014) *Iron Gustav: A Berlin Family Chronicle*, tr. P. Owens, N. Jabos and G. Cramer von Laue, London: Penguin.

Federal Communications Commission (2004) International Telecommunications Data Report. Available online: http://transition.fcc.gov/ib/sand/mniab/traffic/files/CREPOR04.pdf (accessed 14 January 2016).

Ferdowsi, A. (2007) *The Shahnameh: The Persian Book of Kings*, tr. D. Davis, London: Penguin.

Ferry, L. (1992) *Le nouvel ordre écologique*, Paris: Grasset.

Fischetti, M. (2013) The 5,000 mile salad, *The Scientific American*, 309, 3, 80.

Flemish Literature Fund (2015) High impact: literature from the Low Countries. Available online: http://buitenland.vfl.be/en/196/collections/34/high-impact.html (accessed 13 May 2015).

Forsdick, C. (2005) *Travel in Twentieth-Century French and Francophone Cultures: The Persistence of Diversity*, Oxford: Oxford University Press.

Fortier, A.-M. (2000) *Migrant Belongings: Memory, Space, Identity*, Oxford: Berg.

Foster, J.B. (2015) Marxism and ecology: common fonts of a great transition, *Monthly Review*, 67, 7. Available online: http://monthlyreview.org/2015/12/01/marxism-and-ecology/ (accessed 22 January 2016).

Franck, G. (2014) L'économie de l'attention, 55–72, in Y. Citton (ed.) *L'Économie de l'attention*, Paris: La Découverte.

Freedman, D.H. (2013) Are engineered foods evil? *The Scientific American*, 309, 3, 70–75.

Fressoz, J.-B. (2012) *L'Apocalypse joyeuse: une histoire du risque technologique*, Paris: Seuil.

Gamboni, A. (2014) L'Escamoteur: économie de l'illusion et écologie de l'attention, in A. Braito and Y. Citton, *Technologies de l'enchantement. Pour une histoire multi-disciplinaire de l'illusion*, Grenoble: ELLUG.

Garber, M. (2013) Animal behaviorist: we'll soon have devices that let us talk with our pets, *The Atlantic*, 4 June. Available online: www.theatlantic.com/technology/archive/2013/06/animal-behaviorist-well-soon-have-devices-that-let-us-talk-with-our-pets/276532 (accessed 10 December 2015).

García, I. (2010) The proper place of professionals (and non-professionals and machines) in web translation, *Revista tradumàtica*, 8. Available online: www.fti.uab.es/tradumatica/revista/num8/articles/02/02central.htm (accessed 3 June 2014).

García, O. and Wei, L. (2014) *Translanguaging: Language, Bilingualism and Education*, Basingstoke: Palgrave Macmillan.

Garton Ash, T. (2013) From the lighthouse: the world and the NYR after fifty years, *New York Review of Books*, 60, 17, 7–20 November, 51.

Gauchez, M. (1910) *Le livre des masques Belges*, Paris: Éditions de la Société Nouvelle.

Gaultier, P. (2009) L'hypothèse communiste – interview d'Alain Badiou par Pierre Gaultier, *Le Grand Soir*, 6 August. Available online: www.google.ie/?gws_rd=ssl (accessed 29 October 2015).

Gee, H. (2013) *The Accidental Species: Misunderstandings of Human Evolution*, Chicago: University of Chicago Press.

Gerald of Wales (1982) *The History and Topography of Ireland*, tr. J. O'Meara, London: Penguin.

Goldhaber, M. (1996a) Principles of the new economy. Available online: www.well.com/user/mgoldh/principles.html (accessed 12 August 2015).

Goldhaber, M. (1996b) Some attention apothegms. Available online: http://www.well.com/user/mgoldh/apoth.html (accessed 14 August 2015).

Goldhaber, M. (1997a) Attention shoppers!, *Wired*, 12, 5. Available online: http://www.wired.com/1997/12/es-attention/ (accessed 15 August 2015).

Goldhaber, M. (1997b) The attention economy and the net. Available online: www.well.com/user/mgoldh/AtEcandNet.html (accessed 16 August 2015).

Gombrich, E.H. (2007) *The Story of Art*, 16th edition, London: Phaidon.

Grandin, T. and Johnson, C. (2005) *Animals in Translation: The Woman Who Thinks Like A Cow*, London: Bloomsbury.

Greenfield, A. (2006) *Everyware: The Dawning Age of Ubiquitous Computing*, Berkeley (CA): New Riders.

Grötschel, M. (2010) Designing a digital future. Available online: www.whitehouse.gov/sites/default/files/microsites/ostp/pcast-nitrd-report-2010.pdf (accessed 27 January 2015).

Guha, R. (2000) *Environmentalism: A Global History*, New York: Longman.

Hafez, S. (2011) Food as a semiotic code in Arabic literature, 257–280, in R. Tapper and S. Zubaida (eds) *A Taste of Thyme: Culinary Cultures of the Middle East*, London and New York: Tauris.

Hage, G. (1997) At home in the entrails of the West: multiculturalism, ethnic food and migrant home-building, 93–153, in H. Grace, G. Hage, L. Johnson, J. Langsworth and M. Symonds (eds) *Home/World: Space, Community and Marginality in Sydney's West*, Annandale: Pluto Press.

Hahn, M. (2004) *A Basis for Scientific and Engineering Translation: German-English-German*, Amsterdam: John Benjamins.

Hale, S. (2012) *Titian: His Life*, New York (NY): Harper.

Harari, Y.N. (2011) *Sapiens: A Brief History of Mankind*, London: Vintage.

Haraway, D. (1991) *Simians, Cyborgs and Women: The Reinvention of Nature*, London and New York: Routledge.

Hardt, M. and Negri, A. (2005) *Multitude: War and Democracy in the Age of Empire*, London: Penguin.

Hart, S. (1996) *The Language of Animals*, New York (NY): Henry Holt.

Heidegger, M. (1985) Die Sprache, *Unterwegs zur Sprache*, Gesamtausgabe Band 12, Frankfurt am Main: Klostermann.

Heller, M. and Duchêne, A. (2007) Discourses of endangerment: sociolinguistics, globalization and social order, in A. Duchêne and M. Heller (eds) *Discourses of Endangerment: Ideology and Interest in the Defence of Languages*, London: Continuum, 1–13.

Hilty, L.M. (2008) *Information Technology and Sustainability: Essays on the Relationship between Information Technology and Sustainable Development*, Norderstedt: Books on Demand GmBH.

Hopkins, J. (1999) Wittgenstein, Davidson and radical interpretation, in L.E. Hahn (ed.) *The Philosophy of Donald Davidson*, Chicago/La Salle: Open Court, 255–285.

Huang, J., Qian, F., Gerber, A., Mao, M.Z., Sen, S. and Spatscheck, O. (2012) A close examination of performance and power characteristics of 4G LTE networks, *MobiSys*, 12, 25–29 June. Available online: www.cs.columbia.edu/%7Elierranli/coms6998–6997Spring2014/papers/rrclte_mobisys2012.pdf (accessed 15 January 2016).

Humane Society of the United States (2015) Veal crates: unnecessary and cruel. Available online: www.humanesociety.org/issues/confinement_farm/facts/veal.html (accessed 9 December 2015).

Inghilleri, M. (2012) *Interpreting Justice: Ethics, Politics and Language*, London and New York: Routledge.

Inglis, D. and Gimlin, D. (2010) Food globalizations: ironies and ambivalences of food, cuisine and globality, in D. Inglis and D. Gimlin (eds) *The Globalization of Food*, Oxford: Oxford University Press.

Ingold, T. (2000). *The Perception of the Environment: Essays in Livelihood, Dwelling and Skill*, London and New York: Routledge.

Ingold, T. (2011) *Being Alive: Essays on Movement, Knowledge and Description*, London and New York: Routledge.

International Telecommunications Union (2015) ICT facts and figures: the world in 2015. Available online: www.itu.int/en/ITU-D/Statistics/Pages/facts/default.aspx (accessed 14 January 2016).

Issa, T. (2005) *Talking Turkey: The Language, Culture and Identity of Turkish Speaking Children in Britain*, Staffordshire: Trentham Books.

Jacobsen, E. (1958) *Translation a Traditional Craft: An Introductory Sketch with a Study of Marlowe's Elegies*, Copenhagen: Gyldenal.

Jakobson, R. (2012) On linguistic aspects of translation, 126–132, in L. Venuti (ed.) *The Translation Studies Reader*, 3rd edition, London and New York: Routledge.

James, W. (1890) *The Principles of Psychology*, New York (NY): Henry Holt.

Janik, V.M., Sayigh, L.S. and Wells, R.S. (2006) Signature whistle shape conveys identity information to bottlenose dolphins, *PNAS*, 103, 8293–8297.

Jimenez-Crespo, M. (2013) *Translation and Web Localization*, London and New York: Routledge.

Joyce, J. (1993) *Dubliners*, Herts: Wordsworth Classics.

Jullien, F. (2009) *Les transformations silencieuses: Chantiers*, I, Paris: Livre de Poche.

Kato, D. and Allen, B. (2014) Toward an ecocritical approach to translation: a conceptual framework. Available online: file:///Users/michaelcronin/Desktop/State%20of%20the%20Discipline%20Report%20-%20Ecocritical%20Approach%20to%20Translation.webarchive (accessed 11 November 2015).

Kenneally, C. (2008) *The First Word: The Search for the Origins of Language*, London: Penguin.

Kessous, E., Mellet, K. and Zouinar, M. (2010) L'économie de l'attention. Entre protection des ressources cognitives et extraction de la valeur, *Sociologie du travail*, 52, 3, 359–373.

Khalaf, A., Alshebabi, O. and Hanieh, A. (eds) (2014) *Transit States: Labour, Migration and Citizenship in the Gulf*, London: Pluto Press.

Kirby, J. (2011) *Aristotle's Metaphysics: Form, Matter and Identity*, London: Continuum.

Kirkpatrick, E.M. (1983) *Chambers 20th Century Dictionary*, Edinburgh: W&R Chambers.

Klein, N. (2014) *This Changes Everything: Capitalism vs. the Climate*, London: Allen Lane.

Koehn, P. (2009) *Statistical Machine Translation*, Cambridge: Cambridge University Press.

Kolbert, E. (2014) *The Sixth Extinction: An Unnatural History*, London: Bloomsbury.

Kurzweil, R.C. (2005) *The Singularity is Near: When Humans Transcend Biology*, London: Penguin.

Lanchester, J. (2010) *Whoops!: Why Everyone Owes Everyone and No One Can Pay*, London: Penguin.

Language Scientific (2015) Website localization and website translation – what is involved?' Available online: www.languagescientific.com/translation-services/website-localization-services.html (accessed 5 May 2015).

Lanham, R. (2006) *The Economics of Attention: Style and Substance in the Age of Information*, Chicago (IL): University of Chicago Press.

Larsen, P.O. and von Ins, M. (2010) The rate of growth in scientific publication and the decline in coverage provided by the Science Citation Index, *Scientometrics*, 84, 3, 575–603.

Lathey, G. (2010) *The Role of Translators in Children's Literature: Invisible Storytellers*, London and New York: Routledge.

Latour, B. (1987) *Science in Action: How to Follow Scientists and Engineers Through Society*, Cambridge (MA): Harvard University Press.

Latour, B. (2013) *An Inquiry into Modes of Existence: An Anthropology of the Moderns*, tr. C. Porter, Cambridge (MA): Harvard University Press.

Latour, B. (2014) Anthropology at the time of the Anthropocene – a personal view of what is to be studied. Available online: www.google.ie/?gws_rd=ssl (accessed 9 December 2015).

Latour, B. (2015) Telling friends from foes in the age of the Anthropocene. Available online: www.google.ie/?gws_rd=ssl (accessed 14 December 2015).

Laudan, R. (2013) *Cuisine and Empire: Cooking in World History*, Berkeley (CA): University of California Press.

Law, J. and Mol, A. (2003) *Situating Technoscience: An Inquiry into Spatialities*, Lancaster University, UK: Centre for Science Studies. Available online: www.comp.lancs.ac.uk/sociology/papers/Law-Mol-Situating Technoscience.pdf (accessed 30 March 2016).

Lentin, A. (2004) The problem of culture and human rights in the response to racism, 95–103, in G. Titley (ed.) *Resituating Culture*, Strasbourg: Council of Europe.

Levenstein, H. (2003), *Revolution at the Table: The Transformation of the American Diet*, Berkeley (CA): University of California Press.

Lieberman, P. (2006) *Towards an Evolutionary Biology of Language*, Cambridge (MA): Belknap Press of Harvard University Press.

Lionbridge (2016) Software localization: reach a global audience with your software and applications. Available online: www.lionbridge.com/solutions/software-localization (accessed 18 January 2016).

Liu, A. (2011) An eco-translatological perspective on the translator: a case study of Xu Chi, *Theory and Practice in Language Studies*, 1, 1, 87–90.

Lung, R. (2011) *Interpreters in Early Imperial China*, Amsterdam: John Benjamins.

Mac Con Midhe, T. (2015) *Aistí Eorpacha*, Baile Átha Cliath: Coiscéim.

Macfarlane, R. (2015a) From Aquabob to Zawn, *The Guardian Review*, 28 February, 2–4.

Macfarlane, R. (2015b) *Landmarks*, London: Hamish Hamilton.

MacLean, P. (1990) *The Triune Brain in Evolution: Role in Paleocerebral Functions*, New York: Kluwer Academic Publishers.

Maffi, L. and Woodley, E. (2010) *Biocultural Diversity Conservation: A Global Source-book*, London and New York.

Magee, W.H. (1969) The animal story: a challenge in technique, in S. Egoff, G.T. Stubbs and L.F. Ashley (eds) *Only Connect: Readings on Children's Literature*, Toronto: Oxford University Press.

Mahfouz, N. (1990) *The Palace Walk*, tr. W.M. Hutchins, and O.E. Kenny, London: Black Swan.

Malaguzzi, L. (1993) *The Hundred Languages of Children*, New Jersey: Norwood.

Malm, A. (2014) *Fossil Capital. The Rise of Steam Power in the British Cotton Industry, 1825–1828, and the Roots of Global Warming*, Lund: Lund University Press.

Mandel, R. (2008) *Cosmopolitan Anxieties: Turkish Challenges to Citizenship and Belonging in Germany*, Durham (NC): Duke University Press.

Mardarossian, C. M. (2002) From literature of exile to migrant literature, *Modern Language Studies*, 32, 2, 15–33.

Markowsky, J. K. (1975) Why anthropomorphism in children's literature? *Elementary English*, 52(4), 460–466. Available online: www.jstor.org/stable/41592646 (accessed 8 December 2015).

Marlowe, L. (2015) Thousands defy Paris ban to join protest, *The Irish Times*, 14 December, 5.

Marshall Thomas, E. (1996) *The Hidden Life of Dogs*, New York (NY): Pocket Books.

Massey, D. (1991) A global sense of place, *Marxism Today*, June, 24–29.

Massey, D. (1994) *Space, Place and Gender*, Cambridge: Polity.

McCarthy, M. (2009) *The Group*, London: Virago.

McEntyre, M.C. (2009) *Caring for Words in a Culture of Lies*, Grand Rapids, Michigan and Cambridge: Eerdmans.

McIntosh, A. (2008) *Hell and High Water: Climate Change, Hope and the Human Condition*, Edinburgh: Birlinn.

McKenzie Wark, K. (2004) *A Hacker Manifesto*, Cambridge (MA): Harvard University Press.

McKenzie Wark, K. (2012) *Telesthesia: Communication, Culture and Class*, Cambridge: Polity Press.

McKenzie Wark, K. (2013) #Celerity: a critique of the manifesto for an accelerationist politics. Available online: https://speculativeheresy.files.wordpress.com/2013/05/wark-mckenzie-celerity.pdf (accessed 21 January 2016).

McKenzie Wark, K. (2015) *Molecular Red: Theory for the Anthropocene*, London: Verso.

McNeill, J.R. (2001) *Something New Under the Sun: An Environmental History of the Twentieth-Century World*, London: Norton.

Melby, A. (2006) MT+TM+QA: the future is ours, *Revista Tradumàtica*, 4.

Meldrum-Hanna, C. and Russell, A. (2015) Slaving away. Available online: www.google.ie/?gws_rd=ssl (accessed 3 November 2015).

Meylaerts, R. and Gonne, M. (2014) Transferring the city – transgressing borders: cultural mediators in Antwerp (1850–1930), in M. Cronin and S. Simon (eds), special issue on 'The City as Translation Zone', *Translation Studies*, 7, 2, 133–151.

Miller, G., Fogel, M., Magee, J., Gagan, M., Clarke, S., and Johnson, B. (2005) Ecosystem collapse in Pleistocene Australia and a human role in megafaunal extinction, *Science*, 309, 5732, 287–290.

Mitchell, T. (2011) *Carbon Democracy: Political Power in the Age of Oil*, London: Verso.

Mitchell, W. (1995) *The City of Bits*. London: MIT Press.

Montgomery, S.L. (2000) *Science in Translation: Movements of Knowledge Through Cultures and Time*, Chicago (IL): University of Chicago Press.

Moore, G. (1965) Cramming more components onto integrated circuits, *Electronics Magazine*, 38, 8, 19 April, 27–29.

Morton, T. (2013) *Hyperobjects: Philosophy and Ecology after the End of the World*, Minneapolis: University of Minnesota Press.

Moss, S. (2012) *Natural Childhood*, London: National Trust.

Naess, A. (1989) *Ecology, Community and Lifestyle: Outline of an Ecosophy*, tr. D. Rothenberg, Cambridge: Cambridge University Press.

National Geographic Education (2016) Climate refugee. Available online: http://educa tion.nationalgeographic.org/encyclopedia/climate-refugee/ (accessed 12 February 2016).

Nettle, D. and Romaine, S. (2000) *Vanishing Voices: The Extinction of the World's Languages*, Oxford: Oxford University Press.

Ngozi Adichie, C. (2006) *Half of a Yellow Sun*, New York (NY): Harper.

Nicole, P. (1999) *Essais de morale*, Paris: Presses Universitaires de France.

Novak, M. (2010) The meaning of transarchitecture. Available at: www.fen-om.com/net work/2010/03/05/the-meaning-of-trans-architecture-marcos-novak/ (accessed 19 March 2014).

Ó Murchadha, T. (1915) Roimhrádh, in D. Defoe, *Eachtra Robinson Crúsó*, tr. T. Ó Murchú, Dublin: Clódhanna Teo.

O'Connell-Rodwell, C. (2007) Keeping an 'ear' to the ground: seismic communication in elephants, *Physiology*, 22, 4, 287–294.

O'Connell, E. (1999) Translating for children, 208–216, in G. Anderman and M. Rogers (eds) *Word, Text, Translation*, Clevedon: Multilingual Matters.

O'Leary, P. (2004) *Gaelic Prose in the Irish Free State 1922–1939*, Dublin: University College Dublin Press.

O'Sullivan, E. (2005) *Comparative Children's Literature*, London and New York: Routledge.

Observ'ER (2013) Worldwide electricity production from renewable energy sources. Available online: www.energies-renouvelables.org/observ-er/html/inventaire/Eng/con clusion.asp (accessed 16 January 2016).

Office of the President (2009) A strategy for American innovation: driving towards sus-tainable growth and quality jobs. Available online: www.whitehouse.gov/sites/default/ files/microsites/ostp/innovation-whitepaper.pdf (accessed 18 May 2015).

Oliver, J. (2006) *Jamie's Italy*, New York (NY): Hyperion.

Oliver, J. (2012) *Jamie Oliver's Great Britain*, New York (NY): Hyperion.

Oliver, J. (2013) *Save with Jamie: Shop Smart, Cook Clever, Waste Less*, London: Michael Joseph.

Osborn, F. (1948) *Our Plundered Planet*, Boston: Little Brown.

Ostler, N. (2011) *The Last Lingua Franca: The Rise and Fall of World Languages*, London: Penguin.

Page, M. (2002) *The First Global Village: How Portugal Changed the World*, Lisboa: Notícias Editorial.

Pangeanic (2015) What is the size of the translation industry. Available online: http://pa ngeanic.com/knowledge_center/size-translation-industry/# (accessed 26 February 2015).

Pascal, B. (1993) *Pensées*, Paris: Flammarion.

Pater, W. (1893) *Studies in the History of the Renaissance*, London: Macmillan.

Pennycook, A. and Otsuji, E. (2010) Metrolingualism: fixity, fluidity, and language in flux, *International Journal of Multilingualism*, 7, 240–254.

Pennycook, A. and Otsuji, E. (2015) *Metrolingualism: Language in the City*, London and New York: Routledge.

Petrini, C. (2007) *Slow Food Nation: Why Our Food Should Be Good, Clean and Fair*, tr. C. Furlan and J. Hunt, Portland (Or.): Rizzoli ex-Libris.

Petro, P. (1997) *Travels in an Old Tongue: Touring the World Speaking Welsh*, London: HarperCollins.

Phillips, L. (2015) *Austerity Ecology and the Collapse-Porn Addicts: A Defence of Growth, Progress, Industry and Stuff*, Alresford: Zero Books.

Pimentel, A. (2014) Stuffed: why data storage is hot again. (Really!), *re/code*, 10 January. Available online: www.google.ie/?gws_rd=ssl (accessed 19 January 2016).

Plumwood, V. (2007) Human exceptionalism and the limitations of animals: a review of Raimond Gaita's The Philosopher's Dog, *Australian Humanities Review*. Available online: http://australianhumanitiesreview.org/archive/Issue-August-2007/EcoHuma nities/Plumwood.html (accessed 2 December 2015).

Pöchhacker, F. and Shlesinger, M. (2007) (eds) *Healthcare Interpreting: Discourse and Interaction*, Amsterdam: John Benjamins.

Polezzi, L. (ed.) (2006) *The Translator*, special issue on 'Translation, Travel, Migration', 12, 2.

Poole, J., Tyack, P., Stoeger-Horwath, A. and Watwood, S. (2005) Animal behaviour: elephants are capable of vocal learning, *Nature*, 434, 455–456.

Pound, E. (1910) *The Spirit of Romance: An Attempt to Define Somewhat the Charm of the Pre-Renaissance Literature of Latin Europe*, London: Dent.

Pratt, M.L. (1992) *Imperial Eyes: Travel Writing and Transculturation*, London and New York: Routledge.

Pratt, M. L. (2009) Harm's way: language and the contemporary arts of war, *PMLA*, 124, 5, 1515–1531.

Probyn, E. (2000) *Carnal Appetites: FoodSexIdentities*, London and New York: Routledge.

Rackham, O. (2000) *The History of the Countryside*, London: W&N.

Rafael, V. L. (2012) Targeting translation: US counterinsurgency and the politics of language, *Social Text*, 113, 30, 4, 55–80.

Rahman, Z.H. (2006) Hope of escape lost in translation, *The Sunday Times*, 17 December.

Raskin, P.D. (2006) *The Great Transition Today: A Report from the Future*, Boston (MA): Tellus Institute.

Readings, B. (1997) *The University in Ruins*, Cambridge (MA): Harvard University Press.

Richards, T. (1993) *The Imperial Archive: Knowledge and the Fantasy of Empire*, London: Verso.

Robbins, P. (2011) *Political Ecology: A Critical Introduction*, Oxford: Wiley-Blackwell.

Robinson, D. (1997) *Becoming a Translator: An Accelerated Course*, London and New York: Routledge.

Robinson, Douglas (2016) Cyborg translation. Available online: http://home.olemiss.edu/ ~djr/pages/writer/articles/html/cyborg.html (accessed 15 January 2016).

Roden, C. (2011) Foreword, in R. Tapper and S. Zubaida (eds) *A Taste of Thyme: Culinary Cultures of the Middle East*, London and New York: Tauris.

Rogers, W. (1931) Foreword, Beverly Hills Women's Club, *Fashions in Foods in Beverly Hills*, Beverly Hills (CA): Beverly Hills Citizen.

Rose, H. and Rose, S. (2014) *Genes, Cells and Brains: The Promethean Promises of the New Biology*, London: Verso.

Rotondo, J.P. (2011) Literature knows no frontiers: John Galsworthy and the shaping of PEN, *The Daily Pen American*, 11 August. Available online: www.pen.org/blog/?p= 2086 (accessed 22 January 2013).

Rudwick, M. (2005) *Bursting the Limits of Time: The Reconstruction of Geohistory in the Age of Revolution*, Chicago (IL): University of Chicago Press.

Rymer, R. (2012) Vanishing voices, *National Geographic*, July. Available online: www.google.ie/?gws_rd=ssl (accessed 2 February 2016).

Saint-Simon (1830) *Doctrine de Saint Simon*, vol.2, Paris: Aux Bureaux de l'Organisateur.

Sanders, K. (2008) Night of the Grizzly. Available online: www.google.ie/?gws_rd=ssl (accessed 8 December 2015).

Sassen, S. (2005) The global city: introducing a concept, *Brown Journal of World Affairs*, 11, 2, 27–41.

Savage-Rumbaugh, S., Shanker, S. and Taylor, T.J. (1998) *Apes, Language and the Human Mind*, Oxford: Oxford University Press.

Schama, S. (2014) *Rembrandt's Eyes*, London: Penguin.

Schlosser, E. (2001) *Fast Food Nation: The Dark Side of the All-American Meal*, Boston: Houghton Mifflin Harcourt.

Scollon, R. and Wong Scollon, S. (2003) *Discourses in Place: Language in the Material World*, London and New York: Routledge.

Scott, C. (2015) Working with the notion of eco-translation. Available online: https://soundcloud.com/university-of-exeter/prof-clive-scott-working-with-the-notion-of-eco-translation (accessed 26 March 2016).

Seetharam, A., Somasundaram, M., Towsley, D., Kurose, J. and Shenoy, P. (2010) Shipping to streaming: is this shift green? *Green Networking 2010*, 30 August. Available online: http://none.cs.umass.edu/papers/pdf/green07q-seetharam.pdf (accessed 17 January 2016).

Sennett, R. (2009) *The Craftsman*, London: Penguin.

Serres, M. (2003) *Hominescence*, Paris: Livre de Poche.

Seyfarth, R. and Cheney, D. (2003) Signallers and receivers in animal communication, *Annual Review of Psychology*, 54, 145–173.

Shattuck, R. and Arrowsmith, W. (1961) *The Craft and Context of Translation: A Symposium*, Austin (TX): University of Texas Press.

Shubin, N. (2008) The disappearance of species, *Bulletin of the American Academy of Arts and Sciences*, 61, 17–19.

SIL (2014a) Goal 6. Combat HIV/AIDS, malaria and other diseases. Available online: www.sil.org/about/why-languages-matter/language-and-millennium-development-goals/goal-6 (accessed 28 October 2015).

SIL (2014b) *Why Languages Matter: Meeting Millennium Development Goals through Local Languages*, Dallas: SIL International.

Simeoni, D. (2008) Norms and the state: the geopolitics of translation theory, 329–341, in A. Pym, M. Shlesinger and D. Simeoni (eds) *Beyond Descriptive Translation Studies*, Amsterdam/Philadelphia: John Benjamins.

Simon, S. (2006) *Translating Montreal: Episodes in the Life of a Divided City*. Montreal: McGill-Queen's University Press.

Simon, S. (2012) *Cities in Translation: Intersections of Language and Memory*. New York and London: Routledge.

Skelton, R. (2011) *Landings*, Cumbria: Corbel Stone Press.

Slobodchikoff, C. (2012) *Chasing Doctor Dolittle: Learning the Languages of Animals*, New York (NY): St. Martin's Press.

Slocombe, K.E. and Zuberbühler, K. (2005) Functionally referential communication in a chimpanzee, *Current Biology*, 15, 19, 1779–1784.

Slow Food (2012) The central role of food: Congress Paper 2012–2016. Available online: www.slowfood.com/filemanager/official_docs/SFCONGRESS2012__Central_role_of_food.pdf (accessed 28 February 2015).

Slow Food (2015) Slow food: the history of an idea. Available online: www.slowfood. com/international/7/history?-session=query_session:89BFF235076cf2E DA1OX3B436C15 (accessed 12 February 2015).

Smail, Lord, D. (2008) *On Deep History and the Brain*, Berkeley (CA): University of California Press.

Smith, A. (2010) *The Wealth of Nations*, London: CreateSpace.

Sonny, J. (2013) The ten things technology will allow you to do in the next 50 years, *Elite Daily*, 9 May.

Sousa Santos, B. de (2001) Towards an epistemology of blindness: why the new forms of 'ceremonial adequacy' neither regulate nor emancipate, *European Journal of Social Theory*, 43, 251–279.

Spinks, C.W. (1991) *Pierce and Triadomania: A Walk in the Semiotic Wilderness*, Berlin: Mouton de Gruyter.

St. Gallen (2006) *Stiftsbibliothek, Cod. Sang. 904: Prisciani grammatica*. Available online: www.e-codices.unifr.ch/en/list/one/csg/0904 (accessed 16 August 2015).

Stalin, J. (1938) *Dialectical and Historical Materialism*. Available online: www.marxists. org/reference/archive/stalin/works/1938/09.htm (accessed 22 April 2014).

Standage, T. (1999) *The Victorian Internet: The Remarkable Story of the Telegraph and the Nineteenth-Century On-line Pioneers*, New York: Berkley Books.

Steffen, W., Grinevald, J., Crutzen, P. and McNeill, J. (2011) The Anthropocene: conceptual and historical perspectives, *Philosophical Transactions of the Royal Society*, 842–867.

Steinbeck, J. (1997) *Travels with Charley: In Search of America*, London: Penguin.

Stibbe, A. (2015) *Ecolinguistics: Language, Ecology and the Stories We Live By*, London and New York: Routledge.

Stone, A. (2014) Family farmers hold keys to agriculture in a warming world, *National Geographic*, 2 May.

Suddendorf, T. (2013) *The Gap: The Science of What Separates Us from Animals*, New York (NY): Basic Books.

Susam-Sarajeva, Ş., Batchelor, K., McElduff, S., Robinson, D. and Chesterman, A. (2014) Translation studies forum: universalism in translation studies, *Translation Studies*, 7, 3, 335–352.

Swanson, L. (2009) *Norman Borlaug: Hero in a Hurry*, Charleston: BookSurge.

Systran (2015) Quick translation. Available online: www.systransoft.com/lp/quick-tra nslation (accessed 1 March 2015).

Szerszynski, B. and Urry, J. (2006) Visuality, mobility and the cosmopolitan: inhabiting the world from afar, *The British Journal of Sociology*, 57(1), 113–131.

Tapper, R. and Zubaida, S. (2011) Introduction, 2–17, *A Taste of Thyme: Culinary Cultures of the Middle East*, London and New York: Tauris.

Taylor, C. (1992) *Sources of the Self: The Making of Modern Identity*, Harvard (MA): Harvard University Press.

Taylor, T. (2010) *The Artificial Ape: How Technology Changed the Course of Human Evolution*, New York (NY): Palgrave Macmillan.

Tester, K. (1991) *Animals and Society: The Humanity of Animal Rights*, London: Routledge.

Thibodeau, Patrick (2014) Data centers are the new polluters, *Computerworld*, 26 August. Available online: www.computerworld.com/article/2598562/data-center/data -centers-are-the-new-polluters.html (accessed 19 January 2016).

Thomas, C. D., Cameron, A., Green, R., Bakkenes, E.M., Beaumont, L.J., Collingham, Y. C., Erasmus, B.F.N., Ferreira de Siqueira, M. et al. (2004) Extinction risk from climate change, *Nature*, 427, 145–148.

Tymoczko, M. (1999) *Translation in a Postcolonial Context*, Manchester: St Jerome.

Tymoczko, M. (2007) *Enlarging Translation, Empowering Translators*, Manchester: St. Jerome.

UNEP (2011) Towards a green economy: pathways to sustainable development and poverty eradication. Available online: www.unep.org/greeneconomy/Portals/88/documents/ger/ger_final_dec_2011/Green%20EconomyReport_Final_Dec2011.pdf (accessed 21 January 2011).

Unesco, 'Intangible Heritage'. Available online at: http://www.unesco.org/culture/ich/index.php?lg=EN&pg=home (accessed 30 April 2014)

US Environmental Protection Agency (2007) Report to Congress on Server and Data Center Energy Efficiency Public Law 109–431. Available online: www.energystar.gov/ia/partners/prod_development/downloads/EPA_Datacenter_Report_Congress_Final1.pdf?2abe-a80f (accessed 19 January 2016).

Valdéon, R.A. (2014) *Translation and the Spanish Empire in the Americas*, Amsterdam: John Benjamins.

van Parijs, P. (2011) *Linguistic Justice for Europe and the World*, Oxford: Oxford University Press.

Vega, D., Cerdà-Albern, L., Navarro, L. and Meseguer, R. (2013) Topology patterns of a community network: guifi.net. Available online: http://dsg.ac.upc.edu/sites/default/files/1569633605.pdf (accessed 16 January 2016).

Venuti, L. (2008) *The Translator's Invisibility: A History of Translation*, 2nd edition, London and New York: Routledge.

Vogt, W. (1948) *Road to Survival*, New York (NY): Sloan Associates.

Von Ahn, L. (2011) Massive-scale online collaboration'. TED Talk, April. Available online: www.ted.com/talks/luis_von_ahn_massive_scale_online_collaboration.html (accessed 18 January 2016).

Warwick, K. (2011) *Artificial Intelligence: The Basics*, London and New York: Routledge.

Watkin, C. (2015) Michel Serres' Great Story: from biosemiotics to econarratology, *Substance*, 44, 3, 171–187.

Weber, M. (1946) Science as a vocation, in M. Weber, *From Max Weber: Essays in Sociology*, tr. H.H. Gerth and C. Wright Mills, Oxford: Oxford University Press.

Weir, A., Chappell, J. and Kacelnik, A. (2002) Shaping of the hooks in New Caledonian crows, *Science*, 297, 5583, 981.

West, B. (2015) *Re-enchanting Nationalisms: Rituals and Remembrances in a Postmodern Age*, Berlin: Springer.

Wilenski, D. (2013) *Fantastical Guides for the Wildly Curious: Ways into Hinchingbrooke Country Park*, Cambridge: Cambridge Curiosity and Imagination.

Wilks, Y. (2008) *Machine Translation: Its Scope and Limits*. Berlin: Springer.

Willan, A. and Ruffenach, F. (2007) *The Country Cooking of France*, San Francisco (CA): Chronicle Books.

Williams, C.W. (1958) *I Wanted to Write a Poem: The Autobiography of the Works of a Poet*, ed. E. Heal, Boston (MA): Beacon Press.

Williams, E. (2011) Environmental effects of information and communications technologies, *Nature*, 17 November, 354–358.

Williams, E., Ayres, R. and Heller, M. (2002) The 1.7 kg microchip: energy and chemical use in the production of semiconductors, *Environmental Science and Technology*, 36, 5504–5510.

Williams, R. (1979) *Politics and Letters*, London: New Left Books.

Williams, R. (2014) *The Edge of Words: God and the Habits of Language*, London: Bloomsbury.

Wilson, E.O. (1975) *Sociobiology: The New Synthesis*, Cambridge (MA): Harvard University Press.

Wilson, E.O. (2003) *The Future of Life*, London: Abacus.

Winner, L. (2004) Sow's ears from silk purses: the strange alchemy of technological visionaries, 34–46, in M. Stunken, D. Thomas and S. Bell-Rokeach (eds) *The Hopes and Fears that Shape New Technologies*, Philadelphia (PA): Temple University Press.

Wong, R. (2013) The oxygen trade: leaving Hondurans gasping for air, *Foreign Policy in Focus*, 18 June.

WordReference.com (2005) Cream cheese, 1–2. Available online: www.forum.wor dreference.com/showthread.php?t=17827 (accessed 15 April 2014).

World Bank (2016) *World Development Report 2016: Digital Dividends*, Washington: World Bank.

World Resources Institute (2005) *Millennium Ecosystem Assessment Report*, Washington: Island Press.

Wrangham, R. (2007) The cooking enigma, 182–203, in C. Pasternak (ed.) *What Makes Us Human?* Oxford: Oneworld.

Wulf, A. (2015) *The Invention of Nature: The Adventures of Alexander von Humboldt, the Lost Hero of Science*, London: John Murray.

Wrangham, R. (2010) *Catching Fire: How Cooking Made Us Human*, New York (NY): Basic Books.

Xu, J. (2009) *Translation Ecology*, Beijing: Three Gorges Publishing House.

Yengoan, A. (2003) Lyotard and Wittgenstein and the question of translation, 25–43, in P. Rubel and A. Rosman (eds) *Translating Cultures: Perspectives on Translation and Anthropology*, Oxford and New York: Berg.

Yildiz, Y. (2012) *Beyond the Mother Tongue: The Postmonolingual Condition*, New York (NY): Fordham University Press.

Zalasiewicz, J. (2012) *The Planet in a Pebble: A Journey into Earth's Deep History*, Oxford: Oxford University Press.

Ziegelman, J. (2011) *97 Orchard: An Edible History of Five Immigrant Families in One New York Tenement*, New York (NY): Harper.

Zimányi, K. (2005) *Impartiality or advocacy: perceptions of the role of the community interpreter in Ireland*. Unpublished dissertation for MA in Translation Studies. Dublin: Dublin City University.

Zuckerman, E. (2013) *Digital Cosmopolitans: Why We Think the Internet Connects Us, Why It Doesn't, and How to Rewire It*, New York (NY): Norton.

Index

xenophobia 41

Yeeyan (group translation website) 104
Yengoan, Aram A. 49
Yuchi (Native American language) 132
Yusoff, K. 90

Zalasiewicz, Jan 90
zero-equivalence 147
Zhang Lei 104
Zubaida, Sami 53
Zuberbühler, Klaus 75, 76
Zuckerman, Ethan 95, 104